TONGUES OF FIRE

TONGUES OF FIRE

BLACK PREACHING IN THE FACE OF LYNCHING

Edited by AARON M. TREADWELL

Louisiana State University Press
Baton Rouge

Published by Louisiana State University Press
lsupress.org

DESIGNER: Michelle A. Neustrom
TYPEFACES: Calluna, text; Cervo Neue, display

Portions of this book first appeared in "Tongues of Fire: AME Theological Protection in
the Face of Lynching," *Journal of African American Studies* 39, no. 1 (2021): 28–47.

COVER ILLUSTRATION AND FRONTISPIECE: *Portrait of Reverend Davis and Lynching*,
by Ruth Starr Rose (1887–1965), oil, 1933. Water's Edge Museum, Oxford, Maryland.
Reproduced courtesy of the Ruth Starr Rose Trust.

Cataloging-in-Publication Data are available from the Library of Congress.

ISBN 978-0-8071-8490-5 (cloth: alk. paper) — ISBN 978-0-8071-8538-4 (pdf) —
ISBN 978-0-8071-8537-7 (epub)

To my family:

Jade Treadwell
Carter Treadwell
Miles Treadwell
Ella Treadwell

CONTENTS

III. CONSTITUTIONAL THEOLOGICAL PROTECTIONISM

TONGUES OF FIRE

INTRODUCTION

Defining Theological Protectionism

Lord God, this morning—
Put his eye to the telescope of eternity,
And let him look upon the paper walls of time.
Lord, turpentine his imagination,
Put perpetual motion in his arms,
Fill him full of the dynamite of thy power,
Anoint him all over with the oil of thy salvation,
And set his tongue on fire.

—James Weldon Johnson, "Listen, Lord: A Prayer"

In 1927, James Weldon Johnson provided America a glimpse into a social tool that had historical relevance in the fight against terrorism: the Black church. Johnson, born in 1871, lived during America's most dangerous era of racial violence. He also was born in Florida, which was the nation's most dangerous state for lynching crimes per capita. From 1909 to 1923, Duval County in northern Florida experienced six lynchings, which sent physical, mental, and theological reverberations throughout the city of Jacksonville.[1] Surely Johnson and his family were affected by "Judge Lynch," and Johnson's seminal work, *God's Trombones,* helps to poetically expose responses Black people had formed in their fight against racial caste violence.

Those familiar with *God's Trombones* cannot overlook the author's allegorical use of fire. It is of no coincidence that fire-and-brimstone prophetic preaching depicts fire as a threat—a tool that God would eventually use to strike down sinners. Without the full context of Johnson's background, many

1

have interpreted his sermons as recipes for Black "respectability politics." For example, many have interpreted these "sermons" as Black ministers trying to scare the devil, literally and figuratively, out of mischievous Black people. However, a revisited reading of this work provides a nuanced understanding of the overlooked phenomenon of Black resistance theology.

Black resistance theology, now often described as a part of Black liberation theology, is a unique theological development that is attached to the emancipation ethos of Black religiosity. Its historical beginnings can be found in what Albert J. Raboteau calls "slave religion," a tradition of African slaves syncretizing or superimposing their African spiritualism onto Protestant Christianity. This syncretization or religious mixing often utilized a theology and understanding of Christianity that took the side of the oppressed and impoverished. For the slave practicing this faith, Jesus was more than a spiritual savior; he was a provider of a social gospel that fed the hungry, housed the homeless, and healed the sick. Christ died from a kind of lynching, a public and cursed death—a fate similar to that suffered by many in the post-Reconstruction Black Nadir era. The term *Nadir era* was coined by Rayford Logan to refer to the most violent and pronounced period of public execution in U.S. history. Ultimately, because Christ was resurrected and taught his disciples that he would come again, Black believers were promised a level of invincibility over the trials of bondage, while those who terrorized the afflicted would face godly retribution, as their evil ways were forever "charged on the scroll."[2]

This expression of religious syncretism had a distinct makeup in the United States, as tenets like "millennial Ethiopianism" began to superimpose themselves onto the Black church. It represented "a radical break with the Old World . . . and a glorious African past accompanied by God's judgment of white society and Western civilization." Additional tenets included an attack on social and political discontent, spiritual malfeasance against Black souls, and erroneous teachings that contradicted reason, and reforms directed against self-inflicted vices.[3]

Johnson's seven sermons highlighted the perils of sin while purposely overlooking any loopholes of grace and mercy. This particular methodology was often used in Black sermons dealing with the evils of lynching. Many ministers also grappled with God's handling of lynching and its agents, including the enemy's reception of mercy and grace. These particular spiritual conversations were often secretive, but some examples have been preserved in print and are presented in this collection. Exegetical responses within these spiritually protective conversations ranged from "Should we pray for the lynchers' souls to be forgiven?" to "Should we be praying their downfall?" Throughout this collection, all cases will be exposed.

During lynching eulogies and Sunday morning services, ministers could be found preaching fiery disdain and advocating for needed change with regard to racial caste violence. This work on the Black church's strategy for change included diverse methodologies all grounded in an emancipationist ethos, including the concept of Black theological protectionism, or a religious expression of freedom and liberation. It is fair to assert that by examining the use of theological protectionism during the Nadir era, we are exposed to the willingness of Black people to become mediators against the act of lynching, while also highlighting the complexities of Black theological development. The relationship between violence and the development of Black theology must be examined in order to understand the true essence of the Black church.

The goal of this book is to expose unique documents that express the development of African American theology—a concept that ignites the eventual long civil rights movement of the 1930s to 1970s. Within this collection are sermons that support the use of self-defense with firearms, the public shaming and condemnation of white churches, and reparation strategies that pinpoint lynching as a qualifier for federal aid.

The book has two intentions. First, the field of lynching and the historical analysis of Black agency must continue to be highlighted. Early work on lynching studied the cultural reasons for vigilante justice but overlooked the methods Blacks used to fight back. Concisely, lynching was researched as a violent act instead of a social dynamic that created evolving ideologies among all communities.[4] Second, the book will introduce sermons on resistance theology.

There has been lynching scholarship focused on the correlations between internal tensions and lynching. Case studies that have introduced Black communal responses include James R. McGovern's *Anatomy of a Lynching* (1982), a study of Claude Neal's 1934 lynching in Jackson County, Florida, and most recently Kevin W. Young's *The Violent World of Broadus Miller* (2024). These and other case studies provide a window into the methodology of white lynchers and the sociopolitical dynamics that justified killing in the name of racial purity. They also provide insight into the religious and sociological aspects of lynching, like the murder and dismemberment of the "Black beast" to fuel cultlike celebrations of religious burnt offerings.[5] Still, these case studies fail to focus on the agency of Black people and the recourses they used to avoid becoming victims of lynching.

Studies of Black agency and recourse are forever indebted to Jacquelyn Dowd Hall's *Revolt Against Chivalry* (1974), which examined the relationship between lynching and rape. Focusing on the work of the white antilynching activist Jesse Daniele Ames, Hall described the social disconnect between Ames and other reformers and the Black community, highlighting the Black community's need for internal restitution. Robert Zangrando's work on the antilynching crusade of the National Association for the Advancement of Colored People (NAACP) accentuates the Black community's distrust of white reformers in the antilynching movement as well. Zangrando reemphasized the social impact of Black people using their own tool against terrorism and how Blacks sought to systematically fight against lynching.[6]

There also are works in the field of religious thought that address the theological tolls of caste violence on African American spirituality. Timothy E. Fulop argues that that the atrocity of the Sam Hose lynching sent shockwaves through Black religiosity worldwide and created a gulf of religious skepticism and an indictment of white theological credibility during the Nadir era of race relations.[7] Albert Miller argues that Black theology during the Nadir became a mandatory "think tank" of sorts, to address the "physical, mental, economic, and political attacks against African Americans." At the height of racial caste violence, the Black church pulpit proved itself a pivotal tool in the national fight against American lynching.[8]

And while the lynching historiography has produced research in the study of Black agency, few historians have centered their research on the role of Black religiosity and its direct response to lynching. Therefore, the second purpose of this work is to introduce historical sermons from African Methodist Episcopal (AME) ministers and laypeople in order to highlight the prevalence of resistance theology in response to lynching. In the midst of a violent crisis that affected thousands of Black Christians, the field has been far too silent about this institution's response.

My research has pinpointed sermons, conference notes, and autobiographical works from 1877 to 1919 that emphasize the frequency with which Black Christians spoke against lynching. The year 1919 is selected as the ending point, instead of 1905, as it aligns with Stewart Tolnay and E. M. Beck's database on lynching.[9] The study of lynching has grown in historical focus and sociological examination, but the role of the Black church is often overlooked.[10] As an organic institution with a mandate to protect the immediate needs of its community, the theology of the AME Church has frequently morphed around the ambiguities of American racism.[11] When considering the reverberations of lynching and its effect on African American bodies, a study of its effect on Black souls must also receive its due. Simply put, when one studies the theology of Black southerners during the Nadir era of race relations, one finds a manifesto for averting lynchings.

DEFINING BLACK PROTECTIONISM

Black churches during the Nadir era were often at the forefront of the anti-lynching campaign. W. E. B. Du Bois, Ida B. Wells, Walter White, Hubert Harrison, and Elijah Marrs all utilized church pulpits to protest against Judge Lynch.[12] The Black church has historically played a role within its community as a centerpiece for news and knowledge, and its involvement with lynching legislation was no different. In fact, many of the advocates who supported lynching's abolishment were neither politicians nor journalists but Christian ministers who viewed lynching as contrary to Black people's theological right as *imago Dei*, or made in the image of the creator.[13]

When Bishop Henry McNeal Turner addressed the 1897 lynching of John Johnson and Archibald Jointly of Louisiana, the preacher's message used theology as a tool of protection against future terrorism—theological protectionism. Turner's approach needed little imagination, and as a supporter of the tradition of arms, he preached from an AME pulpit that "Negroes should defend themselves with guns against the lynch mob. Black[s] should acquire guns and keep them loaded and ready for immediate use."[14] Black pulpiteers like Turner had historically created safe havens to protect church members from racial terror and disempowerment, in both the physical and the theological sense. In response to varying forms of oppression, these safe spaces cultivated unique and goal-oriented methods of protecting Black bodies through the use of Black theology. These churchgoers believed that by employing their faith as a verb of action, spiritual forces could provide a varying form of protection during one of America's darkest hours. Theological protectionism should also be understood as an organic and fluid development that shifts as communities change in relationships and social mobility. Areas prone to lynching, defined in Stewart E. Tolnay and E. M. Becks's *Festival of Violence* as ex-slave societies that are predominately white in population, often witnessed a shift in their application of protectionism. In response to their environment, Black pulpiteers exercised a theology that was radical, pious, and even constitutionally focused, based on their interpretation of liberation.[15]

Overall, this book covers three theoretical shifts in the practice of theological protectionism, and all of these methodologies, described as "radical," "pious," or "constitutional" theological protectionism, will be shown to be sermonic attempts to thwart and prevent lynchings. Within each section, each sermon will be organized by its historical relation to an actual lynching and given proper context. Overall, this collection of sermons will reveal the complicated roles that Black preachers played during the lynching era in American history. The methodologies of these responses vary in approach, due to the Black church not existing as a monolithic entity, yet a common thread among all of the sermons is that the Black church identified itself as a responsible mediator against the trauma of lynching.

The first section introduces radical theology, historically one of the oldest branches of Black theological protectionism. Preachers in this group believed that obedience to God warrants salvation and liberation. The development of this theology depended on syncretism, including a liturgy in service that sought freedom from racial bondage.[16] Examples of these sermons highlight the protectional immediacy of radical theology and its goal of preservation, including ministers who argued that believers should be "*prey*ing" for change by shooting at terrorists, or outright leaving the country.

The second section includes sermons from the practice of pious theological protectionism. White terrorism in the South adamantly attacked radical theological protectionism—Black churches and institutions that housed political leadership and supported the tradition of arms often faced violence. In response to violence and terrorism, Black pious theological protectionism witnessed major growth in the southeastern states during the Nadir era. By employing a revivalist mindset in which all things are spiritual, users of this theology believed a cloak of protection could avert the increase of violence.

Within this spiritual mind space, practitioners employed internal and external reflection. They often preached for the moral cleansing of Black communities, including the condemnation of vices and a moralism that had "plagued the Negro" since slavery. Many in this community were encouraged by evangelical witness traditions that mirrored the gospel of their enemies. Many believed that this praxis of employing the theology of one's oppressors would ensure a level of protection for the Black church against violent whites. Indeed, statistical research has shown that communities that practiced foreign religious activities often experienced more violence and had greater numbers of lynching victims.[17]

The third section includes sermons from the practice of constitutional theology. From the Emancipation Act to the passing of the Thirteenth, Fourteenth, and Fifteenth Amendments, the Black church has served as the fulcrum for Black political agency in America. And yet the inclusion of constitutionalism in the Black church has been a diverse process. In the southeastern states, Black constitutionalism was often advanced by Black missionaries, who often used the pulpit to boost their political campaigns. Constitutionalism can also be found in the northeast regions of the United States at the turn of the mid-nineteenth century, as Black churches publicly renounced slavery and the Fugitive Slave Acts. Many in the field of Black constitutionalism have argued that the origins of sociopolitical activism should be attributed to the Black church, and more specifically the AME Church. Dennis Dickerson has argued that Black Methodist theology consist of a syncretic identity of African heritage, Methodist theology as established by John Wesley, and a social quest to provide safety for Black people and communities. In many African American communities, safety required political action and the development of an emancipation ethos within the Black church structure.[18]

Lynching's demise in American history has a challenging historiography. Historians like Michael Pfeifer have argued that lynching was a temporary solution to a desolate court system; participants lynched until they believed the courts could exhibit unbiased competence.[19] Other historians have described lynching as an economic system that would gradually prove itself unnecessary when a middle-class racial caste came to fruition. On both sides of the coin, racial caste and white supremacy have historically been married to lynching, and historians have argued that lynching became a temporal tool for the expedited process of reestablishing white supremacy in the New South. With the creation of Jim Crow rule, Black criminal punishment through the courts became an acceptable solution for white racial caste concerns about supposed

Black criminality. Yet the historiography of lynching will continue to miss the mark if it analyzes lynchings without emphasizing the agency of Black victims. Black people in America have always exhibited forms of resistance, and the same can be said with regard to lynching.

This collection provides the reader with evidence that mainline Black churches were willing and ready to address the evils of Judge Lynch head-on. In the fight against lynching's dominion, preachers showed a willingness to utilize a theology that saw beyond the divinity of Christ and also included his humanity as a fellow lynched victim. Theological protectionism highlighted the symbiotic relationship between serving a lynched deity and Black people's motivation to, in the words of the Black hymnist, "make it over." "Making it over" sometimes meant speaking out against the deadly trend of white terrorism, and other times it meant praying prior to shooting your Winchester rifle. If historiography is going to champion the success of Ida B. Wells, T. Thomas Fortune, and Hubert Harrison, the field should also recognize the teachings of theological protectionism that these and other antilynching advocates received on Sunday mornings.

I

RADICAL THEOLOGICAL PROTECTIONISM

INTRODUCTION

Radical theology, one of the oldest branches of Black theological protection-ism, is inspired by the emancipation ethos of Black religiosity and was exer-cised in accordance with the zealot traditions in the Bible. Preachers in this group believed that obedience to God warranted salvation and liberation, and all means were at times necessary to achieve it. The development of this the-ology within the Black community utilized African syncretism, which included a liturgy in service that sought freedom from racial bondage by emphasizing an ancestry of nobility and achievement. This is the train of thought within which the formation of Black nationalism was established.[1]

Religious syncretism, or the foundational supplementation of West Afri-can religions with regional European Christendom, was historically the most violent ideology of antebellum slavery. According to Albert Raboteau, "Revo-lutionary interpretations of the Bible by such slaves as [Denmark] Vesey and [Nat] Turner were proof to American slaveholders that slave Christianity could become a double-edged sword."[2] Slaveholding states as far back as the eigh-teenth century recognized syncretized religious holdings as dangerous and enforced laws to ban Black proselytization and syncretized worship.

By the mid-nineteenth century, African syncretic practitioners witnessed continued growth in their radical theological praxis as the caste traditions of white Protestant America expelled Black people from their congregations. In 1845, the two largest Protestant denominations, the Methodist Episcopal Church and the Baptist Church, experienced schisms over slavery. Both splits had a positive impact on Black worshipers, who were previously content with their membership in a predominately white congregation. By 1870, the ma-jority of Black Baptists and Methodists had left their respective white denominations and affiliated themselves to autonomous Black spaces of worship. It was in these safe spaces that radical theological protectionism truly ignited.

When Black people transferred their denominational membership due to experiences of racial caste theology, radical theology exposed itself as a valuable tool for many Black clergymen in America. One denomination that most frequently utilized this tradition was the African Methodist Episcopal Church. This denomination often taught members that God's overarching goal was to be liberated from oppression, and this included the act of averting lynching during the Nadir era. The list of radical ministers in African Methodism who spoke out against theological control and specifically lynching was long, though Henry McNeal Turner might be the most relevant voice in the nineteenth century. According to hundreds of articles and historical manuscripts, Turner was known for preaching fire "at the head of the M.E. African Church, [and] he has the confidence and affection of the two million colored people who are members and attendants."[3]

Some of Turner's sermons supported emigration as a form of exodus theology. In 1893, Turner penned an article in the AME periodical *The Christian Recorder* (*TCR*) that deemed America unfit for the Black Christian. Instead, he would argue that in order to end lynching, a "one hundred million dollar emigration bill to leave this country" was to be provided. In the bishop's eyes, emancipation anywhere would be improved experience for Black people. "If we can go no further than Canada . . . or over to Mexico, where we are offered a whole State, we will accept it."[4]

Within *TCR*, pastors historically have highlighted the relevance of radical theology. In 1893, Rev. J. M. Lee argued against a pious preacher, Rev. R. S. Quarterman, that Black Christians were being docile in this nation's lynching problem. Instead of praying for change, the minister argued that believers should be "*preying*" for change by shooting at terrorists. According to Lee, "I will admit that the pulpit and the bar are strong hands to start the ball to rolling, but there must be something else done besides expounding from the pulpit . . . The Negro must do like all other races. He must fight for his rights. Nothing shorter than a Winchester or a Gatling gun will stop this lynching."[5]

What shouldn't be overlooked in this theological exposition of radical protectionism is the connection between shooting back and living morally. For Lee, by protecting Black bodies, Blacks were upholding the Passion experience of Christ. As "Christ shed His blood on Mt. Calvary . . . let the preacher have a hand fighting for the stopping of lynching if necessary."[6] The relationship between radical theology and the tradition of arms has been well documented. Historians Nicholas Johnson and Charles E. Cobb Jr. have cited the intimate role guns have played in the protection of Black life, and many of these tactics and approaches can be found within the AME Church. Some ministers preached simple rhetoric, like in 1895, when the *TCR* editor mentioned that the best approach to ending lynching was to use firearms. Accordingly, "the strongest and best forces, however, that have been used against lynching are those of Ohio—bullets for the mob from the sheriff's revolver."[7] Other articles and writers would echo similar sentiments, as in 1902, when an unnamed minister argued that "the families of those murdered men have no redress whatever and yet we as a people must tamely submit to such outrages. It is a blessing that we have plenty of faith and lots of patience."[8]

Rev. B. W. Nance was another minister in the AME Church who preached a radical theology supporting the tradition of arms. In 1888, he argued that Blacks must protect their spiritual bodies, and that turning the other cheek was contrary to the teaching of the Bible. Instead, "what we want in the South, is—not to stand and grin—but to meet these unlawful crimes, these enraged lynchers, these infuriated mobs, 'Vi et orrmis' [*sic*] and knock out a few dozen." Radical theological protectionism was not a violent resistance ideology for Nance but a reactive method of protection. According to Nance, Blacks were only to respond with violence in the midst of attacks. For example, violence was appropriate "when our Negro men are lynched and when our sisters and mothers are insulted, and we will not only have 'temporary relief,' but a permanent relief." According to radical theology, ministers would argue that the church had become a neutered figure of its old self. Docile Black ministers and a pacifist gospel preaching within the Black church was applauded by whites, but this methodology was deemed inappropriate by Nance. "If the Negro remains in America, you may preach, you may sing, and shout as much as you desire, but the relief,— the thing that is going to alleviate us from this fearful octopus, this almost insurmountable barrier—is to meet force with force."[9]

Rev. J. L. Lowe was a radical protectionism theologian who touted the legitimacy of fighting back against lynching. Radical theologians like Lowe preached about reactive violence from Black Christians, while warning whites of potential movements. In the *Richmond* (VA) *Planet,* Lowe warned white terrorists that "this kind of thing will never stop till a bon fire be made by the negroes of the home of every man who is thought to engage in lynching a ne-gro."[10] In the *Christian Index,* Lowe would also argue that Black Christians had already started planning for a war against lynching—and for good reason. "The Negroes of this country must have protection from somewhere. It is time that something was done to assure them protection. This thing of mobbing, and lynching, and driving them from place to place cannot always last. The table will surely turn and that at an earlier day than some may think."[11]

1

HENRY McNEAL TURNER

Lynching a Colored Woman in Virginia (*Christian Recorder,* 1878)

HISTORICAL CONTEXT

Charlotte Harris, a Black woman, was lynched on March 6, 1878, in Harrison-burg, Virginia.[12] Her charge was arson, as she was accused alongside a young man named Jim Ergenbright of instigating a barn burning. Jim was acquitted of charges, but Harris was held in Harrisonburg jail awaiting trial. She was subsequently kidnapped from the holding cell at gunpoint by two unnamed men, taken four hundred yards from the cell, and hanged from a tree. Harris's body remained hanging from the tree for two days for all the public to see.[13] There was a search, led by the governor of Virginia, to find the lynchers, but the court was unable to identify any parties responsible for the crime. A striking response to this crime came from the *St. Louis Globe-Democrat,* which described the lynching as "but another leaf in the calendar of lust and lawless-ness of the God-defying and law breaking denizens of the rocky crags of the Alleghenies, many of whom live in the vaces and huts." As for the community, one reporter responded, "It is safe to say, anyone who claimed it [lynching] would be lynched himself. The arrest of negro-killers is not popular down there."[14] This was the only Virginia lynching of 1878, though it was neither the first nor last in the state overall. There are 115 registered lynchings in the state from 1866 to 1930. These troubling statistics surely impacted the many AME congregations that populated the state.

SERMONIC RESPONSE

We would invite the attention of our religious exchanges to the note below, if we had any idea they would notice it. But papers that could not be stirred up to notice the savage lynching of a woman by a Virginia mob, could hardly be expected to give attention to the more decent murder of a man. Now, we suppose it will be told us by these "watchmen," that we are too insulting, but we purpose to quote Scripture, nevertheless. "His watchmen are blind: they are all ignorant, they are all dumb dogs, they cannot bark; sleeping, lying down, loving to slumber. Yea, they are greedy dogs which can never have enough, and they are shepherds that cannot understand: they all look to their own way, every one for his gain, from his quarter." It was thus before the war. You can scarcely get one of the religious papers of the country to touch the question of slavery. So how you can scarcely get one of them to touch the question of our present suffering. That our men are shot down in cold blood, and our women hung to the nearest tree, is nothing in their eyes. Deaf to the cry of the oppressed in the past, they are equally deaf to the cry of the suffering in the present. But, God reigns. The following is written us from Lumpkin, Ga. The safety of the writer will not allow us to give his name:

MR. EDITOR:—Please allow me space in your paper to let our many readers know that one more colored man was killed in our county. He was killed by a white man by the name of Lewis Harris on last Sunday near a church, about five miles from Lumpkin. This murder was in Stewart County. The man that killed went away and stayed one or two days and came back, stood his trial, was cleared, and is loose.

Mr. Editor, this is the second year that I have been here, and this makes four colored men who have been killed and nothing has been done about it. The colored people in this part of the State stand a poor chance.

Mr. Editor, please print this for me, as I want all to know how the people are getting along in this part of Georgia.

Ideas on Solving the Race Problem: Open Letter to Hon. Blanche Kelso Bruce (Christian Recorder, March 27, 1890)

HISTORICAL CONTEXT

The target of this letter by Henry Turner was William F. Butler, who was at one time the president of the Negro Republican Party. Butler had proposed a reparations bill for $5 million. Instead of applauding the bill, Turner thought it undersold the needs of African descendants in America, and he therefore voiced his opinion to Blanche Kelso Bruce, who was the second African American to serve in the United States Senate and the first to be elected to a full term. Due to the increase of lynching in America and the nation's inability to protect Black bodies stateside, Turner suggested that Bruce ask for more money and that it be put toward assisting African American colonization.

SERMONIC RESPONSE

SIR: While passing through Washington, D.C., on the evening of the 28th ult., from my house in Atlanta, Ga., I chanced to purchase a copy of the Evening Star, and very soon my attention was arrested by the head line. "Bruce on the Race Issue." Waiving all considerations of personal friendship which has existed between us for many years, and even admiration upon my part for your personal worth and exalted bearing, your past and present status as a high national functionary entitled your opinions and views to more than ordinary attention. But owing to the Episcopal duties and responsibilities which were then awaiting my presence in some of the Eastern States, I slipped the paper into my grip sack, and have just found time to read the sentiments expressed by you to the reporter.

I am sure you are too generous to regard a dissimilarity of views as an affront, though the writer be less distinguished than yourself. Nevertheless, you may remember telling me some years ago that Senators and Bishops were equals. Therefore, presuming upon your own postulations, I venture upon the quicksands of some meager adverse criticisms of a few of your assertions, as they were reported by the representative of the Evening Star, which I hope will be received as kindly as given by the writer.

You say, "What nonsense all this talking about sending all the blacks back to Africa is." True, you are right, if such a nefarious scheme is in contemplation, for thousands and hundreds of thousands of us are no more fit to go back to Africa than we are fit to go to Paradise. Thousands of us would be a curse to the continent, especially that portion of us who have no faith in the Negro, or his possibilities, who worship white gods, who would rather be a white dog on earth than a black cherub in heaven, who are fools enough to believe the devil is black, and therefore that all are black are consanguineously related to him; ignorant black preachers who will stand up in the pulpit and represent this and that species of crime and vice as being as black as sin; and still another portion of us, who will study for years in college and even graduate, to follow the high calling of a waiter or a bootblack, as though classic lore was a prerequisite to such an exalted occupation; who had rather be a white man's scullion than a black man's prince, who regard Africa as being next door to hades, while it is the richest continent under heaven. And still another class of us, who, while professing to be Christians, will work as hard to dissuade young ministers from going with the gospel to the land of our progenitors as if they were going to leap over a fatal precipice; who pretend to be service God, and have no aim higher than to get to heaven to be white; who profess faith in a bodily resurrection from the dead, and yet expect that resurrected and glorified body to be white; that class of us who would rather go forty miles to hear a white ass bray than a hundred yards to hear a black seraph sing; that portion of our race who will sit in the presence of their beautiful daughters and babble about the solution of the Negro problem being the admixture and intermixture of the races, while Senator Ingalls thunders from the Senate of the nation that there never can be any assimilation and proclaims it blood poison, a term never dreamed by the pro-slavery advocates, but which, coming from that source, clinches every law now existing which forbids intermarriage between the two races, and will be the product of others not yet enacted. I take no issue with Mr. Ingalls, however; he simply voices the white sentiment of the nation, be they democrats, republicans, prohibitionists, or any other party. The issue I am taking is against the folly of too many of our own race.

Now, sir, if these are the kind of Negroes you refer to, I say, with double emphasis, it would be "nonsense" to talk of their returning to Africa. Such prattle would be but the jargon of folly. Every colored man in this country who is not proud of himself, his color, his hair and his general make-up is a monstrosity. He is a curse to himself and will be to his children. He is lower than a brute and does not deserve the breath he breathes, much less the bread he eats. Any man, though he be as black as midnight, who regards himself inferior to any other man that God ever made, is simply a walking ghoul and ought to join his invisible companions at the first opportunity, unless he does it to the extent of his natural or acquired ability.

But who is it, Senator, that has been nonsensical enough to talk about all the colored people returning to Africa? I had not heard of any one worth notice speaking about it prior to reading your interview. The man who is guilty of setting afloat such senseless prattings should be arrested, adjudged insane and sent to the asylum.

Senator Butler indicates nothing of the kind in his $5,000,000 bill, which should have been five hundred million or five billion as a start, for billions will have to come sooner or later. It will take billions of dollars to solve that problem, which the Supreme Court of the United States imposed when it decitizened the Negro in the latter part of 1883, for civil rights and citizenship are one and inseparable, as you told me out of your mouth. Nor does the bill of Senator Butler say one word about going to Africa. True, other senators, such as Morgan, Vance, Hampton and other individuals have brought Africa before the country in their speeches, but not as a part of any definite programme. The gist of every speech that has been delivered upon the Butler bill has been upon the theory that if the Negro went anywhere it must be at his own option.

Possibly no Negro in the nation has spoken more vociferously in favor of the Butler bill than myself, but I have kept in harmony with the spirit of the bill. Let the Negro go if he desires or remain here if he prefers. Let him exercise his own intellect and these would-be censors of his manhood—hands off, unless they are asked for advice. The country is full of toadstool or fungus leaders, giving free advice to the Southern Negro, who know no more about his real condition than they do about Siberia.

The colored men in Charleston, Columbia, Savannah, Chattanooga, Mobile, Natchez, Vicksburg, and Montgomery, do not fully realize the condition of the Southern Negro—I mean in the aggregate. How much less those at a greater distance. The Southern Negro is in the country, not in the cities, and to know their wants, wishes, desires and needs you must go among them, mingle with them, and hear and see for yourself. And when you say they have no desire to go to Africa, I who know the real condition of our race as well as any man who lives, say a million at least of them desire to go somewhere. They want freedom, manhood, liberty, protection or the right to protect themselves. At least a million us have found out this nation is a failure; that it cannot or has no disposition to protect the rights of a man who is not white. Not a court in the nation has given a decision in favor of the black man in twelve years. The Supreme Court is an organized mob against the Negro, and every subordinate court in the land has caught its spirit. Buy a railroad ticket in Washington for the Rio Grande, and I will give you a hundred dollars for every meal of victuals you purchase, unless you go around the back way and enter the kitchen and eat amid filth and smoke, and then pay as much for it as the Queen of England would have to pay. Take your own State, Mississippi. A few weeks ago, I walked up to the ticket window to purchase a ticket for Atlanta, and the agent told me to go out and come around to the back window and I could buy a ticket. I remonstrated against such proscription, and he replied by saying, "We make Senator Bruce go round there, and you will do the same, and all other niggers." This occurred in Jackson, Mississippi. As to the railroad cars, I will say nothing. You know too well. I happen to be used to them, however, and did not get frightened when I saw them.

Much has been said about the politics of Senator Butler, and how, for his democratic proclivities, his bill of five millions should be odious to every black man. I grant that the presumption is that Senator Butler has no special love for the Negro; I shall therefore join in with the presumption and suppose him to be a Negro-hater, for argument's sake, at all events. And who cares if he is? I have the same right to hate him that he has to hate me; the same civil and divine right. I do not seek or want his love. I ask no white man's love the odds of a finger snap, nor black man's either, but if I am hungry or thirsty and my enemy brings me bread or water I shall satisfy my anxiety. If I knew that heaven was so full of democrats that only one seat remained I should seek that seat. If I knew that John Brown, Lincoln, Sumner, Stevens, Chase, Grant, and all the heroes of freedom were in perdition, it would be no temptation for me to go there.

I care not what animus prompted Senator Butler. Immortality enthroned his brow from the moment he offered that bill. He will go down in history as the pioneer of a movement that heaven and earth will endorse in less than fifty years. Heaven indorses it now. Not a bill has been offered in Congress in fifteen years that even contemplated any relief for the Negro as a race. Mobs have broken open jails by scores and by hundreds, and the lynch-law victims could be counted by thousands, and other things too numerous to mention; but beyond a little thunder during Presidential campaign nothing has been done or said about it. But Senator Butler comes forth with a bill, which, if it passes—and grant, O my God, that it may—will enable at least a hundred thousand self-reliant black men to go where they can work out their own destiny, and lay the foundation of a future arena for useful activity; for unless we can find a field for our educated sons and daughters we may burn our colleges in a few years to the ground, for higher education in a few years will be a nuisance unless we can put it to work, and we cannot do it here, shut out, as we are, from every educated business employment by reason of our color. And a race who cannot hew out conditions and manufacture possibilities is a failure. If our inadequacy to such a result is too self-evident to even make the experiment, then the doom of the Negro is sealed, and slavery is his normal sphere.

But while I accept the doctrine of the unity of the human race, I believe the Negro division of it is the junior race of the world, and that this boy race has a long and mighty future before it, and that an enslavement here, while actuated by the cupidity of the whites, is intended to be in the order of Providence the culmination of glorious results. What we will be, no earthly creature can divine; but one thing is sure, we must be put in full possession of every right and privilege here, or their nation must pay us $40,000,000, for our 200 year's service, and let us go where we can have unconditional manhood. I have calculated how much this nation owes the Negro, and it figures out just $40,000,000,000,000. We must have it and will have it, or full manhood here, and we are not going to receive full manhood recognition here. The whites will not concede it. Therefore, as soon as these old slave dwarfs, slave manikins, and slave tools die out, our children and their children will pay a new deal in the programme of the future.

I have not space here to describe the infinite resources of Africa, and show its special fitness to be the future theatre of the elevated and cultured Negro. Let it suffice to say that it is the giant continent of the world. It is the Eden of earth, and will in time be the heart of the globe, sanitarily, commercially and evangelically. No stronger evidence need be produced of a person's idiocy than the presumption that Africa is to remain dormant forever. Such a surmise even is charging the God of nature with folly. Mightier gods than ever graced Olympian thrones will again vacate them, to feast at the banquet tables of Ethiopian Africa, and grander Homers will weave it into song. The land that gave the infant Jesus protection and sent a representative with him to the crimsoned summit of Golgotha, can never be cursed or remain under the shadow of a curse.

Adjutorium nostrum in nomine Domini; and He will put the civilized world under contribution for the enlightenment of that continent, be the agents and actors Republicans, Democrats, Prohibitionists, Negro lovers, monarchies, churches, explorers, diamond-hunters, gold-diggers, ship-sailors, wise-men, fanatics, cranks, enthusiasts, or slave-catchers. If I could believe that God simply made the Negro to remain here and play the scullion for the whites forever, as he is doing to-day, and will do until he gets a flag, founds a nation or does something besides grumble, find fault, and catch a few official scraps (and precious few at that), I would be tempted to waver in my faith that God is just.

Do you not see that race prejudice is on the increase? Instance the case of Hon. Madison Davis, of Athens, Ga., my own State: Mr. Davis was postmaster in Athens before, for eight years, I think, and when myself and all the colored members of the legislature were expelled upon the ground that we were colored, Mr. Davis was allow to retain his seat by the vote of every white Democrat and Republican in the house, upon the ground that his colored blood was too small to constitute him a Negro. Therefore, the State of Georgia declared him white, or accepted him as white. But just look at the terrible excitement which his recent appointment to the same postoffice has provoked, simply because that white gentleman, by the laws of Georgia, has one-sixteenth of Negro blood in his arteries.

Senator Ingalls would possibly pronounce him a hybrid (mule), but he has a house full of children I am not anathematizing the whites about these things. I am not denouncing the South any more than the North, for the decision of a Northern supreme court is the author of it all. I find a white man is a white man and a black man is a black man, be he Northerner or Southerner, and the great question that confronts us is, What will the black man do? You, Senator Bruce, say all of you stay here and wait for better times. I say, let us pray God and man to pass the bill of Senator Butler, and let a line of steamships be started between here and Africa, and let such of us as believe we are not monkeys, and can do something without the white man's domination, go and try the experiment. Give me five millions of dollars, and let the several States turn over to me all the colored penitentiary convicts, and I will carry them to

Africa and inaugurate a republic that your son, Roscoe Conkling Bruce, can be president of some day.

The Roman Empire began with such material, and the sequel you know. Surely Senator Bruce will not object to the penitentiary convicts going, and they will go, too, if you give them a chance.

Pardon the length of this letter. I have just noticed its space, yet it scarcely touches the points I would like to discuss in your interview. I will conclude, however, by saying that Senator Butler may fail in getting his bill through Congress, but, sooner or later, God will raise up a thousand Butlers, black and white, and hundreds of millions will be appropriated for that purpose, and you, Senator Bruce, great though you be, will be left standing as a harmless speck of a writhing negativity.

Let me say, however, what future any man can see here for the Negro, with a head as cool as you possess, and a brain as well balanced as yours, I cannot imagine, especially with every United States court armed to the teeth to crush him out of existence, and in the face of decisions that will run and last as long as the nation shall exist, that simply means his perpetual degradation or ultimate re-enslavement. What could Congress or the President do for us if they had the will to better our condition? What can all the people of the United States do for us when the court, as a last resort, declares that the Negro is a dog, and when no power in the nation can overrule their decision. You may rest your hopes upon the ignis-fatuus of times getting better, but I shall regard the evils complained of above as the voice of God and nature calling upon the Negro to arise and do something for himself, and Senator Butler and his bill as a heaven-send to our race.

H. M. TURNER
Atlanta, Ga., March 12

Colored National Convention Called: A Hundred Million Dollars (1893)

HISTORICAL CONTEXT

By 1893, Turner and other Black radical theologians had tied their faith to the practice of Black nationalism and the back-to-Africa movement. This ideology was accessible to Turner in the early twentieth century, as the AME Church had established and developed missions throughout Liberia. Turner traveled to Africa four times and was dedicated in his fight to raise money for the continent's development. As a military chaplain and state legislator, Turner had even sought out federal funds to aid Black emigration. This particular sermon is not in response to a singular lynching but to a rise in the number of African Americans being lynched. The year 1893 is considered a spike year, or a season in which lynching was very frequent, with more than 116 instances in that year.

SERMONIC RESPONSE

To the colored people of the United States in anguish, Greeting:

On the 18th of July last the undersigned issued a notice through the public press, to the friends of African repatriation or Negro nationalization elsewhere. That owing to the dreadfully, horrible, anomalous and unprecedented condition of our people in the United States, it would seem, that some common action; move or expression on our part as a race, is demanded. The revolting, hideous, monstrous, unnatural, brutal and shocking crimes charged upon us daily on the one hand, and the reign of mobs, lynchers, and fire-fiends, and mid-night and mid-day assassins on the other, necessitated a national convention upon our part, for the purpose of crystalizing our sentiments and unifying our endeavors for better conditions in this country or a change of base for existence.

The history of the world furnishes no analogy for the state of things transpiring in this country. The bloody reign of Queen Mary, the horrible massacre of St. Bartholomew's Day, nor the bloody orgies of the world present no parallel. For they were political, religious or civil persecutions, while ours is upon the plea of most revolting crimes perpetrated.

Therefore, if we are the execrable demons as is alleged through the public press daily, the facts should be impartially investigated and unquestionably established, and we should do it ourselves; and if our guilt is established, and mobs are indispensable to the eradication of our hideous crimes, we should constitute our own mobs and punish our own culprits; and free white men from that villainous task, as a large majority of us have always been law-respecting and law-abiding.

But on the other hand, if after rigid investigation, we find that our race is not guilty of the indictments as charged, we should so inform mankind throughout the world. For as we are now represented we occupy the status of incarnate friends to such an extent that not only civilized man would be justified in loathing us, but heathen savages of the lowest order, might well shun us; and we ourselves might reasonably charge God with folly, if not for cruelty, for creating such monstrosities and perpetuating our existence by supplying us with food to eat, raiment to wear and air to breathe.

At all events, while other people are saying so much about us, and doing so much effecting our destiny we as a free and distinct race should meet in council and say or do something ourselves; otherwise, mankind will rightly decide that we are not only an inferior race, but hopelessly ignorant, woefully degraded and a set of such inhuman brutes that we are not fit to be the vassals of canibals. Further silence upon our part would be an outrage upon our posterity and a scandalous shame upon our race now living.

Therefore, in consideration of the fact that in harmony with the previous proposition, over three hundred letters and postal cards (307) have been received from every state in the Union except Maine, New Hampshire, Rhode Island, Connecticut and Oregon—from Bishops, ministers of the gospel, of judges, lawyers, ex-congressmen and persons, including white and Black, recommending such a Council, most of whom suggested Cincinnati, Ohio, as the most central and convenient point for all parts of the country.

We, in the name of too many persons to mention individually, invite our people in the respective states, territories and District of Columbia to send twenty-five sober, thoughtful intelligent, race-respecting and honorable delegates to meet in National Council at Cincinnati, Ohio, November 28th, at 12 m., and there assemble to review and pass upon our condition patiently, impartially, and to report truthfully our knowledge of every person murdered by mobs and lynchers, and when and what for, with documentary evidence, if possible, for the use of the committee or committees, as will have such matters in hand.

We also call upon such white men as have participated in these mobs, lynchings and lawless murders, to meet us at the same time and place and show the reason why they have thus participated, which they will not hesitate or refuse to do if they are justified by their conscience and are satisfied at their rectitude in the premises, as we desire to inaugurate a reformation among our people if we can be satisfied they are guilty as charged.

We trust all point-of-order raisers, interrupters of persons allotted the floor, cheap notoriety seekers and irritable or hot-headed squallers, will not be sent to the said Council, as we have no time to bother with such persons. Matters are too solemn. It is also presumed somebody will be elected chairman who has judgment and experience enough to preside over the Council intelligently and creditably. The venerable Bishop Payne well writes: "Take care some inexperienced and hot-headed speaker does not say something that will be regarded as the expression of the whole race, and cause much harm." Let us avoid such a contingency, if possible.

As to how these delegates will be selected, we leave to the several states; but should over twenty-five meet the council from any one state, they will only be allowed half or quarter votes according to the number. Scores of letters have requested that a number of select men should be designated from each state to meet in Council; but that would not be a representative body. We need a representative body now, as never before, as we are confronted with awful issues. For if we are so corrupt and infernalize, that we cannot exist here and no reformation is possible, in this country, rather than be exterminated by mobs and lynching assassins, we had better ask Congress, or the Nation, for at least a hundred million of dollars to leave this country if we can go no further than Canada, which Dr. Derrick is so eloquently advocating, and where we are assured we would be so cordially welcomed, or over to Mexico, where we are offered a whole State, if we will accept it. Therefore a representative body is an absolute necessity to enable the delegates not only to speak for themselves and to petition congress of themselves, if found necessary, but for a constituency, even if that constituency should be limited to one million persons. Moreover, it is presumable that a portion of our people, like all other peoples, will take no interest in the Council—for reasons satisfactory to themselves, and we should exercise much reluctance in speaking for them; hence the indispensability of a constituency, that each delegate may know that he speaks and acts for himself and for others at home.

We recommend as much as possible, that each delegate who may expect to occupy the floor, prepare his speech in manuscript before leaving him, so that any attempt to misrepresent him may be thwarted by his written or prepared speech.

This council or convention will have no political character whatever. Those who wish to discuss party politics will please look for another platform for occupancy, as our meeting will be as far above politics as heaven is above earth.

Please allow the immediate writer of this call for a national Council to beg the delegates who may attend, what ought to be the gravest convention ever held by our people in America, to come self-possessed, cool-headed and resolved to mutual respect. Let no man, who uses ardent spirits, dream of attending unless he can promise his God that he will not touch the accursed cup while the Council is in session, for it will be no place for unbalanced men. States, communities or sections sending delegates, we hope, will see they are amply supplied with funds to creditably meet their expenses and return home like gentlemen at the close of the session, which may be a week, or until we get through, at all events. Papers please copy.

"Negroes, Get Guns!" (*Voice of Missions,* 1897)

HISTORICAL CONTEXT

John Johnson, Archibald Jointry, and Gustave Williams were lynched in Tangipahoa Parish, Louisiana, on January 1, 1897. The three Black men were accused of murder but were never brought to court. Instead, they were taken from their cells and their bodies were later found hanging and riddled with bullets. Two days prior, an unnamed person had been hanged in Iberville Parish, Louisiana, ninety-eight miles from Tangipahoa, on the charge of attempted murder and robbery. There is no evidence that connects the two lynchings, though the proximity of the two locations demonstrates cultural support for Judge Lynch in the region. There would be twelve people lynched in Louisiana in 1897, and 360 from 1880 to 1911. Turner, who was familiar with Louisiana and lived in New Orleans in 1857, took these heinous acts personally. When this particular lynching took place, he was but a few miles away conducting a meeting with AME bishops. This is his response.

SERMONIC RESPONSE

The fiendish lynching of John Johnson and Archibald Jointry upon mere suspicion, in Louisiana, while the African Methodist Episcopal Bishops were meeting in New Orleans only a few miles from the scene of blood and death, was most damnable.

Let every negro in this country with a spark of manhood in him supply his house with one, two, or three guns or with a seven or a sixteen shooter, and we advise him to keep them loaded and ready for immediate use, and when his domicile is invaded by bloody lynchers or any mob by day or by night, Sabbath or week day, turn loose your missiles of death and blow your fiendish invaders into a thousand jiblets.

Negroes should defend themselves with guns against the lynch mob. Blacks should acquire guns and keep them loaded and ready for immediate use. Get guns Negros, get guns, and may God give you good aim when you shoot.

We have had it in our mind to say this for over seven years, but on account of our Episcopal status we hesitated to express ourselves thus, fearing it would meet the disapproval of the House of Bishops. But their approval or disapproval has done nothing to stop the fiendish murderers who stalk abroad and are exterminating my race, so we have now said it, and hereafter we shall speak it, preach it, tell it, and write it. Again we say, Get guns, negroes! get guns, and may God give you good aim when you shoot.

The African Question Again (Christian Recorder, June 21, 1883)

HISTORICAL CONTEXT

Turner frequently challenged Black constituents on the benefits of Black nationalism and the importance of the back-to-Africa movement. This letter defends Black emigration as a solution for racial caste lynching violence—and
was warranted until the government or armed Black communities achieved
protection. Turner also described Black people who were unwilling to fight as
having no faith and being "riffraff white-men worshipers," or people who had
become so docile they had no ability to fight against degradation and dehumanization. Instead, to fight against lynching, for Turner, defined true manliness and character. This examination demonstrates the variety of Black uplift
rhetoric in the late nineteenth century.

SERMONIC RESPONSE

Rev. G. W. Offley, I have just read your letter in THE CHRISTIAN RECORDER of
the 10th inst., endorsing my position upon the question of union between
the A.M.E. and A.M.E.Z. Churches, and thank you for your complimentary references to myself, &c. But there are a few sentences in the letter I beg to notice
a little, a thing, however, I seldom do, be they compliments or criticisms, especially when they are so devoid of reason and even thought as several I have
read of late. But to the point; you say, "Bishop Turner says and does many good
things, and I for one do not feel like casting stones at him, because the majority
of our thinkers disagree with him on the African Question." Thank you, sir; I
shall ever be grateful. Again you say, "It (the union) is a much more important
subject than that of emigrating en masse to Africa, for we are not going to do
that," &c. Thank you again. I am glad to know it; for if all the riffraff white-men
worshipers, aimless, objectless, selfish, little souled and would be white Negroes of this country were to go to Africa, I fear it would take a chiliad of years
to get them to understand that a black man or woman could be somebody
without the dictation of a white man. For the truth is, two-thirds of our race
have no faith in themselves, and because they have none in themselves individually, they do not have any in each other. To them the white man is all and
in all, therefore, it is useless to attempt to be any body, especially where the

white man does not hold away; and where he does away the scepter of power, he uses it to the degradation and dehumanization of the black race. The whole tendency of our ignoble status in this country is to develop in the Negro mean, sordid, selfish, treacherous, deceitful and cranksided characteristics. There is not much real manhood in the far more learning and general intelligence, I grant, but far less race patriotism, and wherever race patriotism, and whatever race patriotism does not exist among a people treachery in its worst form does. The American Negro does not possess half the respect for himself today he did fifteen years ago, and it only requires a little sober sense to see it.

You virtually say to the people, "Come, let us hear what Bishop Turner has to say about the union. Do not shut your ears and refuse to hear him because he is an African emigrationist. He does say some good things at times if he is an African monomaniac." Oh, how good you are; I can never forget your kindness. But possibly you do not know that I have been talking and writing in this same strain for twenty three years. Ever since I preached upon "The Redemption of Africa and the Means to be Employed," before the Philadelphia Conference in Bethel Church in the spring of 1860, and received the congratulations of Elders J. P. Campbell, Wm. Moore, Richard Roberson, and a host of other good and great men who are mostly gone to the heavenly land; men, too, who were proud of their race and not ashamed of their color or ancestry; men whose religion was broad and Christ-like enough to comprehend humanity if a portion of it is Black.

You further say, "I for one do not feel like casting stones at him because the majority of our thinkers disagree with him on the African question." Thinkers, thinkers; did you say thinkers? Possibly you meant non thinkers. You remind me of some other correspondents whose letters I read a few weeks since in the CHRISTIAN RECORDER with a list of great names burdened with an array of titles that might have frightened a Bacon, had some of the parties referred to not been distinguished for never giving their race an original idea in their lives. And, what was more ludicrous, Dr. Garnet, who prayed for God to spare his life to reach Africa and die, and Rev. T. McCants Stewart, now on his way to Africa, were referred to as opponents of my position. Thinkers! Thinkers! Thinkers!!

I am inexpressibly pleased to have the endorsement of your able pen on the union question, but when you assume that my African sentiments in the least detracts from my standing in the A.M.E. Church, you are only a little mistaken. I have been ordained deacon, elder, Bishop and D.D.'d, all by the A.M.E.

Church since my opinions and sentiments have been made public, as well as elected General Manager of our Publication Department. Had there been a disposition to caste stones at me on that scale, it would have been done years ago, by men, too, who were able to do it, and at a time and under circumstances that would have hurt. The truth is, they see that something will have to be done, that a revolution is inevitable; that our present status, much less our condition is intolerable; that it never has been endured in peace by any people since time began; that all the hush and be quiet advocates offer no remedy for existing evils; that there must be an outlet, a theatre of manhood and activity established somewhere for our young men and women; that we cannot school and graduate our children eternally to be waiters, sleeping car porters, field hands, boot blacks, wash women, nurses of white children, chamber maids, room sweepers and for such like positions as will ruin our daughters and degrade our sons; that as long as we fill such a station of degradation there will never be accorded us any recognition of us that people will not invite their cooks, nurses, chamber maids, carriage drives and porters into their parlors to associate with their guests. All this, and much more, a large portion of our people see. I travel this country and talk with thousands and know whereof I speak. I have seen men sit down and cry because they were compelled to hire their daughters out as nurses and chamber maids, after spending all they had to give them an education. I have seen beautiful young graduates thus hired return home after a few months of such service well, I will not say, but you can think. The thinkers can think any way.

Now, what is my position? Simply to found and establish a country or a government somewhere upon the continent of Africa, as I see no other place in the world to do it, where our young men and ladies can find a theatre of activity and usefulness, and commence a career for the future that will meet the wants of posterity, at the same time build up a center of Christian civilization that will help to redeem the land of our ancestry. All this jargon about "Bishop Turner trying to get all us colored people out of the United States" is not only nonsense, but absolutely false. But it seems that some people cannot understand how some of us can go, without all going. The same parity of reasoning would imply, because some of us have been hung, all of us must be hung; because some of us got to the jail, penitentiary or hades, all must go. Such persons must think the Negro race is a flock or heard of sheep; because one jumps off the London Bridge, all must jump off and get drowned. No wonder Bishop Campbell says clannishness is the curse of the race. Every solitary writer who has been trying to excoriate me for my African sentiments, have done so under the huddle idea, "He wants us all to go to Africa." The idea of building up a government of a half million civilized Christian people upon the continent of Africa, where we can have our own high officials, dignitaries, artisans, mechanics, corporations, railroads, telegraphs, commerce, colleges, churches &c., &c., has never entered the brain of these maligners and misrepresenters nor have they ever thought of the glory that would accrued to the whole race from such a seat of power and influence. Yet, they are great thinkers, thinkers, thinkers. Strange that a dozen Minervas do not leap from the brain of each one. O, for some Parnassus peak where our sage thinkers could sit in peace and think forever.

Before I close this letter, allow me to revert to a paragraph of one of our thinkers' utterances which I read a few days ago. Shades of death, degradation, scandal, infamy, and all that is vile and mean, listen. Hear it, Erebus, son of Chaos and Darkness, for such stuff only suits thy domain.

"No, We are not going to leave this country, nor are we going to retain our present proscribed position in society. Those who suppose, however, that the remedy for our ills is to be found in national legislation or supreme court decisions, are greatly mistaken. There is a higher and more natural remedy than these. The true and only remedy is to bleach out; to be more specific, we are to lose the caste and features of the African by the absorption of the Caucasian races."

Gracious! What a solution of the Negro problem. Where did the men come from? Can he be a natural man? Let us see, however, how it will stand the test of analysis. Now, to be still more specific, our present proscribed position in society is disagreeable and repugnant, and there will be no ease or comfort while we retain it, and legislation and supreme court decisions cannot give the remedy, for the reason that the Negro is Black, and Black will override all the legislation and judicial decisions of the country forever, and to have our ills remedied, and find peace, happiness and security in this country, as we are not going to leave it, we must all turn white, bleach out by having the white race to absorb us. Now, if this is not a logical analysis of the position assumed above, I will confess my ignorance and will never essay anything of the kind again.

Well, come now and let us start to bleaching. A million of white wives are necessary to commence with. But let the Negro start to get them, and he will want to go to Africa or somewhere else before the sun goes down, for such shooting, hanging, lynching, burning and flow of blood has not been seen since the world began, and such a fuss and bustle as would arise from colored women has never been predicted. The white wives are therefore things of impossibility. I mean in such numbers as would serve the purpose of our thinkers. As it does not appear to be a very healthy job to supply our young men with white wives, suppose we get a million young Caucasian buckras to marry our daughters, sisters, cousins, nieces &c., but without drawing a ridiculous picture, I will just say, if anything, this is a more difficult feat to accomplish than the other. We are therefore left to follow the process that went on in slave times, and the man that advocates it ought to be hung. Now you had just as well open your eyes at once to this abominable doctrine as to wait longer. Every man who advocates the bleaching out of the Negro race, is an absolute fool, or he is a monster in human flesh. Yet I know of men who incline to these absurd opinions, that I believe to be good men at heart, but they are so dwarfed in intellect, so twisted in the idea that white is God, they have thought so narrowly, read so little philosophy, so destitute of a knowledge of the scientific operations of nature, have studied so little about the fitness of things in the economy of race relations, and man's complex unity, that they have no proper conception of the infernalness of their hateful theories. They do not seem to realize themselves as advocators of the meanest form of lasciviousness, and that they are infusing in our young the basest sentiments that were ever distilled in the devil's laboratory. They are worse than cannibals, more to be dreaded than wild tigers; their tongues are a thousand fold more poisonous than the fangs of a rattlesnake. Compared with the theory of the bleachers, emigration of Africa, to the Saharran desert, to the North Pole, to the middle of the sea, is as honey compared to gall for sweetness. They are pirates upon the high seas of life, moral robbers of household happiness, leaders to darkness and quicksands. They would thwart the purpose of God by the foulest treachery to all that makes life worth having; they propose to strip your vessel of its rudder and compass in the midst of a fearful storm, and turn you loose in the whirlpool of lecherous white men.

The above, though horrid in the extreme, is the mildest form in which I can present the teachings of that class of public vipers. Should any one take offence they are welcome to keep it for all I care. I am as much offended at them as they can possibly be at me. You, Rev. sir, will not regard these remarks as applying to you in any respect, for I do not class you as a bleacher, but I do hate the doctrine, and am forced to bitterness whenever I broach it.

2

REVERDY C. RANSOM

The Burning of Sam Hose (July 6, 1899)

HISTORICAL CONTEXT

Samuel Holt, or Sam Hose, was lynched in Coweta County, Georgia, in 1899. He was charged with the murder of his employer, Alfred Cranford, which Hose argued was self-defense. After he was apprehended in Marshallville, a mob captured Hose from officers and took him to a rural location to be tortured. This included severing Hose's ears, fingers, and genitals; removing his skin; and plunging knives repeatedly into his body. Finally, Hose was lynched, his body left in public view.

SERMONIC RESPONSE

Considerable interest has been aroused throughout the country over the action of colored citizens of Chicago, led on by Ida B. Wells-Barnett, to get the facts relating to the burning of Sam Hose in Georgia recently. I have received scores of letters inquiring as to the truth of our reported action. In reply to all interested I would say that we did send a detective to Georgia; that he spent several days at the scene of the lynching; conversed and mingled freely with the person who took part in the lynching, and has reported everything in relation thereto that it was possible for him to learn. He has established the fact that Cranford met his death at the hand of Hose as the result of a dispute over wages; that Hose was not, therefore, a hired assassin, and that assault upon Cranford's wife played no part as a motive to the crime. Any one desiring a copy of this report may secure it by addressing Mrs. Ida B. Wells-Barnett, 2939 Princeton Ave., Chicago, Ill.

While on this subject, I take occasion to refer to some alleged statements of mine in a lecture recently delivered at Cleveland, O. I understand that I have been quoted as advising colored people to use dynamite upon the white people of the South. No man in his senses would urge a race war, or advise the Negroes of the South to attack the whites of the South. But some of my friends informed me that I have greatly injured myself by suggesting that the time would come when colored men would exercise every God-given instinct of self-protection and refuse to yield up human life without protest or resistance.

What I said was that the colored newspaper man who fled from Wilmington, should have stood his ground and died by his press if need be, like Lovejoy did at Alton, Ill.; and that I feared that if mobs continued to lynch and burn Negroes with impunity, as they are doing now, that in time Negroes would learn the use of dynamite and hurl it into the mobs who came to drag them from their homes. Surely there is nothing dangerous in such a statement as this. I had much rather be condemned for standing by utterances that will meet spontaneous approval of a very manly man, than to be damned by the approval and applause which the utterances of some of our time-servers provoke.

Chicago has had the good fortune to have recently within her borders some distinguished Afro-American clergymen. Rev. T. A. Wilson, pastor of Union Bethel, New Orleans, spent more than a week with us and preached two sermons in Bethel, much to the delight of all. Rev. L. H. Reynolds, D.D., of New Orleans, at one time pastor of Bethel church, this city, spent the first Sunday in June with us here.

Dr. J. Albert Johnson, pastor of Metropolitan A.M.E. church, Washington, D.C., returned from Wilberforce commencement with us and took bachelor's quarters at our house, as our family was out of the city. He preached Sunday, June 18th, at both Bethel and Quinn Chapel, two sermons that Chicagoans will not soon forget. If by our union with the B.M.E. Church, we got nothing else except J. Albert Johnson, our connection has been broadened and enriched by the addition of this lofty soul and cultured brain. Dr. Johnson is not a seeker after place, but when the Church knows him and comes to appreciate his work, she will not withhold from him anything in her power to bestow. And if episcopal honors are ever bestowed upon him, they will have to come to him as they did to Bishop Lee; he will not seek them. At our request, he delivered in Bethel church, June 20th, the address which he delivered before the Alumni Association at Wilberforce, the previous week, on "The Testimony of Modern Science to the Christian View of the World." His sermon, the previous Sunday, had so stirred the people that the desire to hear him again was manifested by the audience which occupied every seat in Bethel church and the standing room in the aisles. The address is indeed a masterpiece, the ablest deliverance we have ever heard from a colored man upon the scientific theme.

R. C. RANSOM

The Atlanta Riot: A Philippic on the Atlanta Riot (September 28, 1906)

HISTORICAL CONTEXT

The Atlanta riot started on September 24, 1906, and continued until September 26. Dozens of Black citizens would be killed, while hundreds more would be wounded. The riot was encouraged over a surge in Black population, including job competition among lower-class white workers. The pretext for the riot began with the reported assaults of a local white woman on September 22. Historically, these claims have exhibited themselves to be unsubstantial. Nonetheless, the response was the development of white mobs across the city, and they violently targeted Black-owned businesses. Many notable descriptions of the riot have been recorded, including a depiction by Walter White and W. E. B. Du Bois. Reverdy Ransom also shared his experiences in a sermon.

SERMONIC RESPONSE

A Philippic on the Atlanta Riot. Delivered in Faneuil Hall, Boston, Massachusetts

A few short months have passed since one of the fairest cities of the republic was shaken to its foundations by a convulsion of nature. The sympathy awakened by this disaster was spontaneous and universal.

Today one of the most progressive and populous cities of the South is quivering from an eruption of human passion and the shedding of innocent blood. But for the most part the fountains of human sympathy are congealed. The tongue of public utterance is either palsied or vocal with explanations and apologies for a murderous mob, and advise caution and warning for those who are identified with its innocent victims.

We meet tonight within these walls to express our indignation and horror at the wounding, maiming and slaughter of the innocent and unoffending Negroes of Atlanta, Ga., by the hands of their fellow-citizens. If I could frame sentences which could sting like an adder, and hiss and bite like a serpent, they could not enough express my condemnation of the people who performed these lawless deeds.

For years the South has sought to justify itself before the world, and shield its outrages upon the Negro behind the charge of crimes committed against women. Frederick Douglass declared more than twenty years ago that the South was seeking to rob the Negro of the sympathy of the world by branding him as being peculiarly given to assault upon women.

So persistently and so successfully have they worked this charge that the prophecy of Frederick Douglass has been fulfilled.

The pulpit and press have been largely silenced. The voice of public protest has been stilled, so that today, from the depths of infamy which has been heaped upon us as a people, there arises the voices of timerous and time-serving Negroes, who find that the shortest road to popular approval and applause is to join with the villifiers of their race in denouncing them for crimes which, in ninety-five cases out of one hundred, there is no conclusive evidence have ever been committed by them.

This American butchery is without palliation or excuse.

It was deliberately planned and executed.

Its victims were neither suspected nor charged with a commission of any crime. Their only crime was their color. The men who are guilty before God and should stand convicted before the bar of just public opinion, are the politicians, who in the time of peace and amicable relations between the races, deliberately manufactured the race issue, appealing to the passions and prejudices of the whites against the Blacks for the sole purpose of political effect and to gratify personal ambition.

They brought to their aid the newspaper press and held up the Negro in such an unfavorable light that even the minds of the children were inflamed. Reports sent out by the bureaucracy of Russia are no more false and misleading, no more cunningly devised and shameless, than are southern press dispatches and southern publications wherever they touch the Negro question.

The reason that the race question is so acute today is because there has not been enough plain speaking, of vigorous and courageous action. Self-interest, expediency, cowardice and indifference, have told the Negro when his constitutional rights are invaded that he must surrender with the hope of regaining them at some distant day; when humiliated and degraded by all forms of Jim Crowism he is told that he must meet it with patient submission; when lynched, burned and slaughtered, he is told to keep silent and warned against making any effort at self-defense.

In times of race disturbances it is quite evident that the Negro can expect no protection or defense from the legally constituted authorities. If he is to be credited with the instincts of a brute, much less the impulse of a human being, it is his duty to defend himself.

If the Negro will stand up for himself, a host will stand with him. If he permits himself to be chased, beaten and slain without resistance, he will be left, deserted and despised.

I with others upon this platform here tonight have been solemnly to apologize to a band of murderers; we are not here, almost in the shadow of the victims they have slain, to find any palliation for their crimes; we are not here to give respectful salute to the state militia of Georgia, who have brutally assaulted unoffending Negroes, and fraternized with the mob who slew them, taking from them by force the weapons they had with which to defend their lives, their families and their homes.

Faneuil Hall is no place from which to issue an apology to a lawless community which has trampled law and order beneath its feet, and where the exhibition of brutality is a repudiation the of the Christian spirit and a menace to the very existence of civilization.

The blacks have no hatred against the whites. They are naturally a peaceful people, but if these outrages continue and the authorities fail to protect them, while depriving them of their arms with which to protect themselves, the Negro will learn, as others have learned, the manufacture and use of that instrument. We do not advise retaliation, but we do advise self defense. In the dark days of the nation's history Longfellow reminded us to

Beware! The Israelite of old, who tore
The lion in his path—when, poor and blind,
He saw the blessed light of heaven no more,
Shorn of his strength and forced to grind,
In prison, and at last led forth to be
A pander to Philistine revelry,

Upon the pillars of the temple laid
His desperate hands, and in the overthrow
Destroyed himself, with those who made
A cruel mockery of his sightless woe;
The poor, blind Slave, the scoff and jest of all,
Expired, and thousands perished in the fall.

The growing locks and clearing vision of this black Sampson is making him conscious of his strength and power. If he is doomed to forever grind the Philistines' corn and to be a victim of their cruel sports, he would prefer, like Sampson of old, to lay hold of the pillars of America's temple of Dagon and to die with the Philistines.

Respect for law and justice in the United States is not dead.

To this sentiment we address our appeal. Such events as the Atlanta riot have amply vindicated the wisdom of the men who framed and passed the Fifteenth Amendment to the Constitution.

If this nation has the will, it can find a way to preserve a republican form of government in all the states of this union, and protect the lives and liberties of its citizens. It is the duty of the nation now to see to it that once and for all time the Negro is made secure in the free enjoyment of the elective franchise.

It is only by this he will be able to preserve the respect of his fellow citizens and to guarantee protection to his life and property.

No better illustration can we have of this than the leaders of the Atlanta mob who remonstrated with the chief of the fire department who had turned the hose upon them, to desist upon the ground that they had voted for him for mayor. Until the Negro has a voice in the choice of city, county, state, and national officials, he will continue to be the victim of injustice and oppression.

The Negroes greatest present need is not money and property, it is not even education; it is a voice in the community through the exercise of the franchise with which to make himself secure.

I do not believe that this outbreak in Atlanta is either the last or the worst that is to come. The Negro's chief protection in the South today is poverty. If he were to largely engage in mercantile pursuits, having shops, stores and banks, the mob would find a ready pretext to assail him in order to loot, to plunder and to steal.

It is a fact that the most worthless white man in the South is taught to believe, and does believe, that he is better than the most decent, intelligent and law-abiding Negro.

Nothing that the Negro can do, either through character, intelligence or wealth, will change the attitude of the South toward him. The Negro demands, and has a right to demand of this nation, from the president down, "a square deal."

The present state governments of the South are an oligarchy in this republic. It is they, and not the Negro, who are a menace to the nation.

When the Negro is as free to exercise the right of the ballot in Georgia as he is in Massachusetts he will exercise it there as he exercises it here, in the interest of his community, his state and of his country.

The South is not the natural home of the Negro. A man is most at home where he is free so to enjoy life, liberty and the pursuit of happiness. America was settled, and is inhabited today by people who were either voluntary or involuntary emigrants from Great Britian, Europe and Africa. When white men were the victims of tyranny and oppression, they no longer regarded Europe as their natural home; they braved every peril of land and sea in order to secure to themselves freedom upon these shores.

When their oppressors pursued them to their new home they rose in revolution against them, threw off their yoke and drove them into the sea. They and their descendants have made America their natural home.

There are more than a million Negroes who are happy, prosperous and secure in all their rights, living north of Mason and Dixon line. When the South kills the Negro in the most wanton and brutal manner, degrades him as human being, despoils him of his constitutional rights, compels him to labor for a minimum of pay, and thus defrauds him in the contracts of labor, he cannot regard it as his natural home. When Pharaoh oppressed the Israelites, God did not send Moses to counsel patient submission to their oppressors, but he told him to deliver them out of his hands. God told Joseph and Mary to take the young child Jesus and flee into Egypt for Herod would seek his life.

So we say to our people today, rise and emigrate from Georgia, for Hoke Smith and his mob will seek your life. We say to our people rise and depart from Mississippi for Vardaman seeks your destruction. Leave the rice swamps of the Carolinas while Tillman boasts of your destruction and murder in the Senate of the United States. Millions of Negroes can find liberty, prosperity and peace in the states east, west and north. They could breathe new life into the abandoned farms of New England. Michigan could easily assimilate 50,000. Ohio and Illinois have room for many more. Wisconsin, Minnesota, Kansas and Nebraska and the far west have millions of sleeping harvests in their soil which await the touch of willing hands.

If the European emigrants a short time after their arrival here, can assist in transporting millions of their countrymen to these shores, we can also advise, assist, and encourage millions of our people to leave the South. Why should the Negro save money in a community where it will not pass only under cer-

REVERDY C. RANSOM   43

tain galling limitations? Why should he own land which he cannot control, or possess property where he can neither protect nor defend it, or live where his life is less sacred than the life of a dog?

Our ancestors and our kindred lived in the midst of the largest and most ferocious beasts and reptiles of the earth. They live today in the midst of swamps and marshes and the most unhealthy conditions of the South. If they have survived there, they can survive immigration into the sections of our country where they will at least be protected in life and made secure in the enjoyment of the fruits of their toil.

Heaven cannot look upon us with an approving smile if we remain silent and inactive while our women may be insulted and degraded without rebuke, our children stamped with the birth cubie of inferiority, our kindness and patience taken as a signed subjection, every right guaranteed us by law ruthlessly trampled under foot, while we are hunted down and slain like wild beasts of prey.

Against the storms of passion and prejudices which rage about us, we must throw out our anchor and drag the chain until it touches the bottom, resting upon the principles of equality and justice upon which this nation was founded.

The Spirit of John Brown: A Speech Delivered by Reverdy C. Ransom Before the Second Annual Meeting of the Niagara Movement (August 17, 1906)

HISTORICAL CONTEXT

The Niagara Movement was founded in 1905 in response to the Bookerite conservatism that was growing in influence among African Americans. Led by W. E. B. Du Bois and William Monroe Turner, the organization opposed racial segregation and believed voting rights to be an instrumental need for the Black community. The second national meeting of the organization took place in 1906 in Harpers Ferry, West Virginia, at the site of the John Brown raid. The location was intentional, as Brown had become a hero among African American reformers who sought to take on racial caste oppression in a radical manner. Most of the organization's membership utilized education as their tool of agitation, but religious leadership was also encouraged. Ransom was invited to give the keynote speech at this event, and much of his focus fell on the practice of lynching in the southeastern states. Ransom supported the concept that physical protection (shooting out of self-defense) was an acceptable practice for Christians as long as the violence was not initiated.

SERMONIC RESPONSE

Great epochs in the world's history are hinged upon some spot of land or sea, which becomes historic and sacred forever more. There are Mt. Sinai and Mt. Calvary, the Jordan, the Euphrates, the Nile and Rubicon, Thermopylae, Runnymede, Waterloo, Gettysburg, Appomattox, Port Arthur and Manila Bay; WHILE JOHN BROWN HAS MADE HARPER'S FERRY AS CLASSIC AS BUNKER HILL.

The leonine soul of this old hero saint and martyr proves how important and defenseless are tyranny, injustice and wrong, even when upheld by the sanction of the law, supported by the power of money and defended by the sword.

If modern history furnishes a solitary example of the appearance of a man who possessed the spirit of the prophets of ancient Israel, it is John Brown. The sublime courage with which he met the Goliath of slavery in mortal combat, was not surpassed by that of David, who went forth to meet the Philistine who had defied the armies of the living God. He was commissioned by the same authority, and bore the same credentials as did Moses, who left his flocks in the Midian Desert to go and stand before Pharoah and demand in the name of "I Am That I Am" that he should free his slaves.

John Brown left his flocks and fields at Mt. Elba, New York and fought at Osawatomie to make the soil of Kansas free; at Harper's Ferry where his brave followers fought and fell, he delivered a blow against slavery in the most vital part, and fired the gun whose opening shot echoed the sound of the death knell of slavery.

Melchizedek of Modern World

This old Puritan, whose steel gray eyes gleamed with the spirit and courage that possessed Cromwell at the battle of Dunbar, took literally "the sword of the Lord and of Gideon," as both battle cry and watchword. Men like John Brown appear only ONCE OR TWICE IN A THOUSAND YEARS. Like Mt. Blanc, the king of the mountains, he towers high above the loftiest figure of his time. The place he occupied in the affairs of men is unique. He is the Melchizedek of the modern world. He had no predecessors and can have no successors. Any picture of him which does not have its proper setting amid the background of his time, makes him appear Quixotic, rather than the heroic figure that he was.

A Man of Action

Like Moses, Joshua, Cromwell and Touissaint l'Ouverture, he defies classification. He belonged to no party, was a disciple of no school, he was swayed neither by precedent nor convention. He was a man of achievement, of action. Garrison could write and Beecher could preach, while the silver-toned voice of Phillips pleaded; this man performed the DOING OF IT. He could not choose his course; the hand of the Almighty was upon him. He felt the breath of God upon his soul and was strangely moved. He was imbued with the spirit of the Declaration of Independence, and clearly saw that slavery was incompatible with a free republic. He could not reconcile the creed of the slaveholder with the word of God. While dealing with the border ruffians of Kansas he had seen the slave power seek to justify itself and extend its sway, by the murder of peaceful citizens; he had seen the prairies, illuminated at night by the flames of their burning homes, their crops destroyed and their cattle and valuables stolen.

An "Act of God" Needed

The government was cognizant of this and also acquiescent. Statesmen, and politicians were making concessions and compromises to quiet the demands of the South in behalf of its cherished institution. The nation found itself bound to a body of death whose foul decay was spreading its influence to the highest sources of its life. No time then for Missouri compromises and Kansas and Nebraska acts; what was needed then was an ACT OF ALMIGHTY GOD. Slavery leaning upon the arm of law was defiant, it could only be attacked by appealing to "the higher law." John Brown appealed.

Traitor to Country to Be True to Slave

God sent him to Harper's Ferry to become a traitor to the government in order that he might be true to the slave. This nation was established by men who took up arms to fight against a tax on tea, and the universal verdict of mankind approves their action. When John Brown fought at Harper's Ferry he commanded his immortal band with the SWORD OF FREDERICK THE GREAT, which had been presented to George Washington, and posterity has given him a fame no less secure than that of these two great captains who unsheathed in no worthier cause.

It has been fifty years since Osawatomie, and fifty years, less three, since an old man, whose austere manner and flowing beard gave him prophetic mien, INTRODUCED HARPER'S FERRY TO HISTORY. Since then the armies of North and South have marched across the country in a robe of fire and blood, to fall upon the field of battle locked in the embrace of a death of lead and iron.

Brown a Puritan

The true value and merit of a man lie embalmed and treasured up in the life he lived, and the character of the service he rendered to mankind. The whole life of John Brown was serious and purposeful. He was a descendant of one of the company who landed from the Mayflower at Plymouth Rock, and from ancestors who fought in the Revolutionary war. He had all of the moral uprightness and strict religious character of the Puritan, as well as his love of liberty and hatred of oppression and tyranny.

From a child he loved to dwell beneath the open sky. The many voices of the woods, and fields, and mountains, spoke to him a familiar language. He understood the habits of plants and animals, of birds, and trees, and flowers, and dwelt with them upon terms of familiarity and friendship. His heredity and environment were just such a school as was needed to shape his character and prepare him for his God-appointed task. For he believed himself to be sent upon a MISSION UNDER THE AUTHORITY OF HEAVEN. When he wrought like a mighty man of valor, whether in Kansas or at Harper's Ferry, he believed with all the modesty of his truly great and heroic soul, that he was only doing his duty. He proved the sincerity of his motives, the unselfishness of his purpose and his entire devotion, by sacrificing upon the altar of human freedom his money, goods, wife and children. When God's clock struck the hour, he acted. The friends of freedom cried "ill-timed, premature"; education and respectability shouted, "monomaniac, madman, fool!" Posterity hails him hero, and crowns him martyr saint.

Armed Slave to Free Himself

The distinctive act which has given the name of John Brown to immortality was his attempt to organize AND ARM THE SLAVES TO RAISE AND STRIKE FOR THEIR FREEDOM. This deed aroused the nation and STARTLED THE WORLD. His was not an attempt to assist them to break their chains in order to flee to Canada, but to forcibly assert and maintain their freedom in the Southland where they had been held as slaves.

The Negro will never enjoy the fruits of freedom in this country until he first demonstrates his manhood and maintains his rights here IN THE SOUTH, where they are the most violently protested and most completely denied.

What is to be the final status of the Negro in this country cannot be settled in New England, or settled in the North. There will be no rest or peace, or harmony upon this question until it is settled, and settled justly, ON SOUTHERN SOIL, where the great majority of the Negro Americans make their home.

Rights Must Be Won in South

In the days of John Brown a handful of slaves found freedom in flight to Canada and the North. But this did not change the condition of the enslaved millions, or the attitude of their cruel oppressors, while it did cause the supreme court of the United States to make every white man of the North a detective and an agent of the South, in the detection, capture and surrender of fugitive slaves.

Today Negroes are coming North in increasing numbers. But this does not change or modify a revised constitution in any Southern State, abolish one Jim-Crow car or stop a single lynching. In the days of slavery the Negro had a few devoted friends in the North and also in the South, but those in the South dare not speak or act; while some in the North were outspoken, they were backed by no public opinion which would support radical action. So today, the Negro has sympathetic friends and helpers, but public opinion nowhere sustains agitation or action against the conditions that prevail.

Nothing New in Country's Attitude

The present manner of dealing with the Negro question is nothing but the old method in a new disguise. The former attitude of the North was to confine the institution of slavery within the boundaries it occupied and to permit the inhabitants of new territory to settle the question among themselves. Today the South is unmolested in its disfranchising constitutions, by which two score seats are occupied in congress in violation of the constitution. The Jim-Crow car is also kept within these borders.

President Never Mentioned Suffrage

While no President has been so voluminous a writer of messages to Congress, or traveled so extensively in every section of the country, speaking freely and at length on a wide range of subjects, the present occupant of the White House has been ABSOLUTELY SILENT on the question of the enforcement of the Fifteenth Amendment; while his Secretary of War has admitted the violation of the constitution, he has recently in a notable address openly condoned it, if not tacitly, indeed, INDORSED it. On the admission of Oklahoma and the Indian Territory, as in the case of Kansas fifty years ago, the Negro question reappears, and it is never to be unconstitutional to separate the races in the public schools, which opens the door for legislation which will discriminate against the Colored citizen.

In the early sixties scores of Northern regiments and 185,000 Negro soldiers went into valorous action, singing as they marched, and fought and fell, "John Brown's body lies mouldering in the tomb, and his soul goes marching on." The dreams of this dreamer at last found fulfillment as his soul went marching on in the Proclamation of Emancipation, in the Thirteenth Amendment to the constitution abolishing slavery, Fourteenth Amendment bestowing citizenship, and the Fifteenth Amendment, giving the elective franchise to the Negro to protect and defend his citizenship and rights under the constitution and laws

It is, indeed, paradoxical that a nation which has erected monuments of marble and bronze to John Brown, Frederick Douglass, William Lloyd Garrison, Charles Sumner and other abolitionists; a nation which proclaims a holiday that all classes, including school children, may decorate with flowers the graves of the men who fought to preserve the Union, and to free the slaves; a nation which has enacted into organic law the freedom and political status of a race which has been bought with blood, now sits supinely down, silent and inactive, while the work of the liberators is ignored, while those who fought to destroy the government, REGAIN IN THE HALLS OF CONGRESS THE VICTORIES THEY LOST ON THE FIELD OF BATTLE, while the constitution is flouted and the Fifteenth Amendment brazenly trampled underfoot.

The Charter of Rights Annulled

It is thus that the charter of the Negroes' rights is being annulled. The North is busy with its money making and money getting. Northern manufacturers think more of the Southern market for their goods than of the rights of the loyal Negro citizen. Every few months a captured battle flag is returned to some Southern State, to be followed by a proclamation that the gulf between the North and South has disappeared and that the wounds of the war have been healed. SOUTHERN MEN are neither CAJOLED NOR FLATTERED—by these overtures. Their determination to refuse to recognize the political equality of the Negro remains unaltered, while their purpose to fix his social status and reduce him as far as possible to a condition of industrial serfdom is firm.

Political Action Needed

The Negro regards the Democratic party as his traditional and hereditary ire. Tradition, gratitude, sentiment, bind him to the Republican party with an idolatrous allegiance which is as blind as it is unpatriotic and unreasoning. TODAY THERE IS VERY LITTLE DIFFERENCE BETWEEN THE TWO PARTIES, SO FAR AS THEIR ATTITUDE TOWARD THE NEGRO IS CONCERNED. While the Republicans do not, perhaps, INITIATE legislation unfriendly to the Negro, neither do they, on the other hand, openly attack, defeat or VETO such legislation. It has been demonstrated repeatedly that a REPUBLICAN cabinet and a Republican Congress will make the Negro's civil and political rights a matter of barter and trade, to secure Democratic votes in the interest of tariff schedules, interstate policy relating to commerce, or some scheme of our expanded republic relating to its possessions and dark-skinned subjects in the islands across the Pacific Ocean.

Taft Calls Us Political Children

Secretary Taft, speaking for the President, chides us by saying that the Negroes are political children, that they have shown their incapacity to maintain their political rights. It is true that the Negro had a CHILDLIKE FAITH IN THE REPUBLICAN PARTY, believing that it would administer the sacred trust which the fortunes of war and the constitution had imposed upon it, and that it would not use him like a gambler's stake in the game of politics.

Scales Falling from Our Eyes

Thank God, at last the scales are falling from the Negro's eyes. He is being disillusioned by the acts of a REPUBLICAN CONGRESS, the speeches of members of a REPUBLICAN CABINET, and the silence of a REPUBLICAN PRESIDENT. He has reached his political majority. It is his patriotic duty to emancipate himself from his political fetich and cast his influence and his vote where they will make for the preservation of his liberty and the welfare of his country. He should not hesitate to REPUDIATE HIS FORMER FRIENDS, who have betrayed him, nor refuse to FRATERNIZE WITH FORMER ENEMIES, who are willing to give him aid. While he remains a political issue he must insist upon making his power felt and his rights respected.

Negroes Divided Among Themselves

There never has been a time when the American people have not sought to fix the status of the Negro in this country, in every phase of its life, within limitations and boundaries more or less definitely defined. But our fathers have told us that in the darkest days of slavery, when this nation fancied that they were contented with their lot, which they bore with much patience and submission, they secretly cherished the hope of some day reaching the goal which was set before their white fellow-countrymen.

There is not now, and never has been, any division among the Negroes as to the place they hope to occupy within this nation. But there is division among them as to methods and the choice of ways leading to the coveted goal. It was one of the defensive weapons of slavery to keep the Negroes divided among themselves, lest they unite to the injury and. destruction of that institution.

The race has not wholly survived this heritage, nor have the whites ceased in their efforts for division among us by pitting one Negro against another, and the condition in which, we are placed tends to make this practice more or less effective. The 10,000,000 Negroes in this land, despite their seeming acquiescence in the inequalities and restrictions placed upon them, are determined, if it takes a thousand years, to enter, as an equal, every avenue of American life.

Today two classes of Negroes, confronted by a united opposition, are standing at the parting of the ways. The one counsels patient submission to our present humiliations and degradations; it deprecates political activity, ignores or condones the usurpation and denial of our political and constitutional rights, and preaches the doctrine of industrial development and the acquisition of property, while it has no word of protest or condemnation for those who visit upon us all manner of fiendish and inhuman indignities.

This form of teaching is alike acceptable to the North and to the South. It tends to keep the Negro in his preconceived place, and eliminates him, both as a factor and a cause of irritation in politics and all that vitally relates to civic and social affairs.

Position of the Agitators

The other class believes that it should not submit to being humiliated, degraded and remanded to an inferior place. It neither seeks nor desires that a special place be made for it within this nation, separate and apart from other people. It believes in money and property, but it does NOT BELIEVE IN BARTERING ITS MANHOOD FOR THE SAKE OF GAIN. It believes in the gospel of work and in industrial efficiency, but it does NOT BELIEVE IN ARTISANS BEING TREATED AS INDUSTRIAL SERFS, and in laborers occupying the position of a peasant class. It does not believe that those who toil and accumulate will be free to enjoy the fruits of their industry and frugality, if they permit themselves to be shorn of political power.

Founded as this nation is it does not believe that submission to injustice, the surrender of rights for the sake of an opportunity to labor and save, is the road to the goal of the manhood and equality which we seek. It believes the Negro should assert his full title to American manhood, and maintain every right guaranteed him by the constitution of the United States, and having these, all other things will be added.

The White South Frank

However we may regard them, with most respect the frankness and honesty of the Southern people. They do not disguise their attitude. They boldly declare that they seek not to deceive the Negro, the nation or the world. However high the Negro's character and education, however large his accumulation of money and property, however industrious and efficient as a laborer, they do not intend to permit him to enjoy with them political equality, or any other kind of equality. They are not deceived by the Negroes who are seeking to DELUDE THEM BY SUBMISSION TO present conditions, in the hope of outflanking them by a circuitous march. The Negroes who are aggressively fighting for their rights have the press against them and the weight of public opinion. They are branded as disturbers of the harmony between the races, but they have the same spirit that animated the founders of this nation. IN THEM THE SOUL OF JOHN BROWN GOES MARCHING ON. Unless the Declaration of Independence is a lie. and the throne of Almighty God breaks down, they will at last take their place in our national household as an equal among their brethren.

Need Unusual Voice and Issue to Arouse Nation

Like the ghost of Hamlet's father, the spirit of John Brown beckons us to arise and seek the recovery of our rights, which our enemy, "with witchcraft of his wit. with traitorous gifts" has sought forever to destroy. John Brown was thought by many, even among his friends, to be insane. But an exhibition of such insanity was required to arouse the nation against the crime of slavery and to bring on the Civil War. NO WEAK AND ORDINARY VOICE CAN CALL THE NATION BACK TO A SENSE OF JUSTICE. A commonplace movement or event cannot influence or change the present attitude and current of the public mind.

Rights of Citizens the Battle-Cry

The rifle shot at Harper's Ferry received defiant answer from the cannon fired upon Fort Sumter. This nation needs a saint to be aroused. The friends of truth and justice must be rallied. But men cannot be rallied without a rallying cry: and even with this upon their lips, there must be a lofty standard to which they may resort. Can the hearts of men warm as earnestly to the cry of the rights of an American citizen, as they did to that of the freedom of the slave? Will the nation which could not tolerate the enslavement of human beings sanction the disenfranchisement of its citizens?

Abraham Lincoln set before this nation in its darkest hour the preservation of the Union as the standard for all loyal men. Can the men of the present take higher ground than to make secure the life and liberty of the black men who helped to sustain it when it was tottering to its fall?

The game of battle has been thrown down. The lines are clearly drawn; the supremacy of the constitution has been challenged. In fighting for his right the Negro defends the nation. His weapons are more powerful than pikes and Sharp's rifles which John Brown sought to place in his hands at Harper's Ferry. He has the constitution, the courts, the ballot, the power to organize, to protest and to resist. The battle before us must be fought, not on the principle of the INFERIORITY OF ONE RACE AND THE SUPERIORITY OF THE OTHER, but upon the ground of our common manhood and equality.

Socrates drained the cup of hemlock to its dregs; Jesus Christ suffered crucifixion on a cross; Savonarola was burned in the streets of Florence; and John Brown was hung from a gallows. But the cause for which they willingly became martyrs, the principles they advocated, and the truths they taught, have become the richest and most glorious heritage of mankind.

Before the strife and hatred of race and class have vanished, many will be called upon to wear the martyr's crown. A new birth of freedom within a nation is always accompanied with past suffering and pain. How much greater, then, the travail through which humanity must pass to bring forth its last and highest birth, for which all preceding ages have worked and waited until now.

We see it in the tyrant's face, in the oppressor's cruel wrongs; we read it in the statute books of every unjust law; we hear it in the strife of human conflict; we feel it in the universal aspiration of the soul; it comes to earth by many signs from heaven. The spirit of human brotherhood is unbarring the sprites of life to admit a civilization in which it can reign incarnate, while out of the many threads of human life upon this planet we are weaving the royal garments it shall wear.

Lynching and American Public Opinion (1926)

HISTORICAL CONTEXT

In this sermon Ransom takes a rather shocking stance on how to thwart Black lynching, which was for Black people to shoot back. According to Ransom, "Mobs do not quail when there is no fear that their wild brutalities will be answered by a volley of bullets." This particular ideology was also frequented by his church member, Ida B. Wells, who had made a history of suggesting the positives of Black Second Amendment rights.

SERMONIC RESPONSE

When Truth desired a hearing and Liberty a voice, men have in the past looked to Faneuil Hall. These walls have been articulate with the cry of the oppressed, not only of our country, but throughout the world. No spot on earth is more sacred to the cause of freedom and justice than the ground upon which we stand. While one stone rises above another here, Faneuil Hall will remain a standing challenge to tyrants and tyranny. By the high ideals it has championed, Faneuil Hall doctrine has done more than any other to make this country's history worth recording. The acts of Faneuil Hall audiences have done more to influence American public opinion in the right direction than have the acts of Congress.

With the flight of years a great transformation has been wrought in public sentiment and the personnel of the audiences assembled here. In the old days white audiences thronged these walls to hear white men, representing the best heart and brain of the nation, plead for liberty and justice for the poor oppressed blacks. Today the burden rests upon black men and women to come here and appeal to a public opinion and a public press, which is, for the most part, indifferent or hostile. Our appeal is for the supremacy of civilization over barbarism and savagery.

We are here not in the spirit of anger or of that discouragement which has abandoned hope. We are here not so much to denounce and assail, as to appeal to this nation to forsake its sins, to cast off its bloody robes of murder, to throw back into the deepest abysmal pit of hell its lyncher's torch and seek that righteousness that exalteth a nation.

The question that confronts us is older than the Declaration of Independence, the Magna Charta, or the laws of Moses upon the tables of stone; it goes back to the time when God beheld the blood of Abel crying from the ground. Can this nation, consecrated to freedom, afford to face the future with the mark of Cain branded upon its brow?

Lynching, which is fast becoming a national crime, reaches far beyond the helpless victim who perishes horribly by the fury of the mob. The question that most vitally concerns us is not one of race antipathy or sympathy; it concerns our Christianity, democracy and civilization itself. Some who object to protests of this kind tell us to make our people cease committing crimes against women, and then lynching will cease. But in eighty per cent of the lynchings this crime is not even alleged.

In approaching a question like that of the freedom with which Negroes may be put to death by mobs, we should seek for causes. We have not far to seek. Primarily, it sprang out of the desire of the former slave-holding states to repress the Negro. The South, in order to justify itself in these barbarities, began by blackening his character, by painting him as a monster who menaced the safety of women. By continually dinning this into the ears of this country and of the world, they have finally so quieted the public conscience that now a Negro charged with any crime, and sometimes with no crime at all, may be lynched with impunity anywhere in the South and occasionally in the North. The conscience of the nation has become so seared that it is no longer horrified when in the state of Pennsylvania or Georgia a human being is burned to death at stake. The newspaper press does not use its powerful influence to arouse public opinion against this iniquity, while the pulpit, which should be the first to lead in an attempt to purge the nation of this foul blot, is, for the most part, silent.

Negroes themselves are largely to blame for the contempt in which they are held and the impunity with which their liberties and their lives may be invaded. Sheriffs, mayors, courts, governors, will not take seriously into account the interests of a people who have lost or surrendered the right to retaliate or call them to account at the ballot box. Mobs do not quail when there is no fear that their wild brutalities will be answered by a volley of bullets.

I am unwillingly, but slowly, coming to the conclusion that the only way for the Negro in particular, and the dark-skinned peoples in general, to win and hold the respect of white people is to mete out to them a white man's measure in all the relations of life.

In at least seven of the states of this Union the Negro holds the balance of political power. He should use this weapon in an effort to stir the national government against lynching. We are all familiar with the argument that the national government can do nothing to put down lynching in the Southern States. The national government can do anything it desires to do when the public welfare or interests demand it. The national government found a way to interfere when the boll weevil was destroying the cotton crop in Texas and other Southern States. The national government found a way to legislate on the question of marriage in relation to the Mormon Church, and would immediately take steps to nullify any action the State of Utah might take on this subject contrary to the prevailing public opinion.

Are not the rights of human beings as sacred as the cotton crop? Is not the doctrine of the inviolability of human life more sacred than this nation's attitude toward the doctrines of the Mormon Church?

But the action of this government in abrogating the treaty with Russia furnishes a still more striking example as to how the lynching evil can be combatted. The treaty was abrogated because American citizens of the Jewish race visiting in Russia did not receive the same treatment accorded to other American citizens. Now, the treaty of the United States with Great Britain contains the clause, "the most favored nation."

We would advise that Negro subjects of the British Empire who come to this country numerously from the British West Indies travel freely throughout the Southern States and when they are Jim Crowed and otherwise assaulted and degraded, that they appeal to the British Government on the ground that their treaty rights have been violated. Let them urge that England abrogate its treaty with the United States, unless the government of the United States guarantees to British subjects of the Negro race the same treatment as is accorded to other subjects.

Why were American public opinion and American statesmen aroused to such a height of indignation on behalf of the Jew? Is it because they are in love with the Jews, or rather is it because of the Jewish vote? One of the reasons why the Negro's cause in this country has in recent years sadly gone from bad to worse is because misguided Negro leaders have counseled them to an attitude of submission, which is both unmanly and un-American. He has largely lost or surrendered his right to vote to the nullification of the Fifteenth Amendment.

To demand the enforcement of the Fifteenth Amendment today is to be branded as "an enemy of both races," "a fanatic," "a mischievous agitator." To all outside interference the South says: "Leave the Negro to us, we understand him, and know best how to deal with him, both for his own good and the welfare of the South." President Taft, who has boldly committed himself to the doctrine of race discrimination, pipes his grand diapason in harmony with this sentiment by declaring, that the Negro "ought to come and is coming more and more under the guardianship of the South!"

With far more justification, we reply on behalf of the Negro, leave the Southern white people to us. We have lived among them for two and a half centuries, we both know and understand them. We have nursed their children, built their homes, and for more than two hundred years we have fed and clothed them. When they took up arms to destroy the Union in order to bind us in perpetual chains, we did not fire their cities with the torch, nor rise in violence against them, but protected their property, their helpless women and children. Leave them to us. We have imbibed not the ideals of feudalism, but of democracy; we are Americans filled with the spirit of the twentieth century. Leave them to us, and we will make the free public school universal throughout the South and open alike to all, without regard to race, creed or color. We will make free speech as safe in Mississippi as it is in Massachusetts; we will abolish lynching and usher in a reign of law, of courts and juries, instead of the shot gun, the faggot and the mob. We will abolish peonage, elevate and protect labor and make capital secure. Leave them to us; our chivalry shall know no color line, but our womanhood shall be protected and defended, and our citizens, regardless of race or color, shall be permitted to participate in the government under which we live. Leave them to us, and we will make them know their place and keep it, under the Constitution as amended. We will remove the last vestige of Jim-Crowism under the forms of law, and make the places of public necessity, convenience, recreation and amusement, open alike to all without respect to race or color. We will make intelligence, character and worth, instead of race and color, the sole test of recognition and preferment for all. Thus as North and South divided over the Negro, so would the Negro unite them in the only bond of union that can stand the test of time fraternity, justice and righteousness.

3

IDA B. WELLS

Excerpt from "At the Hands of a Mob" (written 1926),
in *Crusade for Justice: The Autobiography of Ida B. Wells*

HISTORICAL CONTEXT

Tom Moss, a friend of Ida B. Wells, was lynched in Memphis, Tennessee, on March 9, 1892. Moss, who was the owner of People's Grocery, had a brawl break out in front of his store. The racial nature of the fight caused "jealous whites" to make an example out of Moss. Although innocent, he was abducted by a lynch mob and publicly executed with gunfire.

SERMONIC RESPONSE

Although I had been warned repeatedly by my own people that something would happen if I did not cease harping on the lynching of three months before, I had expected that happening to come when I was at home. I had bought a pistol the first thing after Tom Moss was lynched, because I expected some cowardly retaliation from the lynchers. I felt that one had better die fighting against injustice than to die like a dog or a rat in a trap. I had already determined to sell my life as dearly as possible if attacked. I felt if I could take one lyncher with me, this would even up the score a little bit. But fate decided that the blow should fall when I was away, thus settling for me the question whether I should go West or East. My first thought after recovering from the shock of the information given me by Mr. Fortune was to find out if Mr. Fleming got away safely. I went at once to the telegraph office and sent a telegram to B. F. Booth, my lawyer, asking that details be sent me at the home address of Mr. Fortune.

In due time telegrams and letters came assuring me of Mr. Fleming's safety and begging me not to return. My friends declared that the trains and my home were being watched by white men who promised to kill me on sight. They also told me that colored men were organized to protect me if I should return. They said it would mean more bloodshed, more widows and orphans if I came back, and now that I was out of it all, to stay away where I would be safe from harm.

Because I saw the chance to be of more service to the cause by staying in New York than by returning to Memphis, I accepted their advice, took a position on the New York Age, and continued my fight against lynching and lynchers. They had destroyed my paper, in which every dollar I had in the world was invested. They had made me an exile and threatened my life for hinting at the truth. I felt that I owed it to myself and my race to tell the whole truth.

So with the splendid help of T. Thomas Fortune and Jerome B. Peterson, owners and editors of the New York Age, I was given an opportunity to tell the world for the first time the true story of Negro lynchings, which were becoming more numerous and horrible. Had it not been for the courage and vision of these two men, I could never have made such headway in emblazoning the story to the world. These men gave me a one-fourth interest in the paper in return for my subscription lists, which were afterward furnished me, and I became a weekly contributor on salary.

The readers will doubtless wonder what caused the destruction of my paper after three months of constant agitation following the lynching of my friends. They were killed on the ninth of March. The Free Speech was destroyed 27 May 1892, nearly three months later. I thought then it was the white southerner's chivalrous defense of his womanhood which caused the mob to destroy my paper, even though it was known that the truth had been spoken. I know now that it was an excuse to do what they had wanted to do before but had not dared because they had no good reason until the appearance of that famous editorial.

For the first time in their lives the white people of Memphis had seen earnest, united action by Negroes which upset economic and business conditions. They had thought the excitement would die down; that Negroes would forget and become again, as before, the wealth producers of the South—the hewers of wood and drawers of water, the servants of white men. But the excitement kept up, the colored people continued to leave, business remained at a stand-still, and there was still a dearth of servants to cook their meals and wash their clothes and keep their homes in order, to nurse their babies and wait on their tables, to build their houses and do all classes of laborious work.

Besides, no class of people like Negroes spent their money like water, riding on streetcars and railroad trains, especially on Sundays and excursions. No other class bought clothes and food with such little haggling as they or were so easily satisfied. The whites had killed the goose that laid the golden egg of Memphis prosperity and Negro contentment; yet they were amazed that colored people continued to leave the city by scores and hundreds.

In casting about for the cause of all this restlessness and dissatisfaction the leaders concluded that the Free Speech was the disturbing factor. They were right. They felt that the only way to restore "harmony between the races" would be to get rid of the Free Speech. Yet they had to do it in such a way as not to arouse further antagonism in the Negroes themselves who were left in town, whom they wished to placate.

Months passed after the lynching before the opportunity came in which they appeared to be "defending the honor of their women" and therefore justified in destroying the paper which attacked that honor. I did not realize all this at that time, but I have come to know since that that was the moving spirit which dominated the mob in destroying my paper.

Like many another person who had read of lynching in the South, I had accepted the idea meant to be conveyed—that although lynching was irregular and contrary to law and order, unreasoning anger over the terrible crime of rape led to the lynching; that perhaps the brute deserved death anyhow and the mob was justified in taking his life.

But Thomas Moss, Calvin McDowell, and Lee Stewart had been lynched in Memphis, one of the leading cities of the South, in which no lynching had taken place before, with just as much brutality as other victims of the mob; and they had committed no crime against white women. This is what opened my eyes to what lynching really was. An excuse to get rid of Negroes who were acquiring wealth and property and thus keep the race terrorized and "keep the nigger down." I then began an investigation of every lynching I read about. I stumbled on the amazing record that every case of rape reported in that three months became such only when it became public.

4

ELISHA WEAVER

Going to Africa (*Christian Recorder*, December 21, 1893)

HISTORICAL CONTEXT

While Henry McNeal Turner became an international voice for Black nationalism, many AME preachers vocalized different methods to fight lynching. One of these voices was the Rev. Elisha Weaver, who used the AME Church's paper to articulate his beliefs. Lynching was still an American issue in 1893, and Weaver was historically influential for his analysis of America being a land full of genocide battles. When describing the violent history of the Pilgrims and the Indians, Weaver issued a challenge to Black Americans to persevere and fight for the same freedoms as the English colonists had struggled for in New England. What is not noted is the methods of genocide used by the Pilgrims, whereas it can be assumed that his audience was aware that fighting included acts of strategy and, at worst, violence.

SERMONIC RESPONSE

If by agitation years ago, through the press and before the people, we have survived slavery in the South, mob violence, prejudice and murder in the north, why not by the same means overcome the troubles of today? If they have lynched our people in some of the states, we should not become discouraged, it is the same experience of the Pilgrim fathers and their contact with the Indians, which was but the crystallization of their present civilization, and as it is today with the fathers of the first-generation after freedom, the lynching is the trials and hardships which precedes a future civilization to be built up by the egress of the South of the ruins of American slavery. The Pilgrim Fathers did not give up the contest in New England, why should we give it up in the South, especially when the Southern country justly as well as by the laws of tropical clymatology belongs to the Negro. Let him stay here, continue to build it up and develop its resources till he posses it under the same flag that it was governed for and by the old master class who are rapidly disappearing before the march of a new civilization. As for going to Africa, our people will learn after awhile that a man's race or color is no evidence of his purpose nor of what is in his head and will stop allowing themselves to be governed as if it did. Human nature is the same, especially under similar circumstances, in all races therefore we are for the human race. But the colored race of all races, first, only because and in the sense that it is down and needs helping up, of course some one has always made capital off of the helping up business. It is not the fellow who cries the loudest for his party, who serves his party most, but himself best. What we want to do is to quit playing on the credulity of the more ignorant of our people and let them go to work. This unrest only enables the smart fellows to live off the fools by asking them to go where they will not do themselves. There is no Eldorado anywhere. If a man has no money he had as well be on this side of the river as on the other.

Rome was built by her stay-at-homes. It is our duty to stay here and help to make this our native land made and built up and enriched by the sweat of his brow a free country. This is not only our highest duty, but it is the best thing for us to do. I do not question Bishop Turner's sincerity and the reason I speak of him personally is because he is regarded as the leader favoring qualified African emigration. I have no moral right to question his honesty and sincerity of purpose any more than he has mine; but the days of scaring men out of saying what they think are gone, yet I admire the fairness and respect with which he treats those with whom he differs regardless of his position.

Lessons from Two States of Lynching
(*Christian Recorder*, September 18, 1902)

HISTORICAL CONTEXT

In 1902, there were sixty-two documented lynchings, with eleven of them taking place in Mississippi alone. Jim Gaston and Monroe Hallum were both lynched in Attala, Mississippi, on July 17, 1902. William Ody was also lynched on July 17, 1902, in Tunica. John McDaniel was lynched on August 9, 1902, in Amite, and just a few days after Weaver penned this letter, Thomas Clark was lynched, on September 28, 1902, in Alcorn. These five lynchings in Mississippi, all within a three-month span, surely sent shockwaves across America.

SERMONIC RESPONSE

Two Southern States have given recent exhibitions of guiltless lynchings and Mississippi and Virginia must endure the judgment and contempt of the civilized world, until purged of their barbarous crimes of blood-guiltness. In each State mob vengeance has made victims of two innocent colored men lately, and both double butcheries have been deemed of sufficient value as to justify action against members of the mob. In Virginia the trial of the indicted lynchers resulted in their prompt acquittal and the boast of the local press that the verdict was the unanimous expression of public sympathy on the side of the indicted lynchers. In the face of such expressions and the probably farcical trial of the blood stained criminals, would it be accounted unjustifiable for colored men, if innocent when arrested, to defend themselves against mob butchers at any cost?

In both States the offense for which the prisoners suffered death was foreign to the capital offense usually charged against the race. In both cases the offense was against white men, and in Mississippi it was the charge of simply speaking ill of white men. This charge, as weak as it was, on investigation was found groundless. The fact led to the prompt presentation of true bills by the grand jury of Attata county in Mississippi against the men indicted for the lynching of the two colored men. It is said that local sentiment against lynching is so pronounced that it is more than likely that the lynchers now awaiting trial will be condemned and punished.

As yet colored people are not active in the lynching industry nor are many of them provoked to desperation by overbearing deputies or constables. The capacity of the race for suffering is well nigh infinite it seems, but as there is never a lane but has a turning point, this long traveled by the patient black man may lead to the point from which he will look down upon his writhing adversaries with a look.

5

HENRY BLANTON PARKS

The Disabilities and Persecutions of the Negro Race in the South and Our Attitude Towards It (Christian Recorder, July 6, 1893)

HISTORICAL CONTEXT

Preachers in the battle against lynching often included dogmatic clergy like Rev. Henry Blanton Parks. These individuals often attempted to find comfort by using the concept of theodicy. Theodicy justifies wrongdoing with the assumption that a person has previously committed a sin and therefore has reaped what they sowed. Many Black clergy at the time not only rejected these sentiments but also were frequent in their condemnation of those who propagated this theology publicly. When a bishop of the Methodist Episcopal Church, South made a proclamation that all lynched Blacks "ought to die" and that they resemble "gorillas and a demon race that remains stationary," Parks argued it was important to publicly strip any and all credibility from this religious denomination. Failure to fight against these attitudes would be to concede the statement as truthful.

SERMONIC RESPONSE

It is quite an honor to be privileged to present a paper before this distinguished body of Christian teachers upon this subject. It is not without a sense of my inability to do justice to this subject that I appear. I shall, however, to the extent of my ability, present an outline of the true situation as I see it.

While we rejoice to say that slavery, the blackest and most degrading of all institutions known to man, has been put to an end and the once oppressed, dejected and down-trodden slave, according to the Constitution of the Republic, is a free man, clothed with all the rights and immunities common to the citizens of this proud and prosperous nation. It is also true that the institution had its destroying and degrading effect upon this people, to destroy which will take long years of earnest and careful labor.

The "History of Nations" will show that it is by the most careful and earnest effort, not only by those afflicted with moral corruption, but by the undivided support of those by whom they have been surrounded and with whom they have had to do, that they have been enabled to completely overcome this greatest of all maladies. It requires no argument to show that a slavery which destroyed all the teachings of the Ten Commandments given by Jehovah upon the awful summits of Sinai, will destroy the moral character on any people upon whom it was allowed to be practiced, especially when that slavery continued for two hundred and fifty consecutive years.

In the second place, we regret to say that the same determination to continue this disregard is as great today as it was when the immortal Abraham Lincoln signed the ever blessed act of emancipation. The same resistless and determined spirit of licentiousness that gave life and power to concubinage during those dark days, asserts itself in the Southern whites and defends its insatiable desire with the point of the sword.

THE DEPRAVATION OF EVERY RIGHT GIVEN HIM BY GOD AND MAN
WITH WHICH TO OVERCOME HIS CONDITION WHETHER IT BE THROUGH
THE PULPIT, PRESS OR BALLOT

No people can ever be expected to rise to an exalted position in a refined civilization without the right of free speech. Americans have been taught that it is a God given right, and for it they have fought, bled and died. It is the safeguard of the nation's liberty, the corrector and perpetuator of right, honor and dignity.

That this privilege is most emphatically denied us all will admit. He who would attempt in that Southern land to lift up his voice of correction and denunciation against the most flagrant and detestable wrongs and outrages perpetrated upon his race, must die at the stake. All the teachings of the pulpit and press must wink at, or utterly disregard these evils. The ballot must not be used if not in accord with his dictation. To my mind it is clear that unless this people can enjoy the privilege of free speech upon all questions, especially those that are essential to their elevation and welfare—the preaching of the whole gospel of the despised Nazarine—it will be more than hard for them to rise above their present disabilities.

THE LACK OF POWER IN ANY WAY TO PREVENT THE ENACTMENT AN ENFORCEMENT OF THE MOST CRUEL, INHUMAN AND DEGRADING LAWS EVER PERPETRATED UPON ANY PEOPLE

The educational and financial condition of my race, render it impossible for them to overcome the determined mob violence which has been the means resorted to [to] destroy the ballot or disfranchise him. It is no longer a question whether he is disfranchised or not, all have admitted it. The distinguished statesman from Kansas, John J. Ingalls, said in his recent letter to the Omaha "Bee": "The Negro is eliminated from politics. They who frame the laws to govern him in those states are they who took a million lives of the Nation's best sons, to hold him as a bond man."

Any man who reads the separate car law that compels Negro ladies to ride with drunken men who dishonor God, and who are strangers to every principle of decency and honor, will agree with me, that this law is both inhuman and degrading to say nothing of the iniquitous system, that makes it lawful for the landlord to imprison his renter who refuses to accept the twenty-five or thirty-five per cent charge upon the dollar, as legal and as right. To overcome this condition of affairs without a change of public sentiment is simply impossible.

THE INABILITY TO DEFEND HIMSELF, WIFE AND HONOR AGAINST SLANDER, MALIGNITY, ROBBERY, LYNCHING, BURNING, LAWLESSNESS AND MURDER IN EVERY FORM

Without free speech to present, explain and defend his cause, no man can protect himself in this, our democratic form of government. His cause must be presented in all its phases before the people will be competent to render a fair and impartial judgment. Every subject, as you know, has two sides. The white man presents his side to suit himself. The other man is not allowed to be seen. That he can do this, all admit, when they know that the press and state are at his back and completely under his control; that he would slander and belie his opponent is no more than reasonable as an excuse for his crime.

. . .

To persecute is to pursue, to injure, vex, afflict, cause to suffer pain from hatred and malignity, to beset in an annoying way, especially to afflict for adherence to a principle, creed, or set of religious principles. Persecution is the act or practice of persecution or the state of being persecuted.

There is no finite mind that can find language to accurately describe the persecutions of the Negro in the South. He is pursued by day and by night with the most detestable and malignant hatred that ever animated human hearts.

But one asks, is it persecution?

Is it hate?

When, I ask can it be that actuates a man to rob, degrade, debauch, belie and murder his fellow man, at all times and upon every opportunity? Is it righteousness? Is it that love taught by the immortal Jesus?

Two hundred thousand Negro men, woman and children have been mobbed, lynched, burned and murdered by this people since the Emancipation. The day once was when it was thought to be mobbed by a band of masked men, under cover of night, or to be hung to a lamp post or limb, by a band blood thirsty hoodlums, and to have one's body riddled with bullets, and left hanging by the neck in that condition, was sufficient punishment for the Southern Negro; but that day is past and now he is being roasted alive, after his eyes have been burned out with red hot irons.

Oh, think of it, ye men of God!

See yonder, a man accused of a crime, for which he has no form of a trial, bound to a post before a mob of five thousand human beings, stripped of his raiment, beneath the burning rays of the noonday Sun, his eyes being bored out with red hot irons, and while he cries to God, heaven and men for justice, the yells of the murderous mob make the air hideous with blasphemous oaths of denunciation. See them, not satisfied with this, they saturate his body with coal oil and apply the lighted match. The maddened flames rise over his head, and his wild shrieks and cries for mercy are stifled by their terror. Tell me, in the name of God and man, if this is not persecution?

But I must turn from this Black picture of living realities, to the other side of the subject.

By this, I understand the attitude of the Christian Church and ministry of the nation, that is to say, of the Saxon race.

While we rejoice to say that the educational and religious work that has been, and is being done by some of our white churches of the North along this line, it is simply wonderful. Especially is this true of the M.E. Congregational churches. Their institutions of learning, among some of which is the New Orleans University, of New Orleans, La.; Clark University, of Atlanta, Ga.; Gammon Theological Seminary, and the Atlanta University, the faculty of which, refused eight thousand dollars annually from the State of Georgia, before it would allow its institution to refuse admission to children of all races and colors, stands as living monuments of greatness to the churches by whom they were founded and under whose auspices they are controlled.

We regret to say that the church and ministry is not doing anything like what it might and could do, toward changing this condition of affairs.

The Church is a band of men and women whose souls, hearts and lives have been consecrated to God; a peculiar people, zealous of good works. Their mission is, to make the world better. Its ministry is, to preach righteousness and love, to denounce sin of every nature, to cry aloud against unrighteousness. They are His vicegerents on earth; by and through their efforts the world is to be brought to its Savior.

Christ said, speaking to his ministry, "Ye are the light of the world, a city set on a hill." And again he said, "Ye are the salt of the earth." If we have had the proper interpretation of these scriptures, we are forced to the conclusion that they are not doing anything, in comparison with what the world has a right to expect and demand at their hands.

The question under consideration is nothing more nor less than a moral one, thus a christian one. Shall the Church of God teach the oppressive Southerner to love his neighbor as himself, and to do unto all men as he would them do unto him? That he shall not steal, that he shall not commit adultery? If the answer to these questions is given in the affirmative, we reply that she is not doing it. But one asks where is your proof? I ask, where are the words of condemnation of the ministry against the persecutions of this people, these murderers of the most shameful and barbarous nature ever known to man; the reports of which we read every week, more or less, in our daily papers.

They are enough to arouse righteous indignations in every breast of every christian in the land, and cause him to say, "I will do all in my power, in any way, in the name of God and humanity, to put to an end this most accursed sin.

But what are they doing along this line? What are they saying, through the press, upon this subject? Read all the great church papers, their reviews and magazines, in which all other great questions effecting its interests, in this and other nations, are discussed, and what do you find of a condemnatory nature upon this subject? Nothing, save a few words occasionally from the editor.

A few months ago, in Texas, a man was roasted alive. Less than six months ago, in Louisiana, a girl, 13 years of age, was bound to a post and burned to death. Three weeks ago a man in Georgia was roasted alive upon a pine stump. Five months ago, in Arkansas, five hundred men and women witnessed the burning of a man. Two weeks ago, in Kansas, made historic by the immortal and courageous John Brown, a man was taken from the officer of the law on his way to the State Penitentiary, to serve seven years for having assaulted another, and hanged to a lamp post and left strangling to death. It is to be remembered that this man is the only one, out of a number mentioned, and the thousands of others not mentioned who had any form of trial. And up to date, not one word of reproof has come from the Church for this great sin.

One of the Bishops of the M.E. Church, South, has said in so many words, that lynching was right, and that these Negroes ought to die. The following extract from the "Richmond Christian Advocate," organ of the South M.E. Church speaks for itself. He refers here, to the burning of a man at Paris, Texas. In order to justify Southern lynchers in general, and the torturers of this one Black man in particular, the Richmond Christian Advocate, devotes a column of its space to represent the Negro race of Africa and America as a cross between a gorilla and a demon, a race that remains stationary, and has no leverage to rise higher, which even in the South is but a short removal from barbarism of the lowest type. Of these Black brutes and besotted savages it says: "Only fear of their superior neighbors and the certainty of the swift retribution hold down the savage passions of the sons and grandsons of the Voudoo Africans." And it asserts that the extreme and terrible punishment inflicted in the case under consideration was exactly the kind to strike the ignorant, besotted and devilish element of these alien races of the lowest grade of human species, as no other method could.

The eloquent Dr. Talmage, whose sermons are read by the nations of the earth, weekly, and who treats every question of the day, political, social, economical, and even the great labor agitations, has the first time yet to lift his voice of warning against these crimes. In his sermons and lectures before the people of Atlanta, Georgia and Memphis, Tennessee, a State in which three men were taken from jail by a mob, and lynched for defending themselves against the murderous attack made upon them by an infuriated mob at midnight, he congratulates the citizens upon the grandure and growth of their city, the architectural magnificence of their buildings, on the culture and refinement of its dignified citizens, while the innocent blood of their murdered victims was yet fresh upon their hands.

The leading evangelists of the American pulpit of today, such as Mills, Jones, Small and a host of others, they who number their congregations by the teeming thousand and who are loudest in their cries against whiskey drinking, gambling, Sabbath breaking and the like are silent upon the robbings, whippings, killings, burnings and outragings of Negro women and girls in the South.

The Irish cause has had no greater adherent, even at home, than the American Church and pulpit. By their assiduous efforts the press had been brought under its control, and it is a fact that she is never silent in her pleadings for the oppressed Irish. I am unable to say why this is the attitude of the Church.

It cannot be that the Negro is not loyal to the country. His record in the days of peace, as well as upon the field of battle, speaks for itself. Indeed, he loves America. Of the stars and stripes he is proud. The South, with all its horrors, is still dear to him. He loves the cool bracing zephyrs of the recuperative atmosphere, so common to that land of flowers; its fertile soil, green woods, delightful groves, clear cool water, and the song of its birds, as well as its beautiful forests, all go to make it "Home sweet Home."

It cannot be because it is not a question that effects the church. Every man who knows anything, knows that if it is allowed to continue, it will destroy the morals of the nation. No one evil has spread with greater rapidity, and with a more disastrous effect than has this one.

Nearly every state in the Union has disgraced itself by countenancing or committing this form of lawlessness within the past five years. Last week, in the city of Chicago, in the face of the assembling multitudes of the nations of the earth, to witness the greatest event in American history, an attempt was made to commit this awful crime. Its effects will be more severe, by far, than was slavery. Nothing did more to disgrace labor, in this country, than did slavery, the injurious effects of which, is being felt by church and state the nation over.

That the continuation of the present his disabilities and persecutions of the eleven millions of Negroes will be more than disastrous, to both church and nation, is a fact that none can deny.

It is not because the church cannot change this condition of affairs. They are the powers that can, in any effective way, reach it. It belongs to the church, and by the church it must be settled.

6

WILLIAM HENRY HEARD

The True Conditions of the Negro in America
(Christian Recorder, October 10, 1889)

HISTORICAL CONTEXT

Here elder William Henry Heard is writing directly to the press about their role in reporting lynchings. His was one of many voices at the time that charged media outlets with playing a role in racial caste violence in America. Cries of "Race wars," "Riots," "Negro rising," "Assaulting in missing girls, &c." can be found in these editorial pages, while the press "created the sentiment, which caused the whipping" and lynchings overall, according to Heard. There were eighty-one lynchings in 1889, and ten in the state of Georgia. The two major newspapers of that state, the *Atlanta Constitution* and the *Savannah News,* were cited in Heard's sermon as main agitators.

SERMONIC RESPONSE

When we read history we are wont to compare the past with the present. The enslavement of Israel and its emancipation is not like that of American Negro. The children of Israel were delivered from the hands of their enemies. Their taskmasters did not persecute them as the American Negro was persecuted. The Russian serfs were given land at their emancipation; homes thus being given them, they were in a measure independent. The American Negro was released without money, homes, raiment and even food and left in the midst or other enemies. Kuklux, White Leaguers Bush attackers, regulators and rifle clubs, were all organized to persecute the Negro and intimidate him and prevent his exercising his right. The state legislatures enacted laws against him. Democratic senators and representatives strove to vote away his right and to take from him what the United States Constitution guaranteed.

Two hundred and fifty years of slavery unfitted the Negro for citizenship and refined his society in many cases, but there were those who had the benefits of refined society in education; many of these were kuklux and murdered.

The training of the 250 years has been of the sort that taught the Negro that he was inferior to his white Brother by creation, and that to hate and undermine his fellow, were honorable, and to be a coward in the presence of white men was his position.

The new friend of the Negro did not understand him, so he undervalued his manhood and only used in as the cats paw to pull out the political chestnuts.

The Negro suffered for his own ignorance and the sins of others. He toiled and paid the taxes of the poverty-stricken Southern states. Being the laboring class, therefore the producer, he paid directly his own tax, and indirectly the taxes of others.

While the Negro was an inhabitant of every state in the Union, yet he was not free until the constitution of the United States was adopted for nearly every state that had bad laws upon its statutes to exclude the Negro from rights enjoyed by other citizens. He could not enjoy the civil and political rights of his brother, and though a man he was not a man.

During the dark days of the rebellion he was only called into ranks and recognized as a soldier as the enemy was about to overpower the government—yet he was never fully recognized as other soldiers though he proved himself just as worthy. Yet not a single Negro commanded a company on the battlefield. What race under heaven would have furnished the same number of men to save the Union and not a captain to command a single company? It is a disgrace to the government that accepted his services. Colored soldiers have more difficulty today in establishing a pension plan that any other class. Yet with Lincoln's proclamation and the amendments to the United States Constitution the Negro is not free.

In many parts of the South he does not enjoy any civil or political rights. He is whipped and driven as in the former days, and paid starvation wages, and yet forced to work for A.W.B. After he has once agreed to work for him, he cannot leave, for he is always kept in debt, being paid only a pittance and that in checks representing money which can only be exchanged at the plantation store, and then at a discount of from 20 to 25%, for this check is payable 12 months after date. Wilkes, Lincoln, Columbia and Elbert counties, Georgia; Berkeley, Williamsburg and Colleton counties, South Carolina; and in many parts of Alabama, these things exist to my knowledge.

In many parts of the South, materially the Negro is doing well. But he does not enjoy civil rights fully anywhere in the United States. There is no valley so secluded nor mountain so lofty that he can escape prejudice. In the south his civil and political rights are taken; in the North, East and West he is shut out of factories, shops and stores because he is a Negro. With these odds he is being educated and is gaining property. But while education and wealth are powers with other races, they do not exert the same influence for the Negro in America. He is run off from the property and that is burned down and the authorities cannot protect him. Yet the Negro is said to be worthless and shiftless. He is prevented from working and then it is said he wants work. He is excluded from capital and yet it is said we have no moneyed men amongst us. He is not allowed to run a machine and then it is said we have few inventors.

These avenues being closed causes young men and women to be unconcerned about the future. Politically he can aspire to office in the South, but he is counted out and there is a little opportunity for him when his vote is five to one. In the north he holds the balance of power in several states, but it is told by his white brethren that he would have no influence in office. So in wards where he has a majority someone else manages to represent him, he being assured his rights are safe in the hands of another. He has been educated not to trust himself but the white man. Physicians, lawyers, preachers and teachers are not allowed to exert the influence for good they might, but they are run off as rioters and conspirators. The leader is always shot or whipped first.

The press of the country is not as friendly to the Negro is it should be, for it is controlled by his enemy, so the dispatches of the Associated Press have flaming headlines of "Race wars" "Riots" "Negro rising," "assaulting in missing girls, & c." The governor orders out a company of Negro slaughterers and they go to the community and arrest and lynch them. Some papers come out and condemn the lynching when they should have published the first as a "tempest in a tea pot." The courts being organized, the Negro if he is brought to trial, in nine cases out of ten is sent to the "chain gang" where men, boys and women, in many cases, are chained together to grade railroads or work on farms to make the State rich and then be forever disfranchised.

We are made to feel vengeance should be wreaked on our enemies. With this black picture of facts still we are hopeful. The sentiment in many newspapers is quite favorable. We have seen the *Atlanta Constitution* and *Savannah News*. The editorials were strong condemning the whipping the innocent Negros. But the same papers created the sentiment, which caused the whipping. Many northern papers, as the *Press of Philadelphia, Inquirer,* and *Ledger* speak out, but none stronger than the *New York Independent.* The position and condition of the Negro in America, North, East, South and West are very unfavorable. He is a man without being allowed to enjoy manhood; a citizen without enjoying citizenship; law-abiding without being protected; a taxpayer without representation. The State, County, and citizen governments demand of him allegiance but do not guarantee him protection of life, or property. His true condition is that of a weaker in the hands of a stronger, who is unfriendly.

7

EMMANUEL KING LOVE

Lynch Law and Raping (1893)

HISTORICAL CONTEXT

As self-proclaimed "sensible Negros," ministers like Emmanuel King Love were not immune to the broad reach of white terrorism's network of misinformation. By 1893, lynching was widely publicized in many circles as an act of vigilante justice against Black sexual immorality. Rape was often cited as the catalyst for lynching support, though this propaganda has been easily disproved. Of the 2,807 lynchings cataloged during the Nadir era, only 788 (28 percent) were a response to rape or sexual assault. Outside of the revisionist lens, this particular letter does exhibit the impact that racial stereotypes would place on both sides of the racial caste experience in America.

SERMONIC RESPONSE

The author is satisfied that abuses will not stop these lynchings, nor will lynchings stop the rapings. Lynching revenges and raping increases. The remedy is in law and reason. Outrages on the one hand beget outrages on the other hand. This is in accordance with the well-known fact that like begets like. Our southern people are a reasonable people and naturally kind-hearted, especially toward the Negroes. In many things they have no superiors on earth for kind-heartedness. Perhaps no people on earth would have done better than these southern white people under the same circumstances. They are simply mistaken in their idea that lynching is the best remedy for raping. This mistake is, perhaps, intensified by the atrocity of the crime—rape, which provokes the lynchings. The author endeavored to take a fair, honorable position and shall beg no pardon for the position taken in this discourse. The sensible Negroes and conservative whites should unite and frown down these outrages. This can best be done by conservative talk, fair reasoning, confidence and patriotic co-operation. Let us appeal to these white people as our friends. As long as we stand off and scold them and regard them as our bitterest enemies, we can never reason any subject of difference with them. The author presents this discourse to the fair consideration of both white and black wherever it shall be read. Praying the blessing of the Lord upon this discourse and all who read it, I am yours in Jesus,

E. K. Love

8

S. PHILIPS BOUGHTON

A Word (*Christian Recorder*, August 3, 1893)

HISTORICAL CONTEXT

Rev. S. Philips Boughton, a radical pastor, echoed a growing sentiment in this work to encourage Black self-defense. This particular message identifies the pulpit as his "weapon of choice," whereas many radical ministers did include additional methods (such as armed protection). For reference, there were 116 recorded lynchings in the year 1893.

SERMONIC RESPONSE

I wish to speak a word to the ministers of our several churches, in regards to the duty to themselves and to their race about lynchers and lynching, every day we read in papers printed by white men, a negro lynched, burned or shot. Now in view of all of this is it not time for the ministers of our race, to speak out from their pulpits Sabbath after Sabbath, until like Sumner, Garrison, Parker and others arouse the sleeping conscience of a guilty nation.

Sir this can be done, and it ought to be done, will our ministers see to it, as a part of their duty, as I trust God I do, and go at once to work. The man or race of men who would be free must strike a blow like Patrick Henry, I know not what others may say or do, but as for me give me liberty or give me death, what does the Constitution mean when it says no person shall be deprived of life, liberty or property, without due process of the law of the state where crimes are committed daily, they refuse to do anything. The General Government seems to be afraid of the states where these brutal outrageous crimes are being committed daily, I think the time has come for us to act, and that at one, with pen and tongue, the white man has said, he has done all that he is going to do, therefore the time has come for us to do our part. Sir, if the fourteenth amendment means nothing, and the Declaration of Independence is a lie, then let us as a race compel the American people to say so, it is for us to keep the question of our lives and liberty before them. Charles Sumner once said, what is life worth without activity, and I say, what is freedom worth to us as a race without its full enjoyment?

Ministers speak, God help you to speak.

S. PHILIPS BOUGHTON,
July 29th '93
New York City

9

JACOB ISRAEL LOWE

Help Brethren (1893)

HISTORICAL CONTEXT

Rev. Jacob Israel Lowe, like many Black nationalists at the time, uses the analogy of "going to war" when describing the battle against lynching of the Nadir era. A cry for a collective effort included a plea to unionize the AME Zion and CME denominations with the AME Church. These Black Methodist groups had previously discussed merging, whereas strengthening Black denominational delegations against racial caste violence was never a talking point.

SERMONIC RESPONSE

I am free to confess that I don't understand the situation, if it is as dangerous as stated in the warnings given; but let us come down to business and look the lion square in the face, and see the whole affair in its true light, and see if any good can be accomplished by this union; or, if there is any need for it. I have no hesitation in answering, yes there is great need for this union, not only with the A.M.E. Zion Church, but the C.M.E. Church as well, and every other branch of Methodism controlled by colored people. We need this union for the accomplishment of the great work before us. The giant of ignorance guards the walls of prejudice and holds the keys of vice, immorality, intemperance and every other destructive implement; and within those walls he has enslaved a goodly number of our race. It is our duty to meet this giant and wrench from him the keys of the gates of his den and liberate our people. Therefore, we need every man that is able to go to war, from 21 years old and upward; we need a united host, for the foe is strong; let us unite. The people are in favor of the union.

The lynching, burning, white capping, ballot box stuffing and other modes of oppression all speak to us in language too clear to be misunderstood, and say, let us unite; and the man or men who stand in the way of this onward flood of unity will be swept under; it will not help the aspiration of any one to any position in the church, by opposing this union. May the Lord of light and life help these dear brethren, both of the A.M.E. and A.M.E. Zion churches who are opposing this union, to see this matter in the light and spirit of Christ, and fall in line and march to the battle cry of union, for in union there is strength and beauty.

10

BUTLER W. NANCE

The Other Side (June 29, 1893)

HISTORICAL CONTEXT

Rev. Butler W. Nance's sermon is in response to the lynching of John Peterson in Denmark, South Carolina, on April 24, 1893. Peterson's charge was rape, and as the *Charlotte Observer* noted, his life was "put in the Governor's hands and under his protection." This was unfortunate for Peterson, as Governor Benjamin Tillman had already noted that "as governor of the State of South Carolina, [I] will head a mob to lynch a Negro who assaults a white woman."

According to the paper, Peterson guaranteed the governor that "he was sure he could prove his innocence and only asked that certain witnesses whom he named should be collected for him." The paper goes on to argue that Tillman sent reporters out to find witnesses, but also sent Peterson to Columbia, South Carolina, without proper protection. Once in the hostile city, Peterson stood trial, and it was said to be clear to many that he was not guilty. The accused, a young white woman named Ms. Mayfield, was questioned, and she responded that she couldn't identify Peterson as the assailant. "I don't know him, sir; that don't look like him at all. He is the same color, that's all. He don't talk like the man; he is thinner in the face, and as dark as this man, but his eyes don't look like him." Even her brother, Mr. Mayfield, responded in trial that Tillman was not the criminal. According to him, "If the right man was here I would know him," but according to him, this was not the man. Finally, according to the paper, "There was clear evidence that Peterson was not the guilty man. The only two eyewitnesses of the crime acquitted him."

With all of this evidence, the fate of Peterson remained grim. During the trial, he was taken to a town calaboose, which can best be described as an unmanned temporary jailing facility. Left without any protection, it was then easy for "four to five hundred men" to forcefully take Peterson from the facility and quickly publicly murder him. Peterson was "hanged and shot—after jerring and insulting him and making frightful jokes upon the poor, ragged, ignorant, helpless man who could nothing but beg every now and then for 'one more chance to see Harve.'"

Governor Tillman's connection to the lynching caused controversy, and he was held under public scrutiny for allowing the lynching to take place. According to ex-governor John Peter Richardson, "He had always believed the doctrines enunciated by the Tillman administration were of such a character as must eventually lead to disregard of law." It was from this meeting that "Colonel John C. Haskell and W. A. Clark both passed a resolution denouncing Gov. Tillman and citing him as a participant in the crime."[15]

SERMONIC RESPONSE

Seeing in the issue of June 8, an article headed "Halt There," written by the Rev. J. W. Randolph, of where he did not say, I wish to say that I am not encouraging the hellish lynch law which is pervading our country from the Lakes to Florida, from the Atlantic to the calm waters of the Pacific.

I know that the Governor of South Carolina has caused the outside world to be shocked by his infuriated stump speeches, under the same oaks at Barnwell, S.C. where that host of Negroes were lynched a few years ago, when he said: "I as governor of the State of South Carolina, will head a mob to lynch a Negro who assaults a white woman, etc." This, no doubt, has caused, to a certain extent, the great insurrection in South Carolina. We are all allowed our honest convictions. Conscientiously, I do not believe that the governor should be censured for the lynching of that Negro at Denmark, Barnwell Co., S.C. It was reasonable to suppose that as the lynchers had released fifteen or more Negroes, who were not identified, that the lynchers, would release this one. The governor asked this Negro: "Are you guilty?" The reply was: "No sir." The governor then said, "Will you face the girl?" The Negro answered, "I will, and can prove an alibi." I do positively think that the effort being made to hold the governor responsible in any criminal or intentional way for the lynching is unjust to him. I think the governor made a serious mistake, as he readily admits, by sending the Negro to Barnwell County, without sufficient protection. You are cognizant of the fact, that to err is human. He says the citizens of Barnwell "abuse his confidence," and to hold him as "particepts [sic] criminis," is not justice. "Give the devil his dues." As a citizen—native born—of South Carolina, and defense of what is right, and for the vindication of the good name which the State has once had, I write this article. I know that the governor has uttered many rough, acrimonious and indecent sayings; I know that a multitude of Negroes have been lynched, and in other States, too, in South Carolina. I know that the female "Klu-Klux Clans" have brought a host of poor, pitiful and innocent Negroes to untimely graves, then when we look at all these merciless perpetrations and count the damnable deeds which have been inflicted upon us, who are, as a rule, a law abiding people within the confines of South Carolina, her record seems marvelous. Where shall we go? The reverand sir suggested, "spread yourselves." Says he: "Go East and North." For what? They are killing Negroes in the East; in the West they are driving them from their homes and lynching them by the wholesale. In the North they are lynching them because white women "get stuck" on them and express their sincere admiration by writing a note to them. "What is the need to jump from pot into the fire." To point out the evil doings of these sections pointed out by our brother it would take volumes to hold them. "To count them all it would take ten thousand tongues, a throat of brass and adamantine lungs."

"A temporary relief" will to come from spreading. In one sense we are spreaders too much now. We need more knowledge and union.

"Home, city and country—a race as well—are prosperous round. When by the powerful link of union bound." What we want in the South, is—not to stand and grin—but to meet these unlawful crimes, these enraged lynchers, these infuriated mobs, "Vi et orrmis [sic]" and knock out a few dozen, when our Negro men are lynched and when our sisters and mothers are insulted, and we will not only have "temporary relief," but a permanent relief.

If the Negro remains in America, you may preach, you may sing, and shout as much as you desire, but the relief,—the thing that is going to alleviate us from this fearful octopus, this almost insurmountable barrier—is to meet force with force. You may say not, but listen to this ode:

In the beauty of the lilies,
Christ was born across the sea,
With a glory in his bosom,
That transfigured you and me.
As He died to make men holy
Let us die to make them free.

When you say Africa, my heart is made to leap for joy. The Negro will never rise to that high standard in the intellectual world, and in the political arena in America, where the aegis of protection is not thrown around us, and where we are denied the rights of free men.

Sir when you teach aright from your pulpit, and other ministers do likewise, we will not go to Africa "Nolens Volens" but every root and branch of us will go "Volens." As a citizen of South Carolina, I am ever ready to raise my hand in her defense as I am in the defense of my people, when I see she or her Governor has been criticized from a prejudicial standpoint, thereby casting vituperations upon her good name, and causing dampness, ill feeling; etc., to circumnavigate her borders. The State where Hons. Eliot, Straker and Stewart once reigned, yea, the State which gave to us the greatest man in America today, Bishop Turner, the State of which I am son, has been made to shed tears by casting upon her too many reflections and illogical dictions. Come again. "Dum spiro spero spes."

Hazlehurst, Ga.

11

J. M. LEE

Is There No Redress for the Negro in America?
(*Christian Recorder*, May 25, 1893)

HISTORICAL CONTEXT

Rev. J. M. Lee is but one of many AME clergymen who promoted the use of armed self-defense against lynching. His use of both theology and history to justify this claim masterfully utilized stories of John the Baptist, France against Germany, and the Spartans who chose to "conquer or die." Finally, it is Lee's argument that only the bloodshed of the Civil War caused the liberation of Blacks that poetically highlights his call for all Black people to use "a Winchester or a gatling gun [to] stop this lynching."

SERMONIC RESPONSE

In your issue of May 4th, I saw an article by Rev. R. S. Quarterman, headed "How Lynching Can Be Stopped." I really think that the Reverend is sadly mistaken. I will admit that the pulpit and the bar are strong hands to start the ball to rolling, but there must be something else done besides expounding from the pulpit, that "out of one blood God create all men to dwell together upon the face of the earth" and at the bar, that justice must be done to all men alike.

The Negro must do like all other races. He must fight for his rights. Nothing shorter than a Winchester or a gatling gun will stop this lynching. The pulpit in ante-bellum days cried for the freedom of the Negro, but it did not come until millions had been slain and thousands of gallons of blood shed. Nothing is accomplished that is worth much, in this world, without the shedding of blood.

The prophets of old prophesied, and John the Baptist preached of the coming of a Messiah, but the plan of Redemption was not wrought until Christ shed His blood on Mt. Calvary. If the Negro is not willing to fight for his standing in the social world, let him leave America and go to Africa where he rightly belongs. Too much do the Negro refer to the third chapter of Zeph and 12th verse, "I will also leave in the midst of the afflicted and poor people, and they shall trust in the name of the Lord." God does not mean for us to trust in him any more so than any other afflicted race. Let the Negro show some resentment, and act accordingly, and he will be felt. It is my candid opinion that the Negro will never amount to anything in this country, any more than what he is now, teaching school, preaching, and getting little minor offices from the government to make him a good tool for the white man. Let the Negro rise up like France did a few years ago, when Germany had her down under her feet, and fight for his standing in this commercial world: and be the like the Spartan conquers or die, then he will be felt and not until then. The Spartans have long ago been blotted off the arena; but turn to the dusty pages of ancient history and they will talk to you of their achievements. The only way for the Negro to leave a name behind him as lasting as the seven hills of Rome, is in the pulpit, at the bar, or on the battlefield.

It has become so that nearly every week you can hear of some poor Negro—guilty or not guilty—being lynched. If he is guilty, why not let the law have its course? No, he is a poor Negro, and he must die like a "suck-egged dog." Someone says, that God will intervene by and by, but that statement is not true; for the simple fact we have tried to escape the limb; only by running. "God helps those who help themselves." He has never promised to help a running people. The Negro is denied everything in this country that is decent but hard labor. He is kicked out of the public inn unless he has "Marse" John's valise.

Now the question comes will the Negro stand these insults and onslaughts until the great and final day? If so, he had better pray for the dawn of that day. The Negro has sung too long "you may have all the world, give me Jesus." It seems from the numbers of the inmates in chain gangs and penetentiaries that he is losing the world and Jesus too. Let us pray God to give us heroes as well as preachers. We need them to stop this lynch law business. Men that will do, not that gather in great clusters and talk about what they intend to do, and in a few days the white people have that whole mob in some jail. Then Rev. Quarterman can cry out with his clarion voice from his pulpit, "God is love." May it be the duty of every preacher in America to lift his voice against lynching and if not stopped then, let them do like the old man that tried to break his son from playing cards. After he had done all he could to break him, he went down in the field and found him and another boy playing. He said to his son, "run me off a hand, let me have a hand in this thing." Let the preacher have a hand fighting for the stopping of lynching if necessary.

12

JOHN G. ROBINSON

The Negro Must Go to Africa (*Christian Recorder*, January 10, 1895)

HISTORICAL CONTEXT

Rev. John G. Robinson's call to emigrate back to Africa was in response to the Brooks County, Georgia, race war that took place in December of 1894. According to a *New York Times* article, a Black man named Jerry Jeffries killed a white man named Tip Mauldin. Mauldin, who was a county constable, was said to have reported a group of Black male laborers publicly drinking and gambling. These acts were illegal according to the state Black Codes of Georgia. After Mauldin notified the group that he had called the police, an intoxicated Jeffries shot and killed Mauldin. To make matters worse, it was said that a group of Blacks publicly mocked the death, labeling it a "war dance."

Local whites responded by establishing a posse to hunt Jeffries, and one of the men in the posse was shot and killed by Waverly Pike, a Black male. This caused what some labeled a war, resulting in five Blacks lynched by the posse on either December 22 or 23. It was not mentioned whether the five lynched were connected to the shooting of Mauldin, though Jeffries was tried and executed by hanging on April 5, 1895. Ultimately, at least six people were hanged publicly in Quitman, Georgia, though a larger death toll has also been reported.[16]

The names of the reported lynched were Eli Frazer, Samuel Pike, Henry Sherod, and Samuel Taylor, with one unknown.

SERMONIC RESPONSE

I had just finished outlining a subject for publication for the purpose of strengthening our missionary efforts in foreign lands when I received a paper containing the sad news of the killing of nine helpless innocent and defenseless Negroes near Quitman, Ga., who were shot down like so many dogs. This should be a silencer to the governors of the Southern States whenever they attempt to defend the civilization of the South. When they are displaying their eloquence some one ought to cry out to the top of his voice, "Quit, Man!"

The whites of this country, North and South, are doing all in their power to show to the Negro that he is an unwelcome citizen in this great "Land of the brave and home of the free" (?). To the credit of the Negro (though he is called a "raper") there is not a Negro within the bounds of the United States who will "kill a man and go into his house and outrage his family in the presence of children and suckling babes, as did those human beasts near Quitman, Ga." My God! My God!!! What will become of the Negro in this country?

I believe in the Providence of God and I also believe that one of His attributes is justice and that he will avenge every evil perpetrated upon any of His creatures. While that is true, we must try to do something ourselves in order to prove to the world that the Negro is a man. The killing of nine Negroes and outraging their families is only a signal or a finger upon the tressle-board of time pointing to the day, when like the Indian, the Negro will be driven from this "white man's country" and murdered like beasts; that is, unless the wealthy and educatedness will go somewhere, build a government, shape laws and build up a nation and prove to the powers of earth that the Negro is a factor in the greatness of the world. Lynch law and mob violence are so common that the newspapers have only to predict that a lynching is probable and it take place in every nine out of ten cases. The conditions that confront the Negro today are signals telling him: "This is not your home." Bishop H. M. Turner, the fearless champion of African colonization, is right in his efforts to develop the resources of Africa and build up a black nation whatever else may be said in contradistinction to his plans. "Jim-Crow Cars," "Bobtail Juries," "One Gallows Governors," "Ballot box thieves," "Lynching crews," "social Caste," "Negro haters," etc., will forever keep the Negro in the background of American greatness. The verdict in the noted Tennessee lunching case and the horrible slaughter of Negroes near Quitman, Ga., should forever silence the mouth of those who have been trying to uphold civilization, and should be a warning order that the white man is only the friend of the Negro for his labor and money. How and in what way can these conditions be remedied? The Negroes have shed their blood upon the fields of mortal combat and suffered in the armies that made this nation great. They have helped in every conceivable manner to build up the resources of this great land. They have bowed to every law passed by the lawmakers, which were enacted for no other purpose but to degrade them and delude their manhood. They have quietly submitted themselves to every indignity that could be conceived by the devil himself. Yet day by day the cloud thickens and the vapor gets wider, so much so that today we find ourselves helpless and almost hopeless without a friend among forty millions of whites in this country. Our ladies and gentlemen of refinement and culture receive the same treatment, at the hands of the "Negro haters" as does the dirty boot-black on the streets of the crowded cities; yet they are treated worse!

13

JOHN HENLEY ROBINSON

Adversity and the Negro (*Christian Recorder*, March 4, 1897)

HISTORICAL CONTEXT

Rev. John Robinson's sermon is full of allegory and history. His words address the unspeakable experiences of African Americans in various communities crushed under the foot of intolerable empires. Robinson's dialect of true American Christendom places Blacks on the side of the "Prince of Peace," who came into the world not just to suffer but also to oversee "the glory and power of Rome fad[ing] away." The modern-day Roman Empire, America, was painted as an "Anglo-Saxon rulership" bound to a similar fate of destruction and damnation, due to its support of tyranny over the oppressed. These and other metaphors offer a strong depiction of Black theological protection.

SERMONIC RESPONSE

The civilized world today, stands against with uplifted hands and condones the barbarous treatment that the American Negro receives. Recent decisions rendered by the highest tribunal of this nation, are acts unparalleled in the history of law and civilized countries. Outrage after outrage is committed, until "Judge Lynch" has control of the South, i.e., when the Negro's cause is in question.

Swinging from telegraph poles, bridges and upon heaps of fire, hundreds of inoffensive and innocent Negros have died and it is needless for me to attempt to name the thousand and one mean and diabolical proscriptions that are meted out to the Negro, the world has been told; it is my aim to show in this article that the Negro is undergoing an iconoclastic process that will prove an eternal blessing to him and place his sons in the front ranks of the greatest of the great. When we pull back the curtains of the past and walk amid the civilization of gone-by ages, we find that it was through iconoclasm that nations were exalted and civilization attained to any magnitude.

The world has found all of its best blessings veiled in sorrows. The blacksmith, hammering away on the hard iron and steel, after it has gone through fire, brings out carriages, plows and many other objects helpful to man and beautiful in their make up; just so, races are carried through the process after process of pain, sorrow and trials until eventually they stand out before the gaze of the world's mighty nations handling art, science and literature. Seed is never sown on unoccupied ground, grass, weeds etc., have their roots tied and tangled around the clods of the field, but the farmer digs and ploughs away, plants his seed and later on cuts away the grass; the labor brings on fatigue and sweat, yet he continues and by and by he is rewarded with an abundant supply of breadstuffs, etc.

The many things that the world enjoys today in the realm of civilization are but the products of the calamitous processes that preceded them. Assyria, great and grand, mighty in her day flourished, faded, and died. Egypt, arrayed in grandeur, planting her domain upon the fertile banks of the Nile, sending out to the remotest parts of the then known world great lessons in philosophy and morals, was a mighty nation. Egyptian mythology and civilization have given so much study and painstaking by the student in history, because of the sojourn of the Jews within her borders and the writings of Moses.

Her pyramids kissing the skies and the recent discoveries of the later day investigator, develope the fact, that Egypt arose to her highest attitude through an iconoclastic process that may have gone on for centuries. In passing through one process after another, she became tyrannical; she filled her mission and faded away amid the wreck of ages, and after playing her part in the great drama of the world civilization, she became oppressive sinks down, and is buried, her doom being sealed, and her tombstone erected, which was as some say the great Babylonian Empire, Babylon! Her mighty men fought, her musicians set to note almost the whisperings of the winds; her swinging gardens presented such magnificence, that walking beneath them and looking up, it would appear that the heavens were in bloom. Her high towers, beautiful streets great walls and costly temples, were grand beyond description! Oh!

Babylon! But when her rules defied the powers that be, and attempted to wipe from the race of the earth, the teachings of Jehovah, an unseen balance was let down from the courts on high, and out from the thick darkness on the night of Belshazzar's great feast, appeared an uncovered hand and in bald letters wrote Babylon's doom on the walls of the temple wherein they had attempted to defile the vessels that came out of house of God.

Out from the fires of national adversity arises Persia. She too made an enviable history, but she perished. Then comes Greece; for a long time Grecian glory filled the world; her Masters of Art carved in statuary the forms of their illustrious dead, and left the impress of their feet upon the "sands of time" to never be erased. Her mighty philosophers, orators, poets and artists left a legacy to the world, that will be shared by all the lower of civilization throughout all time to come. Corinthian revelry and other wicked devices unpleasant to God, drives her from the face of the earth, and only the names of her Socrates, Homers, Platos and Senecas are to be found recorded on the side of right.

Rome, the great military nation, steps upon the stage to do better and die. She dips her sword in human blood her senators reel and rock, live in opulence and argue for territory until their charter covers the face of the globe. She divides up the earth and appoints a ruler, and when the Prince of Peace came into the world she suffered a crown of thorns to be placed on His head and to see Him nailed to the cursed tree. The glory and power of Rome have faded away into many nations, kindred and tongues.

Without noticing the changes that followed the down-fall of Rome to the present, we find ourselves standing face to face with Anglo-Saxon rulership. When we look upon the bosom of the great deep and see the mighty vessels plying their faces, we behold Anglo-Saxon wealth; look if you please at the pictures of the rulers of the world and you see the Anglo-Saxon face. But ah! the mightiest century of the world's history is dying, she goes to her death-bed with a tale of sorrow and sighing; she bears to the historian of the future the innocent blood that has been spilt by the hands of the tyranny and oppression. The dawn of the twentieth century peeps in upon the world and with her comes notes of joy from the builder of nations that will inaugurate and install nations yet undreamed of by many of the world's most profound scholars.

Warfare, bloodshed and cruelty, perpetuated by this American nation dim her sky and the groans of the innocent, will be heard, must be heard. God's great plow, that has ploughed nation after nation beneath the surface, will ere long swing around this way and Washington will be in confusion and her doom will be seen written on the wall. Lay it down as a truth, the word of God never changes.

God builds from eternity to eternity; nations may rise and glare for a while but when they depart from justice and right, God lets the nation fall but preserves humanity and establishes another, once and forever. Don't be disturbed, God lives and mankind will be preserved. Through calamity God has developed mankind; suffering makes the world kin and keeps the heart of man in touch with his fellow man. Take suffering out of the world and let mankind everywhere be free from sorrow and care, sordidness would carry the world back into barbarism and savagery. Suffering awakens the sympathy of our fellowman and causes him to add to our comfort.

When the great Chicago fire subsided and the thousands of sufferers were exposed to the world, and men who a day or two previous were wealthy, had fallen into poverty, their condition caused the outside world to hasten and send relief; later on when New Orleans was covered with yellow fever, the North forgot the battles of Grant and Lee, and from New York, Chicago and other cities came hasty relief. Out of calamity came peace and just so, will the Negro get relief from the courts on high and obtain standing among the nations of the world.

When the blood of the Negro was being spilt on the tobacco-fields of Virginia, the cotton-patches of Mississippi, the rice-farms of South Carolina, the corn-fields of Georgia, the sugar-plantations of Louisiana and everywhere in the Southland, his sufferings awakened the sympathy of the North and England pronounced her indignation against human slavery. Then kinship sprang up; humanity and freeman stepped from their doors, shouldered their muskets and walked into the face of death and died, that the Negro might be freed.

The Negro was given his freedom, granted a right to vote and allowed to mingle in the affairs of the nation.

Since his liberation, he has copied the examples of the white man and day by day he advances higher in the scale of intelligence.

Prejudice has marked out certain bounds and proscribed certain laws for the Negro's guide.

The Negro keeping pace with the onward march of civilization, has proved a displeasure to the white man, and here in the south he (the negro) is most cruely treated and debared from enjoying a one hundredth part of the privileges given him by the constitution of the nation. The mid-night, and mid-day assassins go high handed through the land and take the life of Negroes with as much ease, and as little notice as does a hunter shoot ducks on a mill pond.

Can this state of affairs exist long? Will the Negro forever remain the subject and object of mob law? No! No!! No!!! Kingship, and humanity will rise up before long some where, and relieve the Negro of his suffering, and place him on equal footing with the rest of mankind.

The bones of Lincoln, Grant, Sheridan, Sumner, Garrison, Douglass, and others whose lives were fired up with sympathy are disturbed in their graves. Heaven's calvary parades the skies and the King of glory gives the signal that there is a better day coming by and by. I don't know, I can't see in what way its coming, but its coming.

Hayti, with her flag, and infant Liberia with her flag, are two representatives of the Hamitic race, stepping into the courts of the world, pleading for the rights and privileges of full fledged manhood.

Cuba's dashing Maceo, who went down fighting for liberty, won the sympathy of almost the entire world. Negro suffering in the United States aid Africa's millions who are suffering for the light of the gospel, are loudly appealing to God, and sympathy is coming, sympathy must come.

Mc Kinley, young and vigorous, with the spirit of Lincoln, will close this century by doing many things for equal protection of all citizens alike within the borders of this great country.

When the young king of Spain grows up to realize his position, he will doubtless help to usher peace into the world. England's Queen cannot remain on the throne much longer, and when her body is laid away, and some ambitious ruler takes her place, the spirit of Gladstone will pre-dominate, and Africa will feel the effect; and during the twentieth century the young Negro, who today is wending his way to school, will leap beyond the mighty waters and extend the borders of Liberia to the great distance in Africa, and build out of that baby republic, a mighty nation, and in the mean time, Black faces will be seen in this country, occupying seats in the United States Senate' Congress, and upon the Supreme bench and filling positions of honor and trust in every department of the government.

In sorrow and pain the Negro strives; He toils on, though with ease, and waits; Even he knows that God still; And by and by will make things straight.

14

J. T. SMITH

Where the Negro Now Is, and His Duty
(*Christian Recorder,* January 3, 1895)

HISTORICAL CONTEXT

Rev. J. T. Smith, like Rev. Robinson and many other late nineteenth-century AME pastors, was vocal about his Black nationalism as well as his support for emigration to Africa. Writing in January 1895, Smith had just experienced one of the most violent stretches of caste violence in America's history.

SERMONIC RESPONSE

The majority of our people seem not to know just where we are and the next thing to do. We are in the wilderness and have compassed Sinai several times and are now standing on the banks of the Jordan. We have heard the report of the spies, and our duty is to cross over into the promised land. Our Jordan is the Atlantic and the promised land is Africa. Many of our leading men claim this country to be our earthly Canaan, but time and facts teach the contrary. Now in the name of common sense I would like to know what has been done by us or for us in this country, for the last thirty years that is an evidence of this being the promised land or the country in which the Negro is to be great.

Is it because the nation's congress passed the thirteenth, fourteenth and fifteenth amendments? or because we have purchased and improved a few homes and have built up a few institutions of learning and a strong Christian church? Let us not forget that the Israelites built up a strong religious church in the wilderness, which in many respects was rarely equalled and never surpassed for works of nobility, through the long period of fourteen centuries, from the crossing of the Jordan to the birth of Christ. In short the works of the fathers in the wilderness were the foundation to all of their future greatness, and even in David and Solomon's time were referred to with national pride. But notwithstanding all of this the wilderness was not the promised land.

It is remarkable strange to see how slow man is to accept God's plans for his deliverance and elevation. Not one in a thousand can at first catch the idea. Out of the six hundred thousand men that came up from Egypt, there were only two who accepted God's plan for their deliverance and admired the land that he gave them. As good a man as Moses was, it seems that he didn't fully appreciate God's purpose towards himself and nation. There were some promises made to the Israelites by Pharoah and his people to prevent them from going out of Egypt. The Israelites paid no attention to these promises at first, so they went out, but after trying the wilderness for a while and finding it pretty rough the majority of them wanted to return back to the flesh pots of Egypt. The same thing is true of our people. Many good things were promised to us soon after the war by the white leaders of this country; but at first we paid little attention to them. The watchword with our leaders then was to colonize ourselves somewhere, either in Liberia or in the West. But after a few rash and selfish attempts were made to colonize Liberia and one or two of the Western States we gave it up because some had the fever and some died and others had a hard time. In support of this fact I only need to call attention to the infant days of the Roman republic when poverty, ignorance and other evils swept like an avalanche through the land, but the untiring efforts of Romulus and Cincinnatus caused it to be the greatest government of the ancient world. Even so can we make Africa the greatest of the modern would. I know that Africa has been called by some historians "The dark continent," and therefore many of us have quite naturally formed a bad opinion of it just as the Israelites did of Canaan. But while we have formed a bad opinion of Africa I believe we will soon be made to form a still worse opinion of this country so far as the Negro is concerned. Hitherto I tried to have faith to believe that we would overcome the present prejudice and other evils in the near future, but during this year lynch-lawism has swept around me like a cyclone among the mountains, that with other things have moved every ray of hope from my mind of the Negro's being anything in this country for the next hundred years. Therefore I am ready to start to Africa or some other place as soon as I can raise the means.

15

ALEXANDER WALTERS

Black Self Defense (1898)

HISTORICAL CONTEXT

Bishop Alexander Walters's letter is a direct response to the attempted lynching of Isaiah Lofton in Hogansville, Georgia, and the lynching of Frazier Baker and his infant daughter in Lake City, South Carolina. The men were attacked in 1897 and 1898, respectively, after being elevated to postmaster in their own counties.

Lofton, a schoolteacher and Republican Party organizer, was said to have received the postmaster appointment from the Republican president William McKinley. In response, local whites reportedly verbally and physically harassed Lofton and the site of his post office, and they engaged in a citywide white boycott. When these attempts failed to oust Lofton, "unknown assailants" attempted but failed to lynch the postmaster. He instructually stepped down from the position a mere two weeks later, and would be offered a federal position in Washington, DC. A local beat writer argued that this incident overall proved that "the President preseages [*sic*] a revolution of his former attitude towards the South. The citizens of Hogansville are jubilant over Lofton's resignation."[17]

Frazier Baker was also a recipient of President William McKinley's Black postmastership plan. Baker, like Lofton, was also a Black schoolteacher and active Republican supporter. Baker's post office also received harassment and a boycott, though his space was eventually burned down. When the government attempted to make Baker a second location out of town, it set off white terrorists, who detested Baker's determination. On February 21, 1898, the Baker family, who were at that time sleeping at the post office location, woke up to a burning building and gunfire. In the midst of the chaos, both Frazier and his infant daughter were shot and killed, while his wife and five additional children were able to escape the house, though severely injured. In response to the lynching, South Carolina senator Benjamin Tillman professed that "the proud people of Lake City refused to receive their mail from a nigger."[18]

In 1918, a St. James AME Church was built over the site of the burned post office where Baker was shot. That church was itself burned down, on October 5, 1955.[19]

SERMONIC RESPONSE

On the 10th of March, 1898, I sent the following appeal to the New York Age:

Fellow Citizens:

The late outrages perpetrated against Postmasters Loften of Hogansville, Ga., and Baker of Lake City, S.C., for no other reason than their race and color, and having no reason to believe from past experience that the perpetrators will be brought to justice; and further, because there is a determined effort on the part of the white labor unions of the country to exclude the Negro from the industrial avenues in which he can make an honest living, it becomes absolutely necessary that we organize for self-protection.

I therefore move that T. Thomas Fortune, president of the National Afro-American League, call a meeting of the leaders of the race at an early date, to take in consideration the present condition of affairs and suggest a remedy for the same. All who will unite with me in this request please send their names to this paper.

The greatest problem of America today, is not the currency question nor the colonial processions, but how to avoid the racial war at home. You cannot forever keep the Negro out of his rights. Slavery made a coward of him for 250 years, he was taught to fear the white man. He is rapidly emerging from such slavish fear and ere long will contend for his rights as bravely as any other man. In the name of the Almighty God, what are we to do but fight and die?[20]

16

DANIEL ALEXANDER GRAHAM

A Call Against Lynching (Indianapolis Recorder, 1899)

HISTORICAL CONTEXT

By the year 1899, nationwide protest against lynching was in full force. The African American Council in May of that year asked for all Black people to "fast and pray" in order to receive the judicial liberties they needed to survive. Many churches participated in this event, and Rev. Daniel Graham preached this sermon at Bethel AME in Indianapolis, Indiana, in response to the movement. The intent of this sermon was to overview the many atrocities that had taken place in 1899, including the lynching of Sam Hose in Newnan, Georgia, on April 23, and of Willis Sees in Osceola, Arkansas, on April 30. All of these cases were used to demonstrate the frequency of lynching during the previous decade and the lack of prosecution after the fact.[21]

SERMONIC RESPONSE

The American Negro is afflicted, and the cause of his affliction is a most unreasonable and silly prejudice in the white Americans. If the hatred were reversed it would seem more reasonable, since the Caucasian has suffered nothing from the Negro, while the latter has suffered everything at the hands of the Caucasian.

While this prejudice is greatest in the South, it also manifests itself greatly to the affliction of the colored man in the North. When he wants to buy property or rent a house he is often turned away because of his color. When he seeks employment where help is advertised for, he is told that "Negroes need not apply." Our girls cannot get employment in shops, stores or factories, no matter how well educated, refined and good looking. Naturally, this causes many to fall into evil ways and makes dishonest men of youth who with a man's chance would have become honorable and industrious citizens.

When we cross Mason and Dixon's line the evil shows itself at every turn. Separate waiting rooms, separate ticket windows, separate cars, nothing to eat at any lunch counter. Refused admission to churches, cemeteries and even parks. Parks and cemeteries are placarded "Negroes and dogs not admitted." The effect of such proscription is most baneful as well as inconvenient.

How can the colored youth ever learn to look upon himself as a man when he is constantly treated as a brute? This is one of the greatest causes of vice and drunkenness among the Negroes. To the Southern whites the manly, refined Negro is the most despicable because "he tries to act white," while the ignorant, servile fellow who dances jigs and acts the monkey on the street is the "good old darkey of antebellum days."

The disfranchisement of the Negroes in the South is not the worst evil. If they would require an educational qualification for all voters, we would see no evil in it whatever.

The greatest affliction we have to suffer is the lack of trial by jury when accused of crime. Lynching of Negroes is growing to be a Southern pastime. When reproved for their barbarity they say, "The only way to stop lynching is to stop the crime which leads to lynching." Many Northern people are influenced by this cry and talk about lynching as if it were always for crimes against women. Even some colored people up here have fallen into this error. You will pardon me, therefore, while I give you some plain facts to set you right about this. Since January 1, 1892, 1,226 people have been lynched in this country, principally Negroes. Not one third of these persons were accused of assaulting women.

In 1892, out of 241 lynched, only 46 had such charge against them. In 1893, out of 159 lynched, 39 were so charged. Last year, out of 131 lynched, 24 were charged either with assault or attempted assault. In the face of these figures who can say that we can stop lynching by stopping one crime? The very next day after Sam Hose was roasted and his charred remains divided among the white savages of Georgia for souvenirs, a Negro, Willis Sees, at Osceola, Arkansas, was hung on suspicion of barn burning. In 1894, 10 were lynched for barn burning. Three women were lynched the same year in three different states. Again, I beg you to consider carefully these charges of assault. How many of them are guilty? What is the proof against them? One year ago yesterday in the town of Dorcyville, Louisiana, a man named Will Steak was burned alive upon the charge of assault of one Mrs. Parrish. *The Times Democrat* of New Orleans in its account of the affair said: "Mrs. Parrish identified the Negro almost positively." He died protesting his innocence, but because he was almost identified he was burned alive.

William Offet, of Elyria, Ohio, was fortunate because he was in a Northern state. Being identified by Mrs. J. C. Underwood, the wife of a minister, he was sent to the penitentiary for fifteen years. When he had been in prison four years, this "respectable white lady," conscience smitten, confessed to her husband that she was equally guilty with the Negro. The husband had the prisoner pardoned, and secured a divorce from his depraved wife.

There are many such cases. Ed Coy, who was burned at Texarkana, Arkansas, was another instance exactly similar to that of Offet, and Judge Tourgee obtained the proof that the relatives and husband of the woman who made the charge were fully cognizant of the fact that she was equally guilty with Coy. They compelled her to make the charge and then to set fire to her paramour.

Again, white men often black themselves and commit crime, then lead a mob to lynch some Negro who may happen to be in the neighborhood. In Atlanta, Georgia, about four years ago a black man was discovered in the room of a young white girl of high standing. While attempting to escape he was shot and captured. The black man was found to be the son of a prominent white neighbor with his face and hands blacked. Had he not been captured some poor Negro would have been seized, identified "almost positively" and hung to the nearest tree. A similar case happened in Tennessee a few years ago.

Many innocent men are thus hanged or burned alive just because American prejudice refuses them a trial by their peers. And some court trials are little better than mob trials. The present governor of Georgia, Mr. Candler, while district judge three years ago, sent Ed Aikin, a boy of nineteen years, to the chain gang for ten years on the charge of attempted assault. The only evidence the girl offered against him was that she met him coming down a path and as he did not get out of the path she was afraid and ran. She swore that he was not within ten feet of her, did not speak to her, and did not follow her, but she would make an example of him so that young darkies would get out of the path when they saw white girls coming. Thereupon he sentenced him to ten years in the chain gang. This is an example of attempted assault.

Now, we want it distinctly understood that we are not trying to excuse crime. We contend that the death penalty should be inflicted upon every man who assaults a woman, without regard to the color of the victim or the criminal. This is more than the whites ask or will allow. In fact, there are twenty colored women assaulted by white men for every white woman assaulted by Negroes. Such cases are countless in every community in the South, but there is no redress for the colored women, either by law or by custom. Colored women are absolutely at the mercy of white men in the South, and a man does not lose social prestige or church relationship for ruining colored girls. I compelled a white Southern minister to acknowledge this fact before the ministers' meeting of Minneapolis a few years ago. And yet they talk about the immorality of the Negroes!

Under all these afflictions we have a great work to perform. We must not allow the injustice and cruelty of the whites to divert our attention from our own weaknesses and shortcomings. More attention must be given to the cultivation of Christian character. The morals of the race must be improved. Our women must spend more time in mothers' meetings and clubs for intellectual and moral culture and less on parties, receptions and balls. More money should be spent for good literature and in support of Christian Endeavor, Y.M.C.A., and kindred organizations instead of on Sunday excursions and theaters. If American justice and Christianity have decreed that we must lift ourselves by our own bootstraps let us set ourselves heroically to the task. Measured by the depth from which we have come, we have much to encourage us; casting our eyes to the summits yet to be gained, let us thank God and press on.

17

GEORGE LEE AND ALEXANDER WALTERS

Talk of War on Whites at Negro Conference [1906]

HISTORICAL CONTEXT

In this sermon, Rev. George Lee and Bishop Alexander Walters respond to the Atlanta Race Massacre, which began September 24, 1906, and ended on September 26. The cause of the massacre was a growing Black population—from nine thousand in 1880 to thirty-five thousand in 1900—a growing camaraderie between Black and white working-class populations, and the emergence of a Black elite population. These examples of Black growth and uplift caused political propaganda to target Blacks as a threat to white opportunity, as political leaders began to urge that Blacks "be kept in their place." Alongside this rhetoric of Black economic malfeasance was the spreading propaganda in the *Atlanta Georgian* and the *Atlanta News,* which consisted of continuous citing of cases in which Black males raped white women.

When a paper alleged that four Black men had raped a white woman on Saturday, September 22, 1906, angry white mobs surged into Black neighborhoods, attacking businesses, streetcars, residences, and people. Overall, it was estimated that twenty-five to forty African Americans were killed in the riot, and constitutional chastisement soon followed with a heavier hit. During the same period Blacks were disenfranchised and hit with Black Codes in Georgia.

SERMONIC RESPONSE

I preached peace after the Atlanta riots, but don't misunderstand me, it was prudence, not my religion. If I had the power to stop that kind of thing, even by force, I'd use it. A man told me a short time ago that race prejudice in the South was melting.

It must have begun, I said, since I left Atlanta the other day. I thought it was congealing then.

In the South they are scheming all the time to keep the negro down, but I tell you he is bound to rise. Just so certain as they keep this thing up in the South something is going to happen. The trouble is all one-sided now. Trouble never stays on one side. There's going to be trouble on the other side pretty soon.

Somebody has said that the negro race is dying out. No gentlemen, I have no fear along that line. We're ten million strong, and we're here to register our solemn protest against the treatment we're receiving in this country.

We are discriminated against, not because we're uneducated, not because we're incapable of culture, but it's because we are a distinct race. We were once held in bondage. We're not a criminal class. The negroes have proved their use and loyalty to the American people. Now we ask them to regulate our condition. We're tired of this kind of treatment, and we want to know how much longer the American people are going to scatter to the four winds that section of the Constitution which calls for equal rights for all, regardless of color, race, or previous condition.

If it continues much longer, a terrible conflict is sure to come. It will bring business stagnation and desolation, but it will come, for the sense of justice is no more dead now than it was before the civil war broke out. No one knows this better than Senator Tillman, and if such men as he stir up a war in which the color of the skin is a death warrant, the Nation will cease to be patient. It will certainly act.

The object of our enemies is to make us serfs. It is nonsense to cry peace when there is no peace. We are determined to rise or die in the attempt to obtain our rights. We are determined to leave a heritage to our children which will save them from serfdom. It is silly and wicked to see our people die when action could save them.

Even in the prize ring we have our Joe Gans. I advocate a law which would place the punishment for mob violence under Federal Control. Alfred C. Cowan, a colored attorney of this city, in an address on civil rights, admonished the negroes to violate no law, but if attacked by a man or mob to kill as many of their assailants as possible.[22]

18

TIMOTHY THOMAS FORTUNE

Sermon at an AME Church in Washington DC (1915)

HISTORICAL CONTEXT

Timothy Thomas Fortune was a stalwart antilynching activist in America. This particular sermon was made fresh off the publishing of his fourth book, *The New York Negro in Journalism,* in 1915. Fortune's research in the book, as in this sermon, addresses the value of self-defense by those oppressed by the tyranny of racism. This snippet of Fortune's sermon highlights a logical support for the African American tradition of armed self-protection. There were fifty-eight cataloged lynchings in 1915.

SERMONIC RESPONSE

If the law can afford no protection, then we should protect ourselves, and if need be, die in defense of our rights as citizens. The Negro can't win through cowardice. The Black man's right of self-defense is identically the same as the white man's right of self-defense. Tell me that I shall be exterminated, as you do, if I exercise that right and I will tell you to go ahead and exterminate—if you can. That is a game that two can always play at. And suppose you do exterminate me, what of it? Am I not nobler and happier exterminated while contending for my honest rights than living a low cut that any poor white sneak would feel free to kick.

II

PIOUS THEOLOGICAL PROTECTIONISM

INTRODUCTION

White terrorism in the South vigorously attacked radical protectionism. Black churches and institutions that housed political leadership and supported the tradition of arms often faced violence. Targeting Black churches was a successful tactic for white terrorism, and its outcome caused reverberations for Black theological protectionism.

Some of the earliest slave and Black codes were created to protect white hegemony against the threat of radical protectionism. The frequent attacks against Black people in the Nadir era have been highlighted in Reconstruction historiography, by Eric Williams, W. E. B. Du Bois, Ira Berlin, and in Eric Foner's research on violence and Black emigration. The forced evolution of Black theology is similar to the transformation of the millions of Black emigrants during the Great Migration—violence caused change. Some people shifted their theology to survive, some shifted to thrive, while all remained focused on their social needs.

In response to violence and terrorism, Black pious theological protectionism underwent a major evolution in the southeastern states. Employing a revivalist mindset that viewed all things as spiritual, adherents of this theology believed that a cloak of protection could avert the rise of violence. Within this spiritual mind space, practitioners employed internal and external reflection. They often preached for the moral cleansing of Black communities, including the condemnation of vices, and moralism that had supposedly "plagued the Negro" since slavery. Many in this community were encouraged by Evangelical witness traditions that mirrored the gospel of their enemies. This praxis of employing a theology of one's oppressors was believed by many to ensure a level of protection for the Black church against violent whites. Accordingly, statistical research has shown that communities that practiced foreign religious activities often experienced more violence and had higher rates of lynching.[1]

By employing a theology that was dogmatic and conservative, Black churches often strategically shifted their focus from fighting to surviving. This method of clandestine worship sometimes taught theological uplift in exegetical code and can be perceived as "preaching the mask." Pious theology was relatable to white Evangelical doctrine, whereas the euphemisms still remained grounded in Black protection. One example was published in the *Christian Recorder* in 1884, when the editor issued a mask-wearing devotion for AME membership, suggesting that members let God address the issues of lynching. "While a defense of family, life and friendship should be made, even at the cost of life, the idea of any general peace uprising in any section, is to be deprecated under any and all circumstances."[2]

Pious practitioners also practiced an explicit mission that demanded that white Christians be accountable for their actions. Bad theological interpretation was often cited as the impetus for white terrorism, and these acts could be curtailed by a spiritual refresh. Black pious theology often found itself working through prayer in ecumenical spaces and sermons against violence in integrated congregations. White ministers were also attacked publicly in newspapers by ministers who demanded they preach a true gospel and not overlook lynching in their sermons.

Similar to white Evangelicalism in the South, Black pious protectionism often emphasized the salvific and living presence of God. As long as "the blood has not lost its power," divine intervention could benefit Black people in the war against white terrorism.[3] In the spirit of the pre-Exodus moment in the Hebrew Bible, pious Black Christians pleaded that YHWH should change the hearts of their oppressors and open white eyes as he had the eyes of Paul in the New Testament. Overall, piety was never a method that hid from the lynching dialogue and instead was the most publicly used tool to fight against this deviant act. Pious ministers often used the Bible and their faith as a shield to address dangerous truths in the face of racial caste violence, and during the Nadir era, lynching was frequently the topic at hand.

AME preachers often used pious protectionism as a warning for white terrorist who feared Black resurgence. Rev. Hannibal Thomas once warned whites that cowardly violence can produce enough Black anger for retaliation to come to fruition. Instead, whites were to leave Black communities and their women alone; in similar fashion, Black men should leave white women alone.[4]

Spiritual shaming was another pious protectionism tactic used to avert lynchings, and it employed biblical exegesis that couldn't be disputed as many religious communities in the Southeast heralded the Bible as inerrant and infallible. When Rev. William Yeocum preached to a congregation that had recently experienced a lynching, his words leveled spiritual incrimination against neighboring white Christian terrorists, including a challenge of their manhood: "If these people have the manliness to expect an answer for religious equality and freedom as all Christian people shall do, they are no longer wanted among white people."[5]

Methods of spiritual shaming were also aimed toward Black ministers within pious protectionism. Pastor S. Philips Boughton publicly denounced AME ministers who aired on the side of caution and chose to avoid a lynching discourse in the pulpit. Instead, it was believed that ministers had a spiritual duty to address lynching in order for God to hear their spiritual cry. According to Boughton, "Every day we read in papers printed by white men, a negro lynched, burned or shot. Now in view of all of this is it not time for the ministers of our race, to speak out from their pulpits Sabbath after Sabbath . . . Sir this can be done, and it ought to be done, will our ministers see to it, as a part of their duty, as I trust God I do, and go at once to work."[6] Other preachers followed Boughton's praxis by asserting that white Christianity's failure to protect Blacks from being lynched in the South was an example of poor clergy leadership. According to *TCR*, white churches had a moral responsibility to denounce "crime, whether committed by the multitude or the individual."[7]

Steeped in tenets of Black respectability, some AME ministers and periodical editors refused to point all of the blame at white terrorists. In periodicals and church conference lectures, some laypeople in the denomination taught the concept of theodicy to explain why lynchings occured. When the *Christian Recorder* invited the Dr. Purvis to "expose the root of the present evils" of lynching, ministers and laypeople accepted his premise that often the lynched were criminals. According to his paper, "The factor time is the principal element required in the elimination of both rape and lynching in the Southland, said the speaker. How earnestly do I, too, long for the disturbing hatred of us to die out."[8] Vices of sexual abnormalities, substance abuse, and domestic abuse had integrated themselves into deviant Black circles, according to the doctor. In his mind, gradualism and mission work in a "dark land" were the only cures to curtail Black lynching. Similar sentiments can also be found among Black missionaries traveling to sub-Saharan Africa, seeking to rescue its inhabitants from spiritual "heathenism."[9]

When analyzing the troubles facing Blacks and lynching in the South, pious Black communities were consistent in naming the origins of the blame placed upon them. In the face of Black criminality, the controversial perception of an underdevelopment of the Black person's soul was connected to the evils of the white Christians. Consequently, ministers like Rev. William Yeocum argued that white churches not only were to blame for white terrorism but also should be identified as poor representatives of Christian faith. In light of white atrocities, from slavery to lynching, many would publicly question the legitimacy of any morality existing in these spaces. In order to fix the flaws in American Christianity, pious Black ministers in the AME Church were promoting a racial awaking. The first steps of this awakening began with divine intervention, or as some ministers would describe it, the passing of a morning light. In 1895, one AME minister prophetically claimed that "the morning light is breaking and the darkness of thirty years ago is disappearing. God has raised up the Christian Endeavor to bring together in one grand Christian fellowship and union all Christian men and women in this country regardless of race and color."[10]

When Black prayers couldn't reach white souls through divine intervention, ecumenical services were often had with white congregations. Rev. J. R. Sanders in Arkansas was one of the more vocal ministers against lynching, and his words were supported by the Black pious cause. One of his sermons was published in 1893 by *TCR,* and in it he argued for white religious malfeasance to end. "Sin is ruining this country, Arkansas especially," argued Sanders, and it was due to white pride and the refusal to provide justice and uphold religion in the state. Worst of all, these terrorist acts would "soon throw the white man back into heathenism and bondage" if divine intervention did not take place. Sanders called for a national prayer that God would intervene in this time of need.[11]

Rev. Dr. John Carlisle Kilgo was another minister who was supported by the AME Church for his pious approach to antilynching. As the president of Trinity College in Durham, North Carolina, he was often celebrated in *TCR* for his bravery in condemning lynching in an "unmincing way."[12] Political and military leaders also found their way into the pulpit of pious protectionism.

In Coal Hill, Arkansas, Rev. O. C. Kirtch housed coalitions to publicly charge lynching activity in the area, and in 1899 he invited First Lieutenant J. H. Sykes of Little Rock to "urge the whole people of all charges to offer supplication to their God in behalf the people and against lynching in the South."[13]

Other AME ministers petitioned against lynching through spiritual litmus tests, often challenging Evangelical Christians to abide by the beatitudes of their faith. When Rev. Dr. William B. Derrick, missionary secretary of the AME Church, addressed the annual conference, he made sure to issue an appeal to all "Christian people of this city and State [to] sing hallelujah, and in the midst of famine" to make sure that all people have "enough to eat." If not, he would warn that greed could cause "God's retributive justice [to] place the sword of vengeance into the hand of the Negro."[14]

Pious protectionism might have been deemed satisfactory to white on-lookers, but it was not ignorant to the plight of the Black people. For many, "if these horrible lynchings are continued much longer, a righteous God will curse this whole land, and the civilized world will say: Amen."[15] Pious ministers often addressed the woes of slavery in their sermons, while contextualizing its nuance within their own daily experiences. Rev. William B. Johnson was frequent in his analysis of racism in the South and declared it irresponsible to avoid this subject from the pulpit; he considered it a minister's responsibility to make an "intellectual effort [to] reach the populace."[16]

Henry McNeal Turner, a stalwart defender of Pan-Africanism ideals and an agent of theological radicalism, also wore the mask of pious preaching when needed. His dialogue often cut deep into the hearts of the ashamed, especially in ecumenical spaces. When Turner saw up close a lynching in his home state of Georgia, he soon printed one of his finest sermons on white Christian barbarianism and cowardice. In that work, he argued, "If the churches worshiped in by white men chiefly, and the religious papers edited by white men chiefly, North and South, are afraid to speak for the wronged Negro, in this unparalleled visitation of injustice then we forbid their representatives to call us brother, come into any association with us that implies their Christian birthright or talk of Jesus Christ dying for ALL MEN."[17]

Within pious circles, many believed that "Vegence [sic] will come. Mark how certain is that indiciation [sic]!" Rev. James H. A. Johnson argued in a sermon, "On the heels of every Black man lynched scores of white men by disaster are swept from the face of the earth."[18] For pious ministers like Johnson, the crying stage of grief often transitioned to a call for divine justice, also understood as spiritual vengeance. Many pious ministers believed that white violence would be answered to by the Lord.

This idea of vengeance often operated as an incentive within the "slave religion." Some slaves evoked orishas and other traditional African religious spiritual beings against their oppressors. Poising, conjuring, and revolting all had a religious backing to support their existence within diasporic slavery in the Americas.[19] Black slaves and freedpeople who practiced Christianity in America centralized their belief system around the story of Exodus—sometimes more often than the Passion story of Christ. The saying "Jehovah-Jireh," or "the Lord will provide," has often adhered to the Black theological canon as proof that Christ is a deity that can "make a way out of no way." In the story of Exodus, God split the Red Sea and sent bread from heaven for nourishment. For Black Christians, this meant God would protect them from enemies and supply their human needs. The editor of *TCR* might have put it best when he once prayed that in the midst of "lynchings not yet abated," he was "waiting for God's defense, and was waiting to proceed where God shall direct.[20]

Pious theological protectionism during the Nadir era was no different than the Exodus-based theology that historian Gayraud S. Wilmore identifies within the slave church. In this context, people prayed to God to defeat hate and those who practiced it, and in return many practitioners believed that they now had the right to fight back by any means necessary. Prayers included requests for spiritual intercession alongside physical agency. For pious AME ministers like Rev. Harvey T. Johnson, moral suasion in sermonic form was a dual tool: it could fight against evil spirits and attack those who lynched. In a Church conference, Johnson and others would request that "this body call upon the leaders, organization and members of the race everywhere to set apart a day of fasting and prayer to Almighty God that the hand of the slayer be stayed and that justice be meted out to the guilty and that the innocent and helpless be protected; Resolved, that we resort to moral suasion by enlisting public opinion for the press in the pulpit and seek to secure sympathy and aid of those in a position to help us."[21] Not to be taken as pacifist, Black ministerial calls for lynching were often followed by directions for social agency against lynching. Along with fasting and praying, pious protectionism also made public demands and pushed social change with vigor.

Some pious protectionism ministers issued a strong internal call for focus on moral cleansing. Many of these practitioners would go as far as assuring neighboring whites that Black criminality was not welcome. Pious protectionism defined moral suasion as a tool against individuals backtracking into a deviant state of mind—one that was increasingly relevant among white terrorist populations. A frequently tactic was the public call from Black pulpits to protect white Christian bodies against "relapsing to barbarism." Some ministers and papers sought new national outlets to "denounce with such courage and force the frequent exhibition of the barbaric spirit among the white people of the Southern states." The Black pious ministers believed themselves to be divinely elected individuals interceding for all Americans' souls. In doing so, many Black ministers urged all Christians to fight against the demons that supported lynching. This method of spiritual racial inclusion was used as a tool by Black pious ministers to "save your [white] people from a relapse to barbarism. In such writers must rest, in great measure, the hope of our Christian civilization."[22]

Pious protectionism and moral suasion are also connected to the ideological tactics of Black respectability. This praxis shows a high concern for bringing respect to the Black race and identifies the dangers of white savagery. Periodicals like *TCR* often became organs for pious protectionism as a maturing Black theology. For example, the editor of the *Christian Recorder* often penned strong meditations against lynching, which included directions for Blacks to refrain from mimicking the degenerate ways of white "barbarians." These forms of deviance included the bastardization of Christianity, the teaching of hate, and cowardly actions from weak men. By avoiding these vices, "there would be great hope" for the up-and-coming Negro race.[23]

Many historians have argued that when Blacks lynched other Blacks, they were often motivated by moral deviance and not white interference. By lynching Black criminals, communities were practicing self-preservation by curtailing moral regression. In addition, these acts intentionally assured local whites that guilty actions would not be excused. Some communities are said to have acted in swift and even inhumane ways to display the hatred Blacks had for criminality. Historically, there were even riots and mobs in Black communities that rose up against Black criminals who put the community in jeopardy.[24]

Friends of the race, according to *TCR*, often saw fit to decriminalize the perception of Blackness through pious action. Moral defection was often used to legitimize the lynching of Blacks, whereas pious preachers emphasized the need to reform their communities. This was done to strategically exhibit their morally superiority over their white counterparts. In order to provide agency and protection to Black people, pious ministers strenuously preached against the notions of Black inferiority and denied that Black sexuality was full of an-imal passions. Challenging bigotry and fighting Judge Lynch with pious pro-tectionism included historical analysis and public social construction. Often, the AME Church saw fit to provide public reinforcement of their successes, and the overall progression of the Black race, by enacting pious protectionism.

In pious theology, some mask-wearing theologians approached Black vices and criminality with a hyper focus, some even going as far as to justify Judge Lynch as an act of vigilante justice. For AME minister Rev. John G. Robinson, "outrages committed by lawless negroes and followed by swift punishment at the hands of lynching parties, have called forth much comment by editors of various papers and numerous writers." Social Darwinism had woven itself into Evangelical theology by the late nineteenth century, and many Black minis-ters found themselves trapped. The possibility for mask-wearing theology was possible, but there were pious protectionism ministers who truly perceived the Black person's soul and mind to be damaged. In the words of Robinson, "I do believe that if the white man would consider the numerical, financial and in-tellectual weakness of the negro as a race and give him that cordial support of protection that the law provides, the negro preacher, teacher, editor, etc., will within the next two decades make it impossible to hear of a rape being com-mitted by members of our race."[25]

Rev. Robinson believed sexual deviance to be the downfall of the devel-oping Black soul. Rape was often attached to the metanarrative that justi-fied Judge Lynch, and although studies have discredited the legitimacy to this claim, the creation of white terrorist organizations often was held up by the fulcrum of white patriarchy, or the control over women's bodies.[26] In the midst of publicized Black criminality, pious ministers often faced the Black brute sex-ualization myth with an interesting rebuttal: a sin is a sin. If the Black rapist is to be lynched for committing sexual crimes, lynchers should be held account-able for their crimes—murder. From a Georgia pulpit in the AME Church, one minister made clear to his congregation that "'Thou shalt not kill' is one of the commandments which all churches of the new and old dispensation professes [sic] to obey, but there are many members in these churches in Georgia who have joined mobs and participated in the violation of this commandment."

According to the editor of the *Recorder*, "Until this is done, crime of various kinds will continue to be committed by vicious ones of both races, and will be followed by mob violence, till the hands of this great country of ours will be stained in blood."[27]

Whether Black criminality existed or not, Black pious ministers often presented rhetorical questions about the moral actions of white Christians lynching participants: "What would Jesus do?" When preaching on lynching, pious ministers frequently asked, "Is this the action of Christian civilized people; is this the way some of the followers of the lowly Jesus do? Thou shalt do no murder?" The overwhelming strategy to offset such sins began in the awakening of Black piety led by "the voice of the preachers, especially in this section of the globe, should thunder out vengeance of Jehovah against such barbarism."[28]

"Universal peace, affecting every relation that man sustains to man" was the goal for many pious ministers. Those who preached of the prophet Isaiah, and the metaphoric day when "the wolf and the lamb shall feed together, and the lion shall eat straw like the bullock" (Isa. 65:25), like Rev. Timothy Reeve, argued that God could unite Black victims with the lions of the earth. "No lynching of men would be done, no State riots prevail, nor civil war waged. And this would lead to the recognition of the relation that people sustained to people whom seas and mountains divide."[29] Rev. J. Harvey Jones, when observing the rise of lynching due to supposed Black criminality, asked Black members to "work and govern himself under the same principles of manhood that have characterized and made disguised the success of other nations." Meanwhile, other lay members reiterated the need for an awakening of both their spirits and their voices, as previously mentioned, among Black and white Christian communities. A. S. Bailey once argued in a *Recorder* article, "There was a time when all lynching was laid at the doors of lawless ruffians, but the Louisiana judge says it was not the class at the most prominent citizens of Jefferson Parish who lynched the three men Saturday night . . . God knows the one thing I believe: that colonization or no colonization, Africa or no Africa, protection or no protection from the law, the preachers, teachers and other leading characters of the race, together with the older pants, can do great good in relieving our suffering."[30]

Black pious protectionism also found refuge among the prohibition reformers of the late nineteenth century. The AME Church's discipline and hymnal during this period both included strong stances against alcohol consumption. In addition, bishops in the denomination often made public redress against alcohol and its connection to lynching. "As to the habit of drink, we wish to say a word to our people. No danger of today, equals the danger of the cup. Ballot stuffing and lynching are not to be compared to it. Indeed, it is the one that menaces our future . . . Rum is a deadlier foe than either barbarism or slavery."[31]

One final tenet of pious protectionism included the eradication of Black lawlessness, which included violent retribution. From moral suasion pulpits, ministers often condemned each and every soul that sought to fight crime with crime. According to *TCR*, "Our duty is everywhere to oppose crime and ungodliness and renew our trust in Him who worketh righteousness and avenges his elects."[32]

1

ELISHA WEAVER

The Heathenish, Diabolical and Barbarous Butchery
(*Christian Recorder*, January 9, 1890)

HISTORICAL CONTEXT

Rev. Elisha Weaver's sermon is in response to the lynchings of Black males in rural Georgia and South Carolina, as well as to the silence of white Christian onlookers. In Jesup, Georgia, the pastor acknowledges the area's "barbarous butchery of our people." The small city had experienced a high number of lynchings in just a four-year span (1888 to 1891) and surely had caught the eye of national media. The particular lynchings being addressed were the Christmas murders of Peter Jackson and William Hopps, on December 25, 1889. Their death offense was listed as race hatred, and there was no clear motive for the lynchings.[33] What is recorded is that both men were tied to a tree and shot on Christmas night.

Weaver's sermon also addressed the lynching of eight Black prisoners in Barnwell County, South Carolina, on December 28, 1899. The fate of these men would be tied to the murder of John J. Hefferman, a white merchant, on October 30, 1899. Additional murders of prominent local whites included that of Robert Martin on December 18 and James S. Brown on December 19. These murders caused hysteria in the area, and all of the deaths were attributed to Blacks. The jailed Black men who were lynched for said atrocities were Mitchell Adams, Ripley Johnson, Judge Jones, Robert Phoenix, Peter Bell, Hugh Furz, Harrison Johnson, and Ralph Morrall.[34] According to testimony from the local jailer:

The crowd next roped the eight prisoners, brought them down stairs and marched them through the principal streets, compelling me to go with them. We got seventy yards across Turkey creek, which is about a quarter of a mile away. They stayed there some fifteen or twenty minutes, and the crowd asked the prisoners a good many questions. About thirty minutes after they were gone they commenced firing. It seemed to me they kept firing five or six minutes. I imagine 150 shots were fired in that time. The bodies were lying on the roadside. When we reached there at 9 o'clock the bodies of Johnson and Adams had been removed, but the others were undisturbed. The mob divided the murderers, putting the Hefferman slayers on the left of the road and the Martin murderers on the right. The negroes' arms were pinioned and tightly tied to trees with strong ropes before they were shot. They were not hanged, however. It is impossible to describe how many shots each man received and where they were struck, as their bodies and heads were literally torn to pieces. Some of the negroes were old men, Morrall possibly being 60 years old, and Peter Bell about the same age. Some of the unfortunate men had their eyes shot out, others were wounded in the chest and face. Blood covered the ground upon which they laid, and a more horrible sight could not be imagined.[35]

SERMONIC RESPONSE

The heathenish, diabolical and barbarous butchery of our people at Jessup, Ga., is followed by a heinous lynching at Columbia, S.C., of eight colored men, not condemned, but charged with murder. In God's name, we ask for mercy from the strength of law and religion around us, but for justice; mercy is out of the question. If the churches worshiped in by white men chiefly, and the religious papers edited by white men chiefly, North and South, are afraid to speak for the wronged Negro, in this unparalleled visitation of injustice then we forbid their representatives to call us brother, come into any association with us that implies their Christian birthright or talk of Jesus Christ dying for ALL MEN. There is no sane man who does not believe that the barbarous fiends, to the last man, who are responsible in both the Georgia case and that of South Carolina, can be found. We demand of every Christian paper in the land its influence to discover those despoliations of the fair name of our country or town, that with them the word Caucasian means more than the word Christian, and the dominance of the former is more to be desired than the latter. We will contribute to aid in the condemnation and punishment of the men engaged in these crimes unequaled in Christian communities.

A Word (*Christian Recorder,* August 3, 1893)

HISTORICAL CONTEXT

In 1893, there were thirteen recorded lynchings in the state of Georgia, including three in the Atlanta area. Rev. Weaver addresses these particular atrocities, not for their heinous nature but due to the Black church's unwillingness to take a lead in social protest on the matter. He even argued that journalists in the Democratic *Atlanta Journal* were publicly holding responsible "the Georgia white ministry, on the crime of lynching," more than the Black church was.

SERMONIC RESPONSE

GOD never intended to have upon the earth such an anomaly as an unhappy Christian.

BE content in your present lot. If your religion will not keep you content in your present lot it would not in any other.

NO MAN can teach what he does not know. No man can lead where he does not go. No man really understands the value of what he never had.

WHEN a person who is not a Christian is set to teach others in the Sunday School, who are unsaved like themselves, it is setting the blind to lead the blind, and they are likely to be both found in the ditch.

THE PRESS ABOVE THE PULPIT

WHEN the pulpit and church become patrons rather than moulders of public opinion, the day for truth and righteousness is becoming dark indeed. Happily this condition is not universal and though sadly true of a certain portion of our Southern sections is becoming less so, as the leaven of Christianity enters and permeates the pulpit and pew. It is, however, both a shame and sin that the pulpit should take a back seat and have the secular press read such a lecture to it as *The Democratic Atlanta Journal* reads the Georgia white ministry, on the crime of lynching. Says the paper to the Christian lynchers and pulpit abettors of the same:

"It is time for the pulpit to recognize the existence and prevalence of life crime. 'Thou shalt not kill' is one of the commandments which all churches of the new and old dispensation professes to obey, but there are many members in these churches in Georgia who have joined mobs and participated in the violation of this commandment by helping to slaughter a fellow-creature. The church should be a leader in morality; those who expound the doctrines of our churches should not falter in their denunciation of crime, whether committed by the multitude or the individual. Our preachers inveigh often against offenses far less grave than the taking of human life. Why do they not speak out now, when Georgia is disgraced by the frequent assertion of the power of murderous mobs?"

Visit to "Cyrus" at the Athens of Texas
(*Christian Recorder*, August 24, 1893)

HISTORICAL CONTEXT

Henry Miller, a descendant of a lynched man named Uncle Cato Miller, was hanged on July 28, 1893. Accused of shooting Dallas police officer C. O. Brewer, Miller was targeted by numerous lynch mobs trying to break him out of the county jail. These attempts failed, though he was eventually hanged inside the Dallas County jail after being found guilty of his crimes.[36]

SERMONIC RESPONSE

And now I add concerning this church, "He that hath an ear to hear, let him hear"; drive your stakes firmly down and watch the splinter, for you, are in possession of property of which I think, I know you ought to feel proud. All that is now needed to complete her fullness is to add thirty feet of brick to the rear, neatly and modernly finished internally, with raised chairs, stylish pulpit, etc., which I feel certain the young ladies and gentlemen will assist the Dr. in doing. These things when added will place her out of the reach of her assailants and opposers with the grasp and grip of a Solomon that made Sheba acknowledge and kings and countries tremble. This is the finest property in the state. Quite a drought here at present; cotton worms are feared; corn is plentiful; sickness abundant; deaths not a few including the hanging of one Henry Miller (colored) at Dallas July 28th. Lynchings not yet abated, nor do we know when they will be for every illegal lynching on the one hand, cyclones, storms and other agents in God's hands take hundreds on the other. For my part I am waiting God's defense, waiting to proceed where God shall direct.

Some Lessons on Lynching (*Christian Recorder*, August 16, 1894)

HISTORICAL CONTEXT

Rev. Weaver's sermon here was in response to the lynching of Anderson Holiday on August 2, 1894, in Elkhorn, West Virginia. Known as a "tough citizen," with a "shady reputation" in his own community, Holiday was accused of getting angry and shooting at a man named Bob Calloway but missing. Instead, he struck Wesley Cobbs in the back of the head. What makes this lynching unique is that while Holiday was in custody, both white and Black mobs attempted to break him from the jail.[37] It was ultimately a posse of "about 3,000 armed Negroes" who "made a rush and succeeded in getting him from the officers."[38] Later, it was recorded that this Black-led posse tied Holiday to a tree and publicly shot him by firing squad. A few have debated the legitimacy of a Black armed posse being in the number of 3,000, though the presence of any Blacks at this lynching does exhibit a public response to negate any stereotyping of West Virginia Blacks as unruly. It is fair to assume that these acts were done by Blacks to send "a clear warning to disorderly inhabitants that the newness of their community would provide no opportunity for the erosion of the established values of [respectable Black] civilization."[39]

SERMONIC RESPONSE

Lynching is but an invasion upon the sacred precincts of law and well-ordered society. It is the forcible taking of law out of the hands of the law is nothing short of the rankest insult to the boasted claims of civilization. Its first lesson is an object lesson and it plainly discloses its character, both as virus and epidemic. It first broke out in the South, where its malignant sway is still dominant; but it now spreads its death form across the national body, also that every section now trembles within its clutches and all forms and colors of humanity remain at the mercy of its virulent touch. In imitation of their elders, children not infrequently have lynched each other, while the Black man, so long the sufferer in this ruthless way, has begun to change base from victim to victor. Alas, in too many instances the brother in Black has shown his proficiency as an imitator of the bad example set by the dominant brother in white, but in no respect is this wickedness so appallingly impressive as in the triumph of the former over the latter in the few cases submitted to Judge Lynch for adjustment.

At Elkhorn, West Virginia, an inoffensive colored man was killed by a white man some few days ago. Promptly and after the regulation methods employed by white men, a mob of colored men dispatched their white victim. On short order it was shown that outlawry could be resorted to by Negroes as readily as by white men and that there can be no telling where the thing will and when the game becomes two-handed and universal.

There are those who insist that fire must be fought with fire in the case of colored men whose kind are constant sufferers from the bloody violence of mob. They advocate the gospel of the Mosaic regime which required eye for eye, tooth for tooth, life for life. To do this, whoever would be for the race to believe its past record as a long suffering, hardy and ascendant people. While a defense of family, life and friendship should be made, even at the cost of life, the idea of any general peace uprising in any section, is to be deprecated under any and all circumstances.

Editorial Sparks (*Christian Recorder*, December 20, 1900)

HISTORICAL CONTEXT

In the year 1900, seventy-six recorded lynchings of African Americans took place in the southeastern states. Rev. Weaver's cry for change was not only ringing loudly within the Black church but also became a major cry in the federal government.

SERMONIC RESPONSE

There is no national evil to the overcoming of which the leaders among us should give more earnest and hopeful attention than to that of lynching.

Negroes are the chief victims of the mob and the crime of which its victims are accused by their murderers is one that is charged up against the entire race as a moral defect. It is said that the Negro does not comprehend the duty of chastity and that he knows no moral restraints when his merely animal passions are aroused.

The friends of the race refute these false charges by pointing to such great Negro organizations as the A.M.E. Church and inviting the most rabid Negro-hater to deny that this great Church has produced men, from its bishops down, whose teachings and lives fail to set before the people the purest morals in precept and example. We have resisted with vigor such exceptional references to our religious organizations as have been made by Ridpath, Hoffman and a few others and have ever stoutly stood as the champion of those who regard our churches as centers of high moral influence.

We Know How to Sympathize with Our Friend and Brother (*Christian Recorder*, August 7, 1902)

HISTORICAL CONTEXT

Rev. Weaver's sermon here is in response to the lynching of William Ody in Clayton, Mississippi, on July 16, 1902. It was reported that Ody had attacked the white daughter of a prominent planter and "broke both of her arms and her skull in the attack." On the day prior to the attack, the *New Orleans Daily Picayune* printed an article titled "The Men of Clayton Are Preparing for the Burning of William Ody. He Will Be Disposed of Tonight." That evening, Ody was tied to a tree and burned to death.[40]

SERMONIC RESPONSE

WE KNOW how to sympathize with our friend and brother, the Rev. S. W. White, Presiding Rider of the Jonestown, Mississippi District, who writes touchingly of a barbarous lynching that took place a few days ago on his work at Clayton. We have only the sternest condemnation for the alleged crime which served as a pretext for such brutal savagery and no palliation in the world for wresting proper punishment from the hands of the law. Mob violence can only breed lawlessness and unless the thing is stopped a harvest of bloodshed will be reaped by those who defy the law and exhibit such reckless disregard for human life. Years ago we witnessed three such bloody tragedies while in the saddle as our good brother and know how to feel for him and his dear people who are demoralized in the way he reports. Our duty is everywhere to oppose crime and ungodliness and renew our trust in Him who worketh righteousness and avenges his elects.

2

WILLIAM HANNIBAL THOMAS

The Humanity of Religion (Christian Recorder, January 22, 1885)

HISTORICAL CONTEXT

In the year 1885, sixty-two recorded lynchings took place in the southeastern states. Rev. William Thomas's response to this rising trend is best emphasized by his allegorical critique of anti-Black propaganda in the nation—including employing Black male criminality as an impetus to lynch. In fact, Thomas would argue that the gross ideology of Black immorality had bled itself into the theological beliefs of the African American church. Hence, if they were not careful, the Black man would continue to see himself as "[subordinate] to the Saxon, the habitual deference to whom is the curse of the race."

SERMONIC RESPONSE

The colored race is a strong believer in the hereafter. The spiritual and unseen forces command awe and reverence. We go in raptures over the intangible, the unknowable. The white robe, golden slippers, azure skies and heavenly verdure of paradise, appeal strongly to the serious nature of man, who is often the victim of cold, hunger and nakedness. The people are not wholly blamable. That they should revel in ecstatic joys is to be expected. The best of us are elated when some "master" in Israel depicts, in impassioned eloquence of rich imagery, rapt song and glowing faith, as only a devout colored clergyman can, the future dwellings place of the saints; but the transient exhilaration is too fleeing to produce permanent fruit. There is no maturity of thought or purpose. The inevitable relaxation is not conducive to spiritual growth; the truth is, the imagination is surfeited. We hear too much of heaven and too little of earth. The duties of time are neglected for the fancies of eternity. We should know men and things as they are, the wants and needs of humanity. Our race should be taught the elements of business, what to sow and how to reap. The burning questions of daily experience are the true issues of spiritual needs.

The ministry, to be helpful, must acquaint themselves with the faults as well as the virtues of their people. It will mark an epoch in the history of African Methodism when the ministry is honest enough and brave enough to face the truth. What an immense field the times afford for honest spiritual labor; what a commanding position the Church might take if it was only equal to the occasion; if we had concerted co-operation instead of competitive antagonism; if the efficacy of divine truth was believed in as constantly asserted, the rugged eloquence of John Knox would be tame denunciation beside the fiery philippics hurled from the pulpits of these modern reformers.

A fruitful source of issues of live pulpit themes is at hand. The constant lynching of colored men for alleged crimes in the South too often passed by unrebuked by the press and pulpit, and silence is taken for acquiescence and submission. Some colored men condone and take part in these outrages. The want of race pride, a slavish cowardice that constantly immolates the colored race to the spirit of caste is not sought to be eradicated. The "color-line" among ourselves is a pertinent illustration of conceded inferiority and subordination to the Saxon, the habitual deference to whom is the curse of the race. The gross immorality of many colored women with white men is a natural and logical outgrowth of such training, an evil that is widespread. In keeping with this is a senseless prejudice in existence among ourselves. We denominate a colored female as a woman and a white one as a lady. We are servile to color and deferential to caste, in the church, society and public life.

Our people are showing interest in literature. The young should be taught to discriminate in choosing books; to shun the trash and cull the best in fiction, biography, history and travel. As idleness is a prolific source of vice, they should be taught to believe in the dignity of honest work. Many parents now insist that their children shall not be brought up to toil; in consequence the young men are likely to become dissolute loafers, and the young women to drift into demure courtesans.

Superstition is a curse to all people; the negro has it. It should be eliminated, though comparatively harmless to some grosser vices. The colored race believe in luck in finance. They buy lottery tickets and play policy in all large cities—men, women and children. Christians and sinners. It is estimated by reliable authority that in the city of Philadelphia, $20,000 a week is spent in this form of gambling, of which the colored people contribute at least $3,000, without any adequate return. These devices are sapping the foundations of society. The money enriches the enemy of the race. Those who can least afford it, the poor, are its steady patrons.

Beer drinking is common. The number of reputable women who drink is almost incredible. If the veil was lifted what a revelation; only "sinners" like myself can approximate the number that will not be taken in by the tones of virtue nor the smile of vice. Crimes against motherhood are beginning to lay hold upon the race; its procreative duty is avoided. Recourse is had to every justifiable method. Should not the ministry denounce this crime against the highest functions of womanhood? These and many other evils are widespread and far-reaching in their effects, though not more so than among the white people, from whom our race acquired them. I should like to enumerate, but I may be excluded from the RECORDER for what I have already written. However, if what I have said shall make us no less spiritual in our aims and methods, but more practical and immediate in the means employed, I shall not have spoken in vain.

3

WILLIAM HENRY YEOCUM

The Church Is Responsible (*Christian Recorder,* November 7, 1889)

HISTORICAL CONTEXT

Lynching, according to Rev. William Henry Yeocum, was similar to slavery in
its contradiction of the true teachings of Christianity. Those who lynched, according to the minister, were "hypocritical, Christless and godless professors,
ministers not excepted, [who] quoted the Bible in support of the Institution
of slavery." Yeocum would close this argument with a claim that "we do not
believe God will use the kind of religion processed by the majority of whites
of this country in saving the world."

SERMONIC RESPONSE

"And hath made of one blood all nations of men."

The inspired writers of the Old and New Testaments and theologians of the
present day, have taught that all the families of men are descended from one
origin or stock. Although they may differ in complexion, features and language,
yet they are derived from a common parent. The word blood is often used to
denote race, stock and kindred. Therefore, this passage completely proves that
all the human family are descended from the same ancestors; and that, consequently, all the variety of complexion and the crimp of hair is to be treated
to some other cause than that there were originally different races created.

The design of the apostle in this affirmation was to convince the Greeks
that he regarded them all as brethren and that although he was a Jew, yet he
was not enslaved to many narrow notions or prejudices in reference to other

men. He shows also that no one nation and no individual can claim any pre-eminence over others by virtue of birth or blood or color. All are in this respect to equal in the whole human family, though differing in complexion, customs and laws, are to be regarded and treated as brethren.

It is plain also that one race has no right to enslave or oppress another on account of difference of complexion; nor has any man the right, because, "he finds his fellow guilty of a skin not colored like his own," and having power to enforce the wrong for such a worthy cause to doom and devote him as his lawful prey. Then it is evident from the preaching of the Bible that the true Church of God wherever found should recognize the brotherhood of man however much they need differ in the race-varieties.

This being an outline of the teachings of the primitive church in the opinions of all true believers in Christ. It does seem to me that most of the white religious denominations in America have been derelict in carrying out their mission. During the days of slavery the so-called Christian churches throughout the South supported and advocated the continuance of the Institution. Many of the ministers who claimed to be called of God to preach his word of freedom, salvation and goodwill to all men, with many of their church members, held slaves and traded in human flesh.

This is strictly forbidden in the Word of God, yet many of those hypocritical, Christless and godless professors, ministers not excepted, quoted the Bible in support of the institution of slavery. The Church of Christ should not wait for political parties, or any other organization, to advocate the quality, religious freedom and brotherhood of men of whatever races or complexion. In the South today, in many of the so-called Christian churches, many murderers assembled to worship God with their hands still red with the blood of innocent Black men and women. It is seldom, if ever, we read of a white minister having the moral courage to rise up and denounce the widespread barbarism that is so common in the Southern states. I believe in the day of reckoning when the judge of the whole earth shall come to judge the world, when the secrets of hearts shall be disclosed, God will hold the church responsible for the sins of this nation against its black citizens. White and black Christians in America, just think of it and, the most highly favored nation and country on the face of the globe, with hundreds of churches in many single cities, with missionaries, perhaps, without number in foreign countries; Africa, India, Hindostan, China, and many other places. Think of the millions of dollars of missionary

money sent from this professedly Christian country annually; the many sermons preached to the people every year on the condition of the heathen and
barbarians; many prayers for God's kingdom to come, that his will be done on
earth as it is done in heaven, that the light and truths of the gospel shall soon
cover the whole earth. And yet, here in this land, under the sound of preaching, in sight of many churches, eight millions of its law-abiding citizens, largely
professing Christians, has almost petitioned his white brother to let him to
hear the name of Jesus Christ, while conventions, conferences, assemblies and
associations of professedly Christian ministers and laymen meet, East, North,
West and South; but they never once think of passing strong resolutions condemning the murders, the assassinations, the lynching and whipping of black
Christian men and women, and driving them from their homes and churches.
If these conventions say anything whatever about their colored brethren, it
is of their evangelization of their obnoxious presence in white churches and
assemblies. If these people have the manliness to expect an answer for religious equality and freedom as all Christian people shall do, they are no longer
wanted among white people.

We do not believe God will use the kind of religion professed by the majority of whites of this country in saving the world. It is too narrow and selfish;
like the jug, the handle is all one-sided. The religion of the Bible as taught by
Christ is broad, taking in and equalizing all races and colors of men, and until
the white ministers in this country, from their pulpits, in conferences, associations, conventions, assemblies and synods, rise up and denounce the injustice,
the murdering and oppression of the colored American citizen, those ex-slave
holders of the South will not rest until this nation experiences another bloody
war. For remember that a portion of the white people of this land will not rest
now until the colored citizens enjoy all the rights socially, politically and civ-
illy, that all other citizens enjoy.

Philadelphia, Pennsylvania

AME Church and the Christian Endeavor
(*Christian Recorder*, August 1, 1895)

HISTORICAL CONTEXT

Rev. Yeocum's sermon against Christian hypocrisy echoed a common complaint in the 1890s. In 1895, there were eighty-nine registered lynchings just in the southeastern states, and many believed white ministers were partly to blame. This particular sermon calls out a bishop of the proslavery Southern Methodist Episcopal Church, Bishop Galloway, for practicing "caste prejudice" in his public address. It also identifies white American Christianity as being the progenitor for "race prejudice in the Christian Church in this country." Pious theological protectionism often pointed toward the racial responsibilities of the white church when its voice was silent about lynching.

SERMONIC RESPONSE

After reading the interesting proceedings of the annual convention of the Christian Endeavor Society held in Boston recently we were so pleased with the deliberations and freedom accorded the colored delegates from both sections of the country, we are prompted to write a few thoughts on the above subject.

In the one hundred and eighteen years of advancement and development of the Christian Church, necessity, which is always the mother of invention, as the ages moved on demanded the organization of several powerful auxiliaries to the great work of the Christian Church, which cannot now be dispensed with. The first of these was the Sabbath School, the second was the Young Men's Christian Association, the third was the Salvation Army, the fourth and last, but by no means least, was the Young People's Christian Endeavor Society. Of the three former no one would dare question their importance, power and usefulness to the Christian community where they are supported properly. Their work of soul-saving, uplifting, reforming and rescuing fallen men, women and children cannot be overestimated. The good done by them will be felt and seen in the ages to come. Each of them has its place and work as auxiliaries to the Church. One cannot do the work of the other. God in his own way is making each of them a blessing to the world of Christian civilized communities.

There is also the Epworth League. This organization or so-called Christian auxiliary is peculiar to the Methodist Episcopal Church and the Southern Methodist Episcopal Church. Their annual convention was held recently in Chattanooga, Tenn. There were of course many colored representatives delegates from both sections of the great M.E. Church. Without doubt there were some learned and able speeches delivered to that vast gathering of men. But Bishop Galloway, of the Southern Methodist Church, who preached the sermon of the occasion, got down on his knees, so to speak, and crawled up to the arch idol of the South, "caste prejudice," seen and felt in Church and State, worshipped it as the heathen does his idol. He is reported to have used these words in his sermons "I have nothing but contempt for him who canonizes the man who goes to Africa to save the Negro, and ostracism for the man who stays in Chattanooga to save the Negro." My heavens, I wonder if he read the Sunday School Lesson of a few Sundays ago of the sad taking off of Nadah Abihu for offering strange fire upon God's altar. Those were instructive words from the lips of a Christian bishop to the rising generation of his class. Reading between those lines he virtually says he has nothing but contempt and ostracism for the Lord Jesus Christ, for he came to save the Negro of Africa and of Chattanooga. It is a good thing that God is merciful and forgiving.

The Christian Endeavor moves out upon a higher Christian plane—the principles of Christ—accepting and treating all its members and delegates upon one common Christian level as brethren.

At the convention held in Boston the color line was not drawn. The 5,000 and more Christian men and women there assembled knew no man by his color or the crimp of his hair; all were received and treated alike by the hotels, restaurants and places of entertainment Many of the best families were anxious to entertain the colored delegates. This is Christianity pure and simple and any other is not worthy of being called religion nor Christianity. The religion of the heathen who knows no God is just as good.

My opinion is, that the endeavorers are doing more and will continue to do more to drive away or kill race prejudice than any organization bearing the Christian name. We hope every bishop and minister holding a charge in the A.M.E. Connection will encourage the organization of a Christian Endeavor Society in every A.M.E. Church in the land. An editorial in the Philadelphia Press has this to say:

"One of the best features of the recent Christian Endeavor convention held in Boston was the absence of race distinction. The colored delegates from the South and elsewhere were treated exactly like the white delegates and given the same privileges and opportunities. There were colored singers, colored ushers and colored speakers. The hotels, restaurants and cafes showed no wish to discriminate against the colored people and some of the leading citizens of Boston invited colored delegates to their homes to enjoy their hospitality. The long and short of it was that the colored man and woman were treated according to their merits and given equality of opportunity with the whites. This liberality of the Christian Endeavorers is commendable. It may be that the breaking down of race prejudice will be one of the chief results of the growth of this organization."

There has always been too much race prejudice in the Christian Church in this country. This our brethren in white learn too slowly because there are so many influential ministers in the various denominations who are too weak-kneed to preach against race prejudice when they should know there never was a white or a black gospel. Thus it has rankled in the Church of Jesus Christ until the political institutions and business corporations of the country are effected [sic] by it. If the Christian Church had started out right and kept right on the subject of race prejudice there would have been no slavery, there would have been no civil war and there would not have been so many lynchings in the South. The two former have passed away forever and the latter will have to go, for the morning light is breaking and the darkness of thirty years ago is disappearing. God has raised up the Christian Endeavor to bring together in one grand Christian fellowship and union all Christian men and women in this country regardless of race and color.

4

FRANK J. WEBB

An Evening at Bethel Literary (Christian Recorder, January 3, 1895)

HISTORICAL CONTEXT

Charles Burleigh Purvis was one of the first clinically trained African American physicians in the United States. He was also a founder of the medical school at Howard University. Due to his proximity to Metropolitan AME Church, Purvis was a frequent guest speaker for the church's Literary Society meetings. These gatherings were often devoted to the teachings of Black respectability, as well as Black excellence through intellectual growth. It was the lack of such tenets, according to Purvis, that fueled lynching's continued presence in American culture. Black religious spaces that emphasized pious theological protection often influenced the ideological beliefs of Purvis, including a belief that "the iniquitous power engendered by slavery gave a hereditary tendency towards brutality, bestiality, and crime on the part of whites; but I fail to comprehend a similar rule applied to us for obvious reasons." This reason, for Purvis, included a hereditary practice of Black criminality, including a propensity toward rape.

When Rev. Frank Webb published his retort, he exhibited the theological complexities being argued in intellectual Black churches of the day. This particular argument included the belief that southern Blacks were actually committing crimes, and if Black people were equipped with a proper moral base then lynching would subside.

SERMONIC RESPONSE

On last Tuesday evening the wealth and culture of the Capitol City assembled in the magnificent Metropolitan church in attendance on Bethel Literary to listen to Dr. Charles B. Purvis' address on the "Negro Raper and His Lyncher." . . .

Dr. Purvis was at his best. In personal appearance this great son of a great and grand patriot is all that can be desired. Dignified and pleasing in his address, Dr. Purvis at once captivates his audience with a cheerful humanity irrepressibly strong. It is only necessary that he be heard to capture the thoughtful and the intellectual. With a voice attuned and pleasing, Dr. Purvis uttered arguments and irresistible logic in a manner calculated to win adherents to a just cause. Possessing a greatness of mind verging upon the extraordinary; with vast conceptions remarkable for their profound depth and scientific research. The speaker of the evening during every moment of it held the closest attention of his large audience. Conversations with men and books and politics, learned in the various languages, experienced in the wisdom of statecraft as but few of our leaders are. With all of these advantages and more, Dr. Purvis, notwithstanding, spoke words of wit and wisdom direct from his soul. He spoke the truth as he saw it; not one word tempered by policy. Every line of his eloquent and philosophic oration evinced a free mind above the awards of the learned or the powerful; loving truth more. Not a single earnest sentiment was checked; like a rushing torrent came words of wit and wisdom and scientific research. Listening to him that evening I recognized the beauty of true enthusiasm.

For the first time it came to me strongly that the human mind, no matter how enriched with acquisition, is capable of achieving but little unless accompanied by an ardent and a sensitive heart. Teeming with learned, classical allusions as was the address, the idea of formalized intellectuality, never once occurred to me while listening to it, because of its evident sincerity and inspiring enthusiasm. I realized vividly that the fountain of action is the feeling. Listening to Dr. Purvis, the remembrance came to me of having once met a beautiful woman in the valley of the Rio Grande, and asked among other questions the number of her children. "I have two here and three in Paradise," she calmly answered, in the beautiful language of Spain, with a tone and a manner of grave and touching simplicity. Her heart was the fountain of her faith; there could be no surer. In his every argument and thought Dr. Purvis, like his grand old father always did, spoke the sincerest thought of his heart. The concentrated thoughts of a lifetime were put in an hour's effort, and in every line the undying enthusiasm of a heart unbeguiled by place or power and filled with an unfaltering devotion to his race, was apparent.

With fine scorn and a sarcasm entirely his own he analizes the causes and effects of raping and lynchings. He argued that both crimes were originated by society. That we were all creations of circumstances; our environments made or related us. In eloquent periods . . . pitiless logic in language chaste and elegant Dr. Purvis exposed the root of the present evils. His profound knowledge of science, his wide range of reading rendered his argument well nigh invincible. The factor time is the principal element required in the elimination of both rape and lynching in the Southland, said the speaker. How earnestly do I, too, long for the disturbing hatred of us to die out. There in the tropics of our land, the beauties of nature and their grandeur are most lavishly displayed. The somber robe of winter is nowhere spread with more enrapturing effects than in the land cursed today as no other land, by rapings and lynchings. The woodlands of no clime present so many beautiful tints as this during the dying months of the year. Rich in poetical associations it requires but the heroism of law and order to make it an Eden.

There was one phase in Dr. Purvis' argument which I reckon I did not clearly comprehend; but if comprehending, I must enter my earnest protest. It was the hereditary tendency for crime causing both rapings and lynchings. If that was the idea, I cannot agree with it as I understand our race. There was not advanced a single circumstance warranting the assumption that any raper had a parent guilty of the same horrible crime. It has never come to me where a barnburner had a father or a son addicted to the selfsame propensity. The progenitors of the present national race of lynchers were unknown; indeed if they existed. Lynching was a lost art, providing it is not a new one.

The thoughtful can, however, agree with Dr. Purvis far more readily in the case of the lyncher's hereditary tendency, than in that argument applied to the ex-slave. It is unquestionable that the iniquitous power engendered by slavery gave a hereditary tendency towards brutality, bestiality and crime on the part of the whites; that was but natural; but I fail to comprehend a similar rule applied to us for obvious reasons. Heredity is law. I can never believe a race can acquire beastial habits in a generation. In ante-bellum days, for docility and meekness our race was unparalleled, not a crime of the kind charged against us; as I understand it, it is against all laws, human and divine, for us to change our natures so suddenly and so thoroughly. Therefore, if I understand this particular line of argument, I must beg leave to enter my humble dissent.

It is as impossible for me to write on all the world shades and phases and beauties of Dr. Purvis' paper as to cut a cameo into perfect resemblance of the original gem. I simply cannot do it. It was not more remarkable for the fewness of its faults than for the greatness of its beauties—so evenly balanced, so profoundly philosophical, so deeply scientific was it. Overflowing with greatness of fancy, force, pathos and enthusiasm; unrivalled for comprehensiveness, depth and originality; sagacious, clear and reasonable; no portion cold, timid or superficial, that address on "Raping and Lynching" deserves to stand as the representative of the concentrated thought of 8,000,000 patriots.

The debate, how can I characterize it? The gallant, hoary-headed Douglass opened it and the scholarly grandson of the saintly Payne closed it. Little gleams of pleasantry, sparkles of imagination, flashes of genius radiated through it. The beautiful, sweet-voiced Mrs. Mary Church Terrell spoke with tenderness and such perfect elegance and simplicity as to enrapture, as she always does, her audience. The great Douglass spoke with the old fire and eloquence which captivated and charmed. The sparks of wit and wisdom which he gave out showed that on this night at least, the fuel upon the altar of his genius was of the proper quality. The stately, learned Prof. Kelly Miller with his proverbial delicacy and a scrupulousness, to my mind, this evening lacked his usual fire, originality and earnestness. Exactly why, I am at a loss to say; I only felt that his usual seriousness and force and energy were lacking.

Bethel Literary, in conclusion, has accelerated and confirmed a literary tendency among our race. It has excited profound thought and originality, and familiarized all of us as no other agent could do, with the beauties and value of exact learning. It has brought knowledge and enterprise of other climes home, not close to our imaginations, but to our experience. It has induced a more and effectual demand for thought, less vague.

5

JOHN ROBINSON

A New Thing Under the Sun (*Christian Recorder*, September 7, 1893)

HISTORICAL CONTEXT

Rev. John Robinson's sermon brings light to a "new thing under the Sun," or white southern preachers addressing lynching in their congregations. The particular preacher discussed by Robinson, Rev. J. R. Sanders, was ministering to a congregation in Arkansas, which saw ten lynchings in the year 1893. This number put Arkansas in the top tier of lynchings per capita for the year. Just the month prior, on August 5, a Black man named Will McClendon was lynched 150 miles south of Sanders's location, and it is likely that this act highly influenced his sermon.

SERMONIC RESPONSE

I take this method of informing the many readers of the *Recorder* and especially the A.M.E. preachers of Arkansas, that I have witnessed a new thing under the Sun. I visited the camp meeting ground of the white people of the Camden district last night and was made to rejoice at the words of one of their preachers. The preacher referred to was the Rev. J. R. Sanders, pastor of the M.E. Church, South, at Fordyce, Ark. The Presiding Elder of the district, Rev. Caison, preached a very good sermon, after which the Rev. Sanders arose and said, "My friends, the presiding elder has preached you a good sermon, but there are many things, yes, many things he might have said, which I will say. Sin is running this country, Arkansas especially; Ouachita county most especially. Why? Because at Bearden, where for years harmless and innocent Negroes have been living in sin, has caused the powerful white man to forsake pride, justice and religion and lynch his helpless black brethren with no other cause than that he is black." He told them that such thing as lynching and mistreating the black man would soon throw the white man back into heatheanism and bondage. Many promised that their hands should never be stained with such and other crimes. Thank God there is light ahead. Keep praying, brothers and sisters, God is in the midst of His people and will help them in times of need. The words referred to coming from a Southern white man—a preacher of the M.E. Church, South, a man who lives not more than twenty miles from Bearden, who spoke to a whole congregation of white people, I being the only colored person present, and he did not know I was there; I therefore call it a new thing under the Sun.

6

WILLIAM B. DERRICK

The South: It Is the Home of the Negro
(*Christian Recorder*, August 8, 1895)

HISTORICAL CONTEXT

Dr. William B. Derrick, a southern missionary for the AME Church in 1895, often wrote his findings in the denominational periodical. Many of his responses aligned with the tenets of Black respectability. In the face of lynching, these sentiments included a reminder for the African American to not fight back but to remain in faith, for "God's retributive justice places the sword of vengeance into the hand of the Negro."

SERMONIC RESPONSE

My trip through the South has been both pleasant and fruitful—pleasant as to the splendid reception accorded me wherever I went, and fruitful as to my increased knowledge of the conditions of our people in that portion of the country. The South is, as was Egypt of old, the land of Ham; it is the Negro's home and he is there to stay. He is as indigenous to its soil as is the cotton, the rice, the tobacco and the cane. The sun would feel just as strange in shining upon that land and not kissing the brow of the black man as it would in not seeing its rays reflected from the cotton fields.

The men and women of the race need not be ashamed of the progress their brethren are making in the South, for they are coming to the front with a rapidity that is phenomenal and unparalleled in the history of the world. There are two classes of people in the South among the whites and blacks—the upper or more wealthy and intelligent class, and the middle or more indigent and ignorant class. Of course, these draw distinct social lines on the basis of color; but as to condition, there is no marked difference. The wealthy and intelligent Negro is just as proud and haughty as the wealthy and intelligent white man; and the poor and illiterate black man is no worse off than the poor and illiterate white man. This shows a common humanity and a common original parentage.

There are among these lower classes white thugs and black thugs; but both are thugs. The better class of whites believe in treating the blacks fairly; but they are afraid of the thugs, who are in the majority; they deprecate the outrages perpetrated upon the Negro, but they are in the minority and stand in dread of the mob. In this the North is just as guilty as the South, for what it does not condemn it condones.

The Negro is the life blood of the South; without him the wheels of progress would be stopped. The labor of the South is completely in his hands and should he cease to work there, thousands of white months in Massachusetts and Rhode Island would starve.

The Negroes should combine and form unions and lock the doors against white labor there, as the whites do against black labor here. The Negro is industrious, he is accumulating property, he is becoming more intelligent, he is developing race pride and manliness of character. The teachers must be of their own race, for the whites would teach them that Robert Lee was a greater man than John Brown.

Wiley Jones, a Negro, of Pine Bluff, Ark., owns twenty eight miles of railroad for which he paid $92,000. He gave our conference of that State an excursion over his road. He is treated with the utmost respect by the whites. Where dollars are concerned, the color of the skin makes no difference.

The religious and moral status of the Negro of the South is just as good as it is of the Negro of the North. The reason why the Negro is painted so black in the South is because the abominable press of that section is color blind. That we have a bad element among us is most true; for if we did not have, we would not be as human as the white race. We are not opposed to a discriminating prejudice, but a prejudice that classes us all alike is a product of ignorance. We appeal to the Christian people of this city and State to help stamp out the lawlessness that is rampant in certain portions of the South. Lynchings there should cease, and it is within the province of the people of the North to put an end to them. But in the midst of fire the Negro sings hallelujah, and in the midst of famine he has enough to eat. Some advise him to fight for his rights; but we remember that the Indian fought and is now almost extinct. The Negro has endured punishment and is rapidly increasing. There is a providence in all this, and woe be unto this nation. When God's retributive justice places the sword of vengeance into the hand of the Negro.

7

CHARLES H. SPURGEON

From Our Exchanges: The Law and the Mob
(*Christian Recorder*, July 1, 1897)

HISTORICAL CONTEXT

In 1897, Rev. Charles Spurgeon published this op-ed against journalists and their slanted coverage of racial caste lynching. If change did not happen quickly, Spurgeon warned, "a righteous God will curse the whole land."

SERMONIC RESPONSE

While law is law there can never be any excuse for lynching in any civilized community. This is a declaration that has often been made; but it cannot be too often repeated if it is to be so slightly heeded whenever the occasion occurs for men to exercise their intelligence and control their passions.—*Brooklyn Daily Citizen*

We wish that all leading papers, like the *Citizen,* in this country would thus speak out against the monstrous lynchers.

Lynch law is still rampant throughout the Southland. The Ohio uplands seems to have given a sudden impetus to the industry in the land of its origin. Whither, are we drifting.—*The Appeal*

If these horrible lynchings are continued much longer, a righteous God will curse this whole land, and the civilized world will say: Amen.

To the aged Christian how the glories of the other world gleam through the veil which separates the seen from the unseen! Dr. Nathan Bangs wrote in his journal: "This day I am eighty-two years of age. My peace flows like a river, and I feel content with my lot in the world." "Oh, I have such mighty comfort" said Bishop Hedding, near the end of his pilgrimage. "I have served God over fifty years I have generally had peace, but I never saw such a glory before such light, such clearness, such beauty!"

It is not all unusual for God to make a complete shipwreck of that vessel in which his people sail, although he fulfills his promise that not a hair of their head shall perish (Acts 27:41–44). I should not wonder if he would cause two seas to meet around your barque, so that there should not be more than a few boards and broken pieces of the ship left to you; but oh! if you have faith in Christ, he will certainly bring you safe to shore.

8

WILLIAM JOHNSON

Vox Populi, Vox Dei (Christian Recorder, February 25, 1897)

HISTORICAL CONTEXT

Rev. William Johnson's sermon echoes similar criticism of silent white churches and clergy in the face of caste violence and lynching. For Johnson, America needs more "Daniels," or clergy who will speak out against oppression.

SERMONIC RESPONSE

This ringing thought has been handed down to us immutable from Sinai's burning heights and held inviolate through tradition. In the Forum is an article by Rev. E. M. Royce, Rector of American Episcopal College, in Florence, Italy, captioned the "Decline of the American Pulpit." In question he says why do we have so many inferior men in the pulpit is being repeated from pew to pew and from church to church. Speaking directly, while in every profession men have arisen to a better proficiency correspondingly, for instance, in 1870 there were about 43,000 ordained ministers; in 1880, 64,000, and yet they were no more trained in numbers than the 43,000. Rev. Royce contends that the church and the pastors are not keeping pace with the growth of the nation and that the pulpit is loosing [sic] its hold on the life and thought of the people, because it is loosing its spiritual eyesight.

The question most prominent aside from the spiritual feeling of the flock of Christ and duty of the Afro-American pulpits, irrespective of denomination is the subject of lynching and its dread alarm. If God speaks through man can a united, aggressive and intellectual effort reach the populace. In the dark days of slavery, the pulpit moulded public opinion. As slavery was and is wrong so is these diabolical deeds of mob violence.

No one dare question the Negro's patriotism, no rights are more sacred to him than religion, liberty and law. A thoughtful consideration of duty is paramount. Dare to be a Daniel to our ministry, the perception of unrest and emigration, lead us to consider that he who would be free must strike the first blow.

I hope the shibboleth will be sounded until a convocation of the Negro ministry shall assemble and set a united effort on foot to invite the white clergy to participate. Already our papers are doing their part; we bring up the rear unawed by influence, pledged to religion, liberty and law. These violations of law are menacing to government. Strike now.

9

HARVEY T. JOHNSON

Outrages in the South (*Christian Recorder*, March 30, 1899)

HISTORICAL CONTEXT

Reverend Harvey T. Johnson calls attention to the "recent outrages which have occurred in the south," including twelve lynchings that took place in March 1899 in Little River County, Arkansas; Campbell County, Georgia; and Yazoo County, Mississippi. In Little River, General Duckett was lynched on March 18 for the murder of a local planter, while Edward Goodwin, Joseph King, Moses Jones, and other unnamed men were lynched on the 21st by a mob of over two hundred onlookers. This deadly event would forever be known as the Little River County Race War.

Interestingly, as the mob chaos grew, there were some reports that "a few African Americans who disapproved of Duckett's activities actually participated in the lynching." According to the local Arkansas paper the *Mena Star*, "small parties of white men, varying in number from twenty-five to fifty, are scouring the country for them. Whenever one is found he is quickly strung up, his body perforated with leaden missiles to make sure of their work and the mob hastens on in quest of its next victim." On March 23, the *Mena Star* reported that "seven negro men have been lynched by the citizens of that section. . . . All of the victims that have fallen before the whites were pursued singly over the country and met their fates at different times and in different localities. In the gang that was plotting for a race war there were thirty-three negroes, and it is likely that the entire number have been strung up in the thickets."[41]

The war would continue for multiple days, and reports of additional violence were posted on March 25:

One report states that the whites are still out in organized posses hunting the leaders in the negro revolutionary plot with the avowed intention of hanging them wherever found. Another report states that the negroes are recovering from their panic and terror and are securing arms and threaten vengeance on the whites. . . . A negro who arrived here to-day from Wilton says that every negro in the neighborhood of Rocky Comfort and Richmond has left his home and is afraid to return. A large number of them have crossed Red River and gone into Bowie County in Texas. He says more negroes have been killed than has yet been reported.[42]

SERMONIC RESPONSE

At the meeting of the African Methodist Episcopal Preachers' Association held Monday last at Allen hall, 631 Pine Street, Rev. H. T. Johnson, after calling attention to the recent outrages which have occurred in the South, introduced the following resolutions, which were unanimously adopted, and a committee of seven adopted to put them into practical effort:

Whereas, the jury and lynchings of defenseless colored citizens continue to reach our ears through reports from the Associated Press; and

Whereas, those shocking atrocities are neither detected or punished by the proper authorities; and

Whereas, the pulpit and religious forces in this section where these outrages of her fail to reboot [sic] or refuse to remedy them in any way;

Resolved, that this, the African Methodist Episcopal Preachers' Association of Philadelphia, realizes the grievousness of the situation in the necessity of resorting to divine need as their only redress in this hour of overwhelming peril to our people;

Resolved, that this body call upon the leaders, organization and members of the race everywhere to set apart a day of fasting and prayer to Almighty God that the hand of the slayer be stayed and that justice be meted out to the guilty and that the innocent and helpless be protected;

Resolved, that we resort to moral suasion by enlisting public opinion for the press in the pulpit, and seek to secure sympathy and aid of those in a position to help us.

10

S. R. BRIDENBAUGH

The Awful Crime of Lynching (*Christian Recorder*, May 18, 1899)

HISTORICAL CONTEXT

S. R. Bridenbaugh's lament is a familiar charge against apologetic white presses of the South and their coverage of lynching. According to the author, this particular spirit has even affected the white church and such "ministers as the Rev. Carlyle, Pittsburgh, whose utterances are a reproach to our Christianity and encouragement to the Southern mob."

SERMONIC RESPONSE

Sir:—I cannot refrain from assuring you of my high appreciation of your recent editorials in commendation of lynching. So frequent have become these fiendish acts of the white savages of the South, and so apologetic and the tone of many newspapers in reference to the subject, that one almost despairs for the future. But hope comes with a great paper like *The Press,* voicing as it does the sentiments of thousands of the press people of this country, denounces with such courage and force the frequent exhibition of the barbaric spirit among the white people of the Southern states.

Next to the loathing one feel for the savages that comprise the cowardly mob which shames justice and outrages law and order is the contempt for those intelligent people of the North who condone or seek to apologize for the awful crime of lynching. In molding public sentiment newspapers in the pulpit have a great responsibility. We rejoice in their every utterance against race hatred in the mob spirit. May God spread the church of such ministers as the

Rev. Carlyle, Pittsburgh, whose utterances are a reproach to our Christianity and encouragement to the Southern mob.

May you continue the noble effort to check the spirit of lawlessness as manifest in Southern lynching. Thus will you save your people from a relapse to barbarism. In such writers must rest, in great measure, the hope of our Christian civilization.

11

A. L. GAINES, G. D. ZIMMERSON, AND L. H. REYNOLDS

Report of Committee on the State of the Country
(*Christian Recorder*, May 16, 1901)

HISTORICAL CONTEXT

This committee presentation concerning the state of the country puts the onus of Black lynching partly on the denomination itself. According to the authors, "The church has responsibilities along each and all the above lines in order to make the state of the country salutary and healthful. Attempts are being studiously made by our supported friends as well as by our enemies to hold up that class of our country's citizenship in false and misleading lights." This particular response resides in the construct of Black respectability, as the authors believe that a lack of criminality would spare African Americans from violent outbursts in the South.

SERMONIC RESPONSE

To the Bishop and Conference:

We, your committee on the state of the country, beg to submit the following:

In the light of the history of the long line of evil consequences resultant from the union of church and State, our opinion today is consistent with our position all along, namely, that the maintenance of separation of church and

State is conductive to the best interests both of church and State. And yet notwithstanding this view, there is an important sense in which the interests of church and State are identical, and in which the responsibilities of church and State are great, and among the lines upon which the responsibility of church and State is involved and dependent, it is the purpose of your committee to report.

The state of the country can be seen through a consideration of its administration aspects. This country's President today has devolved upon him responsibilities surpassed only by those that confronted the immortal Lincoln. Rarely does a man become elevated whose actions are satisfactory to all of those whom his labors touch. Much can be said concerning what some have elected to call the President's expansion policy.

More perhaps can be said of the policy of the President in essaying to extend the blessings of liberty to Cuba and of the far-off Philippines while the same blessings are unable to be secured to some of its immediate citizens.

And yet when we consider the complications growing out of our foreign relations and the reasonably friendly relations existing between our country and the other great countries of earth, we are constrained to commend the efforts of the Administration for good and to still pray for the representative of our Administration.

The state of the country may be seen also from a consideration of its fiscal relations. We read with some degree of alarm of the enormous expenditure necessary for the maintenance of the country. And yet when we consider the vast machinery of government and the millions under its fostering care the expenditure is inconsiderable. The industries, both naval and by land, affording means of subsistence and their constant enlargement and multiplication, convince your committee that the fiscal relation of the country is commendable. Not simply by virtue of the above considerations, but by virtue also of its relation to efforts at prison reform can the state of the country be seen. The public sentiment of the country is forcing grand juries and those in authority to investigate prisons as never before. The conditions of prisons in the State of South Carolina by virtue of which many of its citizens are only slightly removed from slavery have not only demanded the attention of grand juries of that State, but the condition has attracted the attention of the country for good. In our own State Penitentiary by Dr. Chas. N. Carrington, an official of that institution, in a paper before the Academy of Medicine and Surgery, said: The cells themselves may be properly dubbed death traps and crime promoters, and there will be a blot on the escutcheon of the fairest State in the Union until this condition is entirely improved. This and all other such statements are unmistakeable signs that the state of the country is improving along the line of Prison Reform. The state of the country may be seen also from the tendency to spread popular education. Some few, and I trust a very few in some States, and I regret to say such is the case in our State, are inclined to legislation that has no justification in accepted statecraft to abridge the privilege of education as it relates to some of its citizens, but it is the hope of your committee that such an unholy sentiment may never be obtained among any considerable number of its ruling classes. The state of the country may be seen also from a growing governmental interest in the ameliorations of tenement conditions. In some States, e.g. New York public sentiment has been so aroused toward the bettering of the condition of tenement quarters that the legislatures have been led to take some action at least by way of investigation. Your committee is of the opinion that when the country becomes thus aroused in the less fortunate, the state of the country is being bettered. The desire to estop mob violence is an indication of the state of the country. Possibly the spirit and tendency toward mob violence in this country received its most stinging blow in recent times from China's representative to this country. Said he: Lynching is an American institution! Mob violence is one thing that puts heathen China above Christian America, and yet it is the belief of your committee that the sentiment against this practice is growing bright. In this the responsibility of the church is two fold. Its responsibility is great as it relates to educating the press to assume a strong and unequivocal position against this foul blot upon America's civilization, its responsibility is enormous in the reformatory effect upon that class from which persons lynched are selected.

The church has responsibilities along each and all the above lines in order to make the state of the country salutary and healthful. The African Methodist Episcopal Church has special work in bringing about this salutary state of the country with reference to that position of the country's population of African descent.

Attempts are being studiously made by our supported friends as well as by our enemies to hold up that class of our country's citizenship in false and misleading lights.

Your committee does not believe such statements as one-third of the negro race is below where it was in slavery, one-third where it was at emancipation and only one-third has made some progress, are statements that are true. The A.M.E. Church is to give standing to the race, and by force of its achievements, refutation to such slanderous charges.

Your committee also desires to express its regrets at the repeated attempts of certain sections of our country to discriminate in regard to the elective franchise as applied to its citizens. Your committee makes no complaint against laws governing the elective franchise applied to all alike. But it regrets all attempts to maintain a property or educational qualification as a necessity for one class of the country's citizens that do not apply to all alike. Your committee considers all such procedure as an encroachment upon human rights and destructive for American institutions, as well as of a large portion of American citizens. Your committee sees in the passage of separate car laws or as they are generally termed "Jim Crow" car laws, a studied attempt to degrade and humiliate the race of African descent, as well as to cut off aspiration toward improvement and self culture, while theoretically the laws are separate but equal, yet no one who has had any experience with this system of car separation, would assert that there are equal accommodations. It is hoped that public sentiment may be aroused to such an extent that this foul blot may be removed. In view of the above considerations, your committee desires to recommend adherence to the principle of separation of church and State in the ordinary sense, but alliance of church and State in efforts to cause the milk of human kindness to permeate the whole people. The State in its attitude to the negro is seen along the above lines and further. The separate car law might be endured, the right of suffrage might be given up, but this country, north and south, is now engaged in the work of denying the negro the right to compete in the hard struggle for bread, when that struggle must be made in the field for skilled labor. And this phase of the negro question is becoming as alarming as are the phases already indicated in our report. Industrial schools will not bring us out of the perplexing difficulty as long as trades unions are permitted to so intimidate capital as make it possible for these unions to exclude negroes from membership in them and yet refuse to work with negroes.

A. L. GAINES, CHAIRMAN

G. D. ZIMMERSON

L. H. REYNOLDS

12

JOHN G. ROBINSON

The Negro on Lynching (Christian Recorder, July 22, 1897)

HISTORICAL CONTEXT

Rev. John G. Robinson has one of the most radical examples of pious theological protection in this collection. As a strong believer in Black respectability, Robinson goes so far as to say that "I do believe that if the white man would consider the numerical, financial and intellectual weakness of the negro as a race and give him that cordial support of protection that the law provides, the negro preacher, teacher, editor, etc., will within the next two decades make it impossible to hear of a rape being committed by members of our race." For Robinson, lynching's demise rests at the feet of Black church missionaries and their ability to curtail Black lawlessness with pious revivalism.

SERMONIC RESPONSE

To the Commercial Appeal:

I have been for a long time, and am still a subscriber to the *Daily Commercial Appeal,* through your local agent.

Recent numerous outrages and attempted outrages committed by lawless negroes and followed by swift punishment at the hands of lynching parties, have called forth much comment by editors of various papers and numerous writers. Leading men of the white race have ventured their thoughts through the columns of the great *Commercial Appeal,* and their thoughts are awakening a sentiment that will ere long bear rich fruit. I deem it a duty (as a negro) to ask the privilege of saying a few words concerning the alarming crimes that are tending to weaken civilization—rape and lynching.

I do not hesitate to say that there are numbers of rapes and other crimes committed by individual members of the negro race, and there is not a thinking negro but what feels keenly the sting of the actions of this thoughtless and lawless element.

The well posted white man, who will take the time to read negro journals, and converse with negro leaders will bear testimony to the fact that the negro is outspoken in denouncing the rapist and all other classes of law-breakers. We feel that we are struggling now as no race has had to struggle since time began—taught for upward of 200 years, the law of obedience and subjection, and then liberated and turned loose to fight life's battles single-handed, so far as the obtaining of morals are concerned, you will admit that we have done well. Political leaders and supposed great men scooped out a canal between the whites and blacks of the South, immediately after the war, which it seems that time will never fill. The young white man and the young negro hardly ever "speak as they pass by."

One has been taught that the other is his enemy; hence the weaker must succumb to the will and wishes of the strong. Therefore, whenever a crime is committed by the weaker, whether that crime be "the unpardonable sin" or a less crime, the stronger will do according to the dictates of their mind, and deal with the weaker accordingly, whether by letting the law take its course or popular uprising of a "lynching bee." Then, whatever public sentiment says will end the whole affair.

In those days of the past, when the negro was in closer touch with the white man, these heinous crimes were unheard of. I do not advocate a social commingling of the races and would be among the last to do so, but I do believe that if the white man would consider the numerical, financial and intellectual weakness of the negro as a race, and give him that cordial support of protection that the law provides, the negro preacher, teacher, editor, etc., will within the next two decades make it impossible to hear of a rape being committed by members of our race.

This protection can only be had by the arousing of as high a public sentiment against lynching as now exists against rape.

I am in favor of putting out of existence, every man who will violently disturb the virtue of womanhood. I am in favor of putting them out of the way in any manner that can be described in the category of punishment, but let that or those manners of punishment be written upon the statute books of our great commonwealths. Until this is done, crime of various kinds will continue to be committed by vicious ones of both races, and will be followed by mob violence, till the hands of this great country of ours will be stained in blood and the underlying principles of our civilization will be undermined and the overthrow of our great republic will be the outcome.

J. G. ROBINSON,
Pastor A.M.E. Church
Durant, Miss., July 6, 1897

13

N. B. STEWART

On Lynching (Christian Recorder, December 1, 1898)

HISTORICAL CONTEXT

Rev. Jesse Johnson is an interesting case study on lynching. The African American preacher was lynched on October 15, 1898, in Landing, Mississippi, by "his own caste." This was not the first time that a Black mob lynched someone in Issaquena County, as Samuel Wilson, a white man, was also murdered by a Black mob in 1884 for assault.[43] There is little detail concerning Johnson's lynching, outside of an article in the *New Light Journal*, published in Columbus, Mississippi. According to that publication, Johnson had been disturbing "the peace of the people," and it was for this that the Black community would enact a "sorrowful imitation" of lynching.

SERMONIC RESPONSE

The subject I am writing about has come to my notice so many times while reading various newspapers, that I have been persuaded through a feeling for suffering humanity, to write in connection with such heroic-minded objectors as Bishops Turner, D.D.; Derrick, D.D.; Dr. Johnson and others, who with the editor of *The New Light*, edited at Columbus, Miss., have been objecting to such barbarous acts. Following is a clipping taken from the aforementioned journal, relative to the lynching of Rev. Jesse Johnson, colored, on the 15th of October at Fitler's Landing, Miss., by people of our caste.

A SORROWFUL IMITATION

A colored preacher named Jesse Johnson, was lynched near Fitler's Landing in that community having stopped over on account of quarantine. The charge against him was that of being a disturber of connubial peace among the colored people, and they say it was by them he was lynched. We say to the black people of Issaquena county what we have always said to the whites. Lynch law is a relic of barbarism and not practiced by the most enlightened and Christian civilized people. This is a most sorrowful imitation you are about to put in practice, which in the end is bound to prove detrimental to your race and it has brought upon the community of Fitlers a disgrace that will last through generations.

Your contemporary makes some justifiable remarks in denunciation of the perpetrators of such an atrocious deed. What a continual phase is seen in the so-called dispensing of justice by the law entitled "lynch law." What a pity it was when Galloway in Ireland, Europe, allowed the power of his Satanic Majesty to have captivated his mind and caused him to have inaugurated such as unholy act.

The clipping will show what caused the victim to be disgracefully dealt with. One will admit that those who break the law of God and man ought to pay the penalty, provided that evidence deduced can convict and then the violator ought not to experience the shameful treatment of lynch law; but the redress should be from the code laid down by the makers of the laws which produce justice to one and all, irrespective of hue or nationality. Well might the editor of *The New Light* describe it as a "sorrowful imitation," and of a truth, if such imitations be not annihilated, it will surely "prove detrimental" to those of our race, and will be the means of causing the non-Christian to ask the question, is this the action of "Christian civilized people"; is this the way some of the followers of the lowly Jesus do? And the result will be if they so illegally execute justice, then it will be better for us to do without the acceptation of faith in Jesus, and through the act of lynching which is mostly done by the so-called workers of the church, others will be hindered from being brought to the fold of Christ.

My suggestive ideas are these: the voice of the preachers, especially in this section of the globe, should thunder out vengeance of Jehovah against such barbarism. The cooperation of the heads of the States and church for destruc-

N. B. STEWART 167

tion of such murderers ought to be effectively carried out; and the warning from the Decalogue, "Thou shalt do no murder." With these cooperators continually protesting against such acts, and the edict of God, "Whoso sheddeth man's blood, by man shall his blood be shed" proclaiming against such murderers, it will not be many years when the law of lynch will be obliterated from the presence of this great province, as was done in the colony where it took its origin.

In conclusion let me say that there are many innocent men, who had been subjected to this painful scene.

Yours for the church,
N. B. Stewart

14

TIMOTHY REEVE

Advantage of Universal Peace (*Christian Recorder*, January 15, 1891)

HISTORICAL CONTEXT

Rev. Timothy Reeve's letter is a Black respectability cry for universal peace. Through evangelism and missioning in the name of peace, Reeve believed, lynching could be made extinct.

SERMONIC RESPONSE

There is no subject known to mankind that affords any more ground for reflection than this one. We have never conceived the advantage there is in individual peace much less that of universal. So I shall not be able to mention but a few of the innumerable advantages of universal peace in this article.

It is true that we have a definition of the term peace that is pretty generally known, and we also have the common understanding of the meanings of the term universal peace, but, however well we may know this, I don't think a refreshing of our minds upon the subject by the way of a reiteration of this definition would be amiss.

The Latin meaning of the word peace coming from the Latin root pax conjuncted with paco, is to press or to stop. In a general sense it means a state of quiet or tranquility.

My subject presupposes the above state of things to be universal. Since man expresses the thoughts of his heart with his mouth by words, let these thoughts be good or bad, peace might as well begin here to exhibit its advantages.

Universal peace, affecting every relation that man sustains to man, would change his manner of expressing himself, no harsh words would be spoken, but universal thought would be expressed in the most pleasing tone and men would approach one another and fully relate their works in pleasing words without the least fear of hurting any one's feelings nor of having their own mortified. Hence, there would not arise disputes between man and man, no law suits had, no unfortunate defendant incarcerated for life or put to death on the scaffold, nor no brother would repeat the rash act of Cain's two men would dwell together in perfect peace, so would a body corporate an organized whole composed of mutually dependent and closely related parts dwell together in perfect concord. No lynching of men would be done, no State riots prevail, nor civil war waged. And this would lead to the recognition of the relation that people sustained to people whom seas and mountains divide.

And as perfect peace and accord are among people who are brought in close and constant contact with each other; so would perfect peace and accord prevail between all nations of the earth. O, who could paint the complexion of a world of mankind where such a state of things prevailed, and who could estimate the good that would follow? Not a single branch of business in the universe would fall beneath perfect development and not a single inhabitant of all the world go cold nor without food. This pure state of social and politic ethics could not exist of pure religious ethics also. And hence man would complete his life of duty under God, which would bring him to that heavenly rest, and to the enjoyment of the infinite pleasure of God in glory.

Mt. Pleasant, Iowa

15

JAMES HARVEY JONES

Texas Siftings (*Christian Recorder*, September 25, 1890)

HISTORICAL CONTEXT

Reverend James Harvey Jones's lament in his sermon concerns a support for African American emigration out of the problematic lynching states. His suggestion is one that was growing in popularity: "Emigrate, colonize, depopulate." For Jones, alongside other Black nationalists of the time, finding a "promised land" or area outside of the oppressive reign of white supremacy was a spiritual desire. For Jones, "coming out of Egypt you will depopulate those States that still hold on to the principles of secession, cut down their representation in Congress, and this will solve the Negro problem; and the solid South will be a thing of the past, and the Negro happy and independent."

SERMONIC RESPONSE

Much complaint (and I think justly, too) is now being made by our race in Mississippi, North Carolina, Georgia, South Carolina and Alabama, concerning their oppression. It is true that for a very long time our people have been crying out against these outrages that have been heaped upon no other people in the world's history like unto ours, the sayings of some that the present oppressed state of the Negro is only a repetition of Jewish hardships to the contrary notwithstanding. 'Tis too true that much of our troubles are the first of our own planting. With regret we reluctantly acknowledge the uncalled for perfidy, deceit and ingratitude now existing among our race, one toward another.

Much of our trouble comes from the unfaithfulness of our own selves. In too many instances are we betrayed and slain in the house of our friends; at times we scarcely know who to trust. How often have we not seen the most honest purpose which would result beneficial to our race, crushed to the earth by some traitor, and the result being in different places, whipping, lynching and such like?

The fact is too patent to be disputed the Negro must think, work and govern himself under the same principles of manhood that have characterized and made distinguished the success of other nations. If I am permitted to originate a word, stickalacity is what our race wants more than any one thing. Compatibility, concentration, a oneness of purpose in the accomplishment of a great end.

By divine will and for a holy purpose, God had permitted us to be located in America, and, too, in the garden spot of the Western hemisphere, and notwithstanding the rapidity with which we have gained education and wealth, yet there is such a multiplicity of men and women who are allowing the most golden opportunity of their lives to pass before their eyes.

Why, there are thousands of our race who are renting land that they have cleared up through the unrequired toil of themselves and families, who pay a rentage of from $3 to $5 per acre. At first the same land could have been bought at $5 per acre.

There are thousands of acres of land as good and as fertile as any that has ever brought forth a stalk of corn, blade of grass or boll of cotton, awaiting our coming and possession; land that can be purchased upon any terms that the purchaser may dictate, and yet our people will remain in huts on land that will not produce a quarter of a bale of cotton to the acre or ten bushels of corn.

What we want is organization; move out of those States whose customs and laws offer no protection to its citizens. I had rather climb a tree, or live among the aboriginees or man-eaters than live in a State like Mississippi, whose recent constitutional convention tries to put a bridle on the elective franchise of her citizens. How does or how can such a country expect the class that in time of peace she crushes, to be loyal in time of war? The veriest worm that crawls will turn its head in resentment when imposed upon. Men, men, men, we are men and as men we should prove our manhood, yet these very same people whose very nature it is to oppress, tries, in the face of such acts as the constitutional convention of Mississippi is honored with the jim crow cars of Georgia, that suffers the cowardly attacks on college professors and editors, to convince the world that they are the best friends of the Negro. Angels and men defend us! If our leading men of the South were a unit, they could very easily change the state of affairs in the so-called solid South. To do this is the work of only a moment. Emigrate, colonize, depopulate.

The idea of men placing our people in the Yazoo Mississippi Delta, or in the sugar farms of Louisiana. What for? Just to be murdered and outraged.

One million of our people can settle on the Brazos, San Bernard, Colorado, Navadad and other tributaries in the South and southwest Texas, where the land is of virgin strength, fat with anxiety for the yeomen of our race to tackle it with their plows, and will laugh in bringing a harvest such as never can be produced in any other Southern State.

The Texas Farmers' Colonization Association has under its control in Brazoria, Fort Bend, Matagorda, Jackson and other counties, over one hundred thousand acres of land for sale at low figures to actual and bona fide settlers, in localities where wood, water and health abound, on water courses that abound with the choicest fish. It would be well for the men who represent our people in localities where they are oppressed to consult Rev. S. H. Smothers, or N. H. Haller or the writer at Brazoria, Texas, should they wish to locate in what will be at no distant day, the very best place for the Southern Negro.

Where good schools and churches are a specialty, where peace among the races is as secure as it is anywhere, it will not be very long before capitalists (some of whom are now prospecting) will open a highway in building the Coast Line R.R. The Pan-American road is now under construction, linking the two Americas together, which will doubtless run in the very heart of the land which is now being offered for a song to our people. Accept these opportunities. Do this my people. Secure for yourselves land, build houses, make home happy. Educate the boys and girls, and by coming out of Egypt you will depopulate those States that still hold on to the principles of secession, cut down their representation in Congress, and this will solve the Negro problem; and the solid South will be a thing of the past, and the Negro happy and independent.

16

A. S. BAILY

The Church and Race (*Christian Recorder,* November 2, 1893)

HISTORICAL CONTEXT

Rev. A. S. Baily's sermon is a bold attack on American criminality, which includes the lynching culture of his time. This is the second of Baily's sermons of the same title in this collection, as he frequented the discussion of religion and race. According to Baily, "There was a time when all lynching was laid at the doors of lawless ruffians, but the Louisiana judge says it was not the class at the most prominent citizens of Jefferson Parish who lynched the three men Saturday night."

The Jefferson Parish lynching took place on September 16, 1893, when Valsin Julian, Paul Julian, and Basile Julian were publicly killed and their bodies presented to 10,000 people.[44] Rosellus Julian, the eldest brother, was said to have political ambitions, and was a "rabid republican." In a public dispute, it was said that he shot and killed Judge Estopinal on September 15. A posse was able to round up the brother (Paul) and his two cousins, but Rosellus was not found. It was said that prior to being lynched, the men prayed aloud, including a "rambling prayer of a negro in distinct tones, while the younger one, who knelt down, recited the Lord's prayer."

The death of the brothers, who were members of a local AME Church, impacted their congregation. Pastored by Rev. Mr. Forrest, the congregation was under great social duress. Due to the proximity to the bodies, the church was forced to "close their doors on Sunday." In addition, "officers were kept constantly going, visiting the different negro churches and halls to see that no riotous language was being indulged in." It was said in an article that Rev. Forrest "threatened to sue the parish for $5000 damages, as a compensation for the closing of his Church, which has ensued, as a natural result of the terror of his congregation. He said he would immediately consult with his bishop in regard to the matter and make all arrangements to bring the matter speedily to the test of the courts."

According to the *Times-Picayune,* the lynching also played a role in "a general exodus of the negro element from that portion of the parish. Yesterday was to be seen the curious spectacle of negroes binding up their bedding and making general and hurried preparation for a speedy departure."[45]

SERMONIC RESPONSE

MR. EDITOR:—

In defense of the church—the AME Church in particular, and the race, please allow me space for the following.

There are two things, for the prosperity of which I have been swallowed up in anxiety—my race and my church. From boyhood these two subjects have been before me and my interest in them have increased as the years go by. When I think of the great number much riper in years and experience than myself, I hardly feel like speaking; but thought it not imprudent speak in defense of these two great causes. Judging from articles which from time to time appear in the paper from observation and experience, I have grave fears that the wheels of African Methodism are being or will be clogged instead of being lubricated, because there seems to be a growing spirit among ministers which is not conducted to godliness and prosperity. This, to some extent, is conveyed to the laity. I have wondered with Bishop Tanner if we were not trying to extend our borders too rapidly, thereby getting to ourselves snares and slanders, which would serve as brake on the wheels.

It seems to me that too much time is being spent in family fighting, worthless displays and alternatively complaining and boasting, and not enough in the earnest work. Would not a more economic expenditure of money and more united efforts in many things at home in the states enable us to extend our borders more rapidly and plant ourselves more firmly?

Glorifying in the past achievements, have we not become too proud, haughty, and selfish in our work? And have we not attributed too much to ourselves? God forbid. Whatever the conditions may be, it has appeared critical enough to me for a careful examination.

Supposing though the church be all right and perfectly safe from calamity, or even hindrance, there is no dodging or explaining away the condition of the black man in America, and is becoming more serious every day, and not better as some have it.

I am not an alarmist or sensationalist or anything; but why call it day when it is night? When it's dark and getting darker, can we believe that the day is breaking? No. So is this case.

A few years ago when lynching began to increase, it was done in the dark and by masked men; but now in the day by unmasked men. They were uncommon then, but now almost as common as Orr's cats. There was a time when all lynching was laid at the doors of lawless ruffians, but the Louisiana judge says it was not the class at the most prominent citizens of Jefferson Parish who lynched the three men Saturday night. What is the real condition when influential men say, "let lynching go one." A judge says, "I will go out to lynch a guilty Negro anytime the people want me to go—go willingly," and when judges, Senators, sheriffs and representatives, and all other officials will he be mob to lynch men? Strange to me why some men—so many will try so hard the whole world forever will find speech and deceitful words.

Mob law has been catered, cherished and encouraged till they find but little need of fear. Though how ever popular it may become some day and God will wreak vengeance upon its advocates, and distress them with dreadful calamities—not by men, but by power which they cannot resist. When no one need to suppose that I favor the criminality and when I do not. I favor severe punishment to every criminal. But punishment by law and not by mobs. Too many loose criminals in the world now is one of its troubles. Now turning the other side of the picture to find the causes of all this trouble, it will be found the black may be the sufferer—must bear a part of the blame. Too many of us are always ready to stoop to them with low a thing, too ready to disgrace to ourselves, too little inclined to elevation, too great lovers of trifles, bad associates and vanities generally; in fact too much inclined to evils, by which we tangle ourselves and deep are much of our needed protection. Hence the cause and effect. Now in the face of all these things it is certain that something must be done. What shall it be, and how can be done? Are we supplied with capable leaders for a race Reformation or are weak capable of side? Would colonialism be our condition? Or would it feel our due to barbarism?

God knows the one thing I believe: that colonization or no colonization, Africa or no Africa, protection or no protection from the law, the preachers, teachers and other leading characters of the race, together with the older pants, can do great good in relieving our suffering by organizing Reform clubs in every community for the purpose of more carefully training the young men and women and infusing into them a spirit of self-respect, race pride, intelligence and high citizenship, getting them on their own ground—on the side of right, honor and true man and womanhood, or protection can come without fear.

Notwithstanding many false accusations have been made against our people, which caused many graves to be filled with innocent bodies, we believe some of them to be true, which battles us in our efforts in decisions in behalf of the accused. Therefore if there be a cause, let's remove it, then we can more successfully treat the effect. Whatever the plans may be, for god's sake let us stop talking so much them with something to be done. If we are men of any period, it seems now the time to put it in action, as we must act or soon be deprived of the power to act.

17

JAMES HARVEY JOHNSON

The Nation's Time for Reflection (Christian Recorder, July 4, 1889)

HISTORICAL CONTEXT

Rev. James Harvey Johnson's sermon masterfully exposes the African American's theological cry for divine justice and retribution. This methodology includes the contextualizing of white tragedies as being works of God. According to the preacher, "On the heels of every black man lynched scores of white men by disaster are swept from the face of the earth. But Jersey Summarily made atonement for the blood of Mingo Jack." Mingo Jack, a falsely accused freed slave from New Jersey, was brutally beaten and lynched outside a jail in Eatontown, New Jersey. The memory of this tragic northern lynching was still relevant for Rev. Johnson and his congregation.

SERMONIC RESPONSE

If ever there was a time for the people of the United States to stop and think, that time is at hand. One minister of the AME Church, Rev. J. C. Embry, says: "God has a controversy with his nation and it is not yet settled." This is true and sooner or later will be made plain.

The sins of this nation are as high as mountains; prominent among them are those against the Indians, the Negro and the Chinese. Time and space will not permit me to dwell at length upon those against Indians and Chinese, and so I will speak of those concerning the Negro.

This nation persisted in holding the Negro in bondage until the Word was about to destroy it upon the mountain slopes of Gettysburg. There was no victory until the Commander-in-Chief agreed to set us free. That was done; but there is intense prejudice North notwithstanding colored men fought, bled and died that the North might live. There is deep hatred South, notwithstanding colored people nursed the babies instead the families of those who were struggling to bind their fetters still tighter on them. And so like grains of wheat between the upper and nether millstone, the colored people are bruised and mangled and almost crushed. In some respects the last estate is worse than the first. Debarred by prejudice from lucrative mechanical and other employment in the North, May, as best they can, have to combat with the hatred of the South. Numerous are the instances in this dilemma of their failing to obtain even shelter, clothing and food which they once did obtain as slaves. And then still worse, crowds of men and even boys (I speak of what my eyes have seen) are loaded down with chains, like the sufferers in Siberia, to be consigned to the fatal coal mines or to some other place of labor and of misery. Let some unconscious philanthropist go and listen to the tales of woe coming from these quarters and he will find every spurt of charity in his breast kindled into a living flame to set aglow even the quiescent spirits of Wendell Phillips, Thaddeus Stevens and Charles Sumner. The hand of oppression in old slave times was made of brass, now it is of iron.

And then within this, awful deeds of lynching. Oh, how much blood, how much innocent blood (for who can tell the degree of a man's guilty until he is first tried) cries from the ground today! Hark! It cries along the southern valleys and that goes through the gorges. It cries for vengeance. Vengeance will come. Mark how certain is that indication! On the heels of every black man lynched scores of white men by disaster are swept from the face of the earth. But Jersey Summarily made atonement for the blood of Mingo Jack. Blessed be New Jersey; she is an exception. Everywhere else, unchecked, the diabolical work goes on. Somebody picks out the victim, says "It is he!" Others cry, "Hang him!" The bloody deed is done. The morning papers proclaimed the poor fellow a brute; hell shouts, heaven droops in sadness. And so it goes until the fathers and mothers, wives sisters and brothers bereaved stand as supplicants before the throne, saying "Oh, Lord how long? How long?" Whilst they are doing this, others of the race throughout the land are clustering around them to increase the volume of their prayer. Others again, appointed for this purpose, are from time to time taking the names and number of those slain, for publication.

The people of this land better stop and consider. I strove to incite them to do so after the Charlestown earthquake, but the medium to which I applied was afraid, I suppose, as the press says, "of losing a few dollars worth of southern trade." Those who have any sense of right better raise their voices against this great crime and lose all such patronage than to incur the inevitable wrath of God.

The sad events of the present day ought to be taken as a warning. He who goes along the banks of the Potomac, where colored men have been lynched like dogs, will see how great has been the recent havoc. Then let him look at Frederick County and consider the balls of fire rolling through the city. The Lord will not always chide. The stormy wind fulfilling his word, cyclones and tempests, snowflakes, swelling tides, sheet-lightning, and bursting clouds will be directed against those defied justice and trample upon that golden rule even observed by the ancient heathens: "Condemn not a man until he is thoroughly tried and proved guilty."

Now, when we consider the other great crimes to be added—the robbing and slaughtering of the Indians, the preclusion of the Chinese from the light of Christianity, the avariciousness controlling corporations, the desecration of the Sabbath day by work and pleasure, the extensive indulgence in inebriation in the whiskey business and blasphemy, the corrupted inclination to countenance gambling, prize fighting and horse racing and other sins like the rank weeds growing, what else can one do but apprehend God's judgments?

It is time now for the pulpit and press to combine in a crying aloud against the evils and dangers of the present and hour. The times require strong preachers—thundering Isaiahs and weeping Jeremiahs. Let them "cry aloud and spare not." Let the people be turned from the error of their way that they may repent and be saved.

Hagerstown, Md.

III

CONSTITUTIONAL
THEOLOGICAL PROTECTIONISM

INTRODUCTION

The foundational seed of Black constitutionalism was planted in the soil of Black America by the Black church. Frederick Douglass and Daniel Alexander Payne, two Black Methodists who were among the first of their race to visit the White House, relied on the tenets of constitutional theology to petition for Black uplift. W. E. B. Du Bois, one of Black America's earliest intellectuals, also exhibited a public fight against racism by examining the hypocrisy of white Christianity. In fact, "Du Bois stood in a long tradition of African American defiance of white Christianity."

> All of the key elements of black liberation theology—God's hatred for exploitation, Christ's alliance with oppressed people of color, and the emancipatory features of Christianity—were present in a wide variety of Du Bois's writings. His regular attacks upon the white Christ and his discussions of a black messiah show that the crucial features of black liberation theology existed in spirit, if not in name, well before the works of Cone, Cleage, Roberts, and Jones.[1]

The AME Church (1816) was founded more than a decade before the early twentieth-century social gospel movement, but the acceptance of sociopolitical activity to enhance Black safety was an original tenet in the discipline. According to James Cone, the Black church in general has always identified Jesus with his trials of social oppression. This mindset aligns with what Howard Thurman describes as a disinherited Christ, or a person who is politically disenfranchised and without political protection. Constitutional AMEs believed themselves to be operating under the same emancipation ethos as Jesus and recognized how in the face of being lynched, Jesus and his followers challenged the oppressive laws restricting liberation.

AME ministers often addressed their lack of constitutional rights, particularly the Fifth Amendment right to due process, when addressing lynching. In the face of lynching spikes, constitutional protectionism saw a rise during the Nadir era, especially in the South. In 1887, when Rev. N. W. Edwards witnessed lynching spikes in Carolina, his request was both theological and political: "We demand in the name of reason, law, humanity and God those rights decreed to us from the foundation of the world." Outside of lynching, additional concerns for constitutional protectionism included socioeconomic and voting rights.

From constitutional pulpits, Fifth Amendment rights were aligned with the Passion story of Jesus Christ. These ministers argued that lynching without a fair trial was a violation of a person's spiritual rights, and if American politicians did not protect people who were lynched, then the blood was also on the nation's hands.

Attacking President Benjamin Harrison became a foundational tactic for constitutional protectionism, and few ministers stood stronger than Rev. William Henry Heard. Born to enslaved parents, the Georgia native worked his way into a state legislative position in South Carolina and eventually became a US ambassador to Liberia. His proclivity for politics was not separate from his theological beliefs. This included demands that elected officials provide Black spiritual and physical protection.

The inability to protect Black bodies motivated Rev. Heard to emigrate to Africa. He was motivated by the nationalist teachings of Henry McNeal Turner and believed physical peace to be a necessity for spiritual growth, though both Heard's and Rev. J. W. Smith's attacks on President Harrison also exhibit the aim of constitutional preaching. This methodology requires a critique of national political matters, including of the press. Rev. Heard would go as far as to depict the press as the enemy to the African American.

Strategic lynching headlines have occurred throughout lynching's historiography, and journalists have been exposed as playing a part in organizing "lynching spectacles." Amy Louise Wood's *Lynching and Spectacle* and Christopher Waldrep's *Lynching in America* are two seminal studies of how some papers helped to create lynching events. These processes included the act of "black crime and moral dereliction dominating southern newspapers," and "narrative representations of lynching . . . reproduced these rituals of white dominance and unity for a larger public." Therefore, when the press was creating headlines and stories that created a national "rhetoric of white unity and moral superiority," it was the AME minister's responsibility to make sure that article wouldn't "make that violence appear socially acceptable, even respectable."[2] The strategies for and dedication to fighting against this process were adroitly emphasized from Black pulpits.

Public challenges against the media were also presented in preaching form. According to Rev. R. S. Quarterman, a missionary board leader for the 11th District of the AME Church, ministers had the responsibility to preach and teach against lynch law until it was classed as a federal crime. When the lamenting ended, political work for constitutional protectionism ensued. Rev. James Townsend, a state legislator from Indiana and an AME minister, often used his position as a recorder at the general land office to emphasize the theological makings of constitutional protectionism.

Some of the ministerial actors within the constitutional protectionism ranks pushed for autonomously Black political conference organizations. W. B. Derrick and J. C. Embry were two of many leaders who organized groups of leading colored men in the larger cities to provide counsel for its political leaders. The plan was to create constitutional protection panels that could take the desires of their communities to "the source of our laws and government, for the correction of every evil now, as we have done in the past. This was the source of emancipation and the maintenance of the Union."[3]

According to constitutional protectionism, "religion means more than the mere preaching, praying, shouting and singing." Many attempts to provide legal protection came in the form of identifying like-minded organizations that sought protection—outside the church structure. In 1894, Rev. J. S. Henderson from Maryland made sure to provide a public endorsement of Ida B. Wells and T. Thomas Fortune of the Afro-American League. At the Bethel Church of Sullivan Street, New York, "Miss Ida B. Wells spoke to the audience. She spoke without paper or notes of any kind for about one hour and the vast audience was held spellbound by her thrilling narrations."[4]

Dual-dimensional partnerships also were established in the AME Church, for the benefit of the secular Black fight against Judge Lynch. Rev. Lampton helped to establish a platform for the Republican Party in the Mississippi Delta. The initiative "condemn[ed] lynching and mob violence. He is justly the leader of our forces in Mississippi. Unassuming, dignified and godlike, he travels and benefits mankind everywhere he goes."[5]

The AME Church also was responsible for its own constitutional programs. In the Thibodeaux District of the AME Church, members and officers sought to create a program that would "protest against the common practice of lynching and call upon the Christians and loyal people of the United States, and especially the Governors and President, to raise their voices in condemnation of the barbarous and inhuman practice of such crime, irrespective of race or color, and pray that the influence of the Higher Power will intervene, and stay the hand of the assassins."[6] The Reverends G. B. Billups, D. Burrell, and L. E. Carter, and Mr. L. Murphy led this program.

Other examples of constitutional theology could be found in the Georgia Conference, led by Revs. C. T. Shaffer (soon to be bishop), H. T. Johnson, and J. H. Bean. The conference minutes record that the leadership pushed a proposal to force Newman, Georgia, to protect Blacks who had been facing "horrible mutilation and [the] burning of [an] alleged murderer and rapist."

AME churches outside of the southern states also were connected to America's lynching problem. Bishop Walters, who oversaw New Jersey, was an avid supporter of a constitutional federal lynch law. According to Rev. G. F. Richings, Bishop Walters once argued, "I am reminded that I'm only a few miles from where the white people mobbed me and left me for dead. But, despite all these awful things I'm hopeful, and I fully believe that the colored man has a great future in the country and will play a prominent part in its development."[7]

By 1899, bishops across the international AME Church frequently addressed the prospect of lynch laws by using constitutional theological protectionism. As a bishop, Henry McNeal Turner would be quoted by Rev. Weaver in an article in August 1899 about the theological ramifications of such a law. This letter stated, "I know ten thousand objects will be raised against the bill and many will say that Congress will not pass it and that it would not be enforced if it were passed, and that the Supreme Court would declare it unconstitutional, etc.; but it has not been tried."[8]

Bishop Arnett's approach to constitutionalism protectionism was simple: stop complaining and be proactive. During an annual conference, the bishop argued that many legal representatives in the South were incapable of creating laws that would protect Black people. Therefore, it was the responsibility of the community to establish and force new candidates and laws. The bishop argued that "he had no faith in a man who would assault womanhood and declared that he was a dangerous character, when referring to local legislators."[9]

In Virginia, AMEs were at the forefront in publicizing the evolution of lynching events. Due to the federal policing of the Ku Klux Klan, lynching turned clandestine in order to avoid the public spectacle tradition of old. The practice of secretive lynching, or a one-on-one murder event, prevented southern towns from being negatively publicized as apolitical spaces.[10] Mrs. Ada Cooper describes her experiences with this trend and the necessity of a nuanced law to protect the shifts of white terrorist activities.

1

IDA B. WELLS-BARNETT

How Enfranchisement Stops Lynching (June 10, 1910)

HISTORICAL CONTEXT

William James was lynched November 11, 1909, in Cairo, Illinois. He was charged with the rape and murder of Anna Pelley but did not receive due process. The large spectacle was said to involve more than ten thousand onlookers and grabbed national headlines. Ida B. Wells's response was printed in the *Original Rights* magazine, with the intention of highlighting the hypocrisy of lynching.

SERMONIC RESPONSE

The Negro question has been present with the American people in one form or another since the landing of the Dutch Slaveship at Jamestown, Virginia, in 1619. For twelve years the founders of the English colony had indifferently succeeded in getting permanently established. The younger sons of the British were miserable failures as pioneers. They would not do the work necessary to wrest a livelihood from the bowels of the earth, and they could not make the Indian do it for them. One such colony perished from the face of the earth and succeeding ones lagged with indifferent success until the coming of those fourteen African slaves, who became the hewers of wood, drawers of water and tillers of the soil. They were submissive, and easily dominated, so they were harnessed to the plow and became the beasts of burden; then the Jamestown Colony began to thrive.

So successful was this first venture into slavery, that the shores of Africa were again invaded. Men, women and children were overpowered, captured, crowded into the holds of the slaveships, brought to this new country and made the slaves of the colonists. For two hundred and fifty years this condition obtained. The original fourteen slaves became four millions. Their unrequited toil had made this country blossom as a rose, created vast wealth for the masters and made the United States one of the mighty nations of the earth, ere the American people harkened to the voice which commanded, "Let my people go." When the mighty upheaval came which almost rent the American nation in twain, it struck the shackles from the Negro slave, and did not stop until he was not only a free man, but a citizen.

The flower of the nineteenth century civilization for the American people was the abolition of slavery, and the enfranchisement of all manhood. Here at last was squaring of practice with precept, with true democracy, with the Declaration of Independence and with the Golden Rule. The reproach and disgrace of the twentieth century is that the whole of the American people have permitted a part, to nullify this glorious achievement, and make the fourteenth and fifteenth amendments to the Constitution playthings, a mockery and a byword; an absolute dead letter in the Constitution of the United States. One-third of the states of the union have made and enforced laws which abridge the rights of American citizens. Although the Constitution specially says, no state shall do so, they *do* deprive persons of life, liberty and property without due process of law, and *do* deny equal protection of the laws to persons of Negro descent. The right of citizens to vote is denied and abridged in these states, on account of race, color and previous condition of servitude, and has been so denied ever since the removal of the United States troops from the South. This in spite of the fifteenth amendment, which declares that no state shall do this.

These rights were denied first by violence and bloodshed, by ku-klux klans, who during the first years after the Civil War murdered Negroes by wholesale, for attempting to exercise the rights given by these amendments, and for trusting the government which was powerful enough to give them the ballot, to be strong enough to protect them in its exercise. Senator Tillman told how it was done in a speech on the floor of the United States Senate, when he said, that he and the people of South Carolina shot Negroes to death to keep them from voting. This they did till Congressional investigation of Ku-Klux methods turned the limelight on the unspeakable barbarism of those wholesale murders.

The South changed its tactics after that investigation, but never once let up on its aim to nullify and finally abrogate these amendments and rob the

Negro of the only protection to his citizenship—his ballot. Again, we have the testimony of the United States Senator, on the floor of the Senate, as to how this was further done, when Senator Tillman defiantly told how he and his compatriots stuffed ballot boxes and threw out those of that remnant of the black South, which still tried to register its gratitude at the polls.

When this bewildered race turned in dazed appeal to the Government which gave it freedom and the ballot, awaiting explanation and beseeching protection, it was told that the Government had made a mistake in enfranchising them; that it had offended the South by so doing, and was now busy repealing the civil rights bill, affirming Jim Crow legislation, upholding disfranchising state constitution, and removing in every way possible the constitutional guarantees to life, liberty and the pursuit of happiness, removing everything, in fact, which was offensive to those who had fired on the flag and tried to break up the union, and the Negro must now look out for himself.

This he has done for the past thirty years as best he could. He was advised that if he gave up trying to vote, minded his own business, acquired property and educated his children, he could get along in the South without molestation, But the more lands and houses he acquired, the more rapidly discriminating laws have been passed against him by those who control the ballot, and less protection is given by the law makers for his life, liberty and property. The Negro has been given separate and inferior schools, because he has no ballot. He therefore cannot protest against such legislation by choosing other law makers or retiring to private life those who legislate against his interests. The more he sends his children to school the more restrictions are placed on Negro education, and he has absolutely no voice in the disposition of the school funds his taxes help to supply. His only weapon of defense has been taken from him by legal enactment in all of the old confederacy—and the United States Government, a consenting Saul stands by holding the clothes of those who stone and burn him to death literally and politically.

With no sacredness of the ballot there can be no sacredness of human life itself. For if the strong can take the weak man's ballot, when it suits his purpose to do so, he will take his life also. Having successfully swept aside the constitutional safeguards to the ballot, it is the smallest of small matters for the South to sweep aside its own safeguards to human life. Thus "trial by jury" for the Black man in that section has become a mockery, a plaything of the ruling classes and rabble alike. The mob says: "This people has no vote with which to punish us or the consenting officers of the law, therefore we indulge our brutal instincts, give free rein to race prejudice and lynch, hang. burn them when we please." Therefore, the more complete the disfranchisement, the more frequent and horrible has been the hangings. shootings, and burnings.

The records show that beginning with 1882, in which year there were fifty-two persons lynched, there was steady increase until 1892, when two hundred and fifty persons were lynched with the utmost cruelty, publicity and barbarism. Public sentiment condoned and approved this method of disposing of Negroes suspected or accused. of misdemeanor or crime against white persons. The custom spread to the North, East and West and lynchings and burnings occurred in any community in which a crime was committed and suspicion put on the Negro. An effort made in 1803 to get these facts before the conscience of the world, proved by statistics based on charges made by the lynchers themselves, that less than one-fourth of the persons hanged, shot and burned by white Christians were even accused of the usual crime—that of assaulting white women.

From the year 1894 lynching decreased year by year for the next decade. The conscience of the situation was again lulled to sleep and the record of the past ten years shows a surprising increase in lynchings and riot even in the North. No Northern state has more frequently offended in this crime than Illinois, the State of Lincoln, Grant and Logan. Since 1893 there have been sixteen lynchings within the State, including the Springfield riot. With each repetition there has been increased violence, rioting and barbarism. The last lynching, which took place November 11th of last year in Cairo, was one of the most inhuman spectacles ever witnessed in this country.

The Negroes of Illinois have taken counsel together for a number of years over Illinois' increased lynching record. They elected one of their number to the State Legislature in 1904, who secured the passage of a bill which provided for the suppression of mob violence, not only by punishment of those who incited lynchings, but provided for damages against the City and County permitting lynchings. The Bill goes further and provides that if any person shall be taken from the custody of the Sheriff or his deputy and lynched, it shall be prima facie evidence of failure on the part of the Sheriff to do his duty. And upon that fact being made to appear to the Governor, he shall publish a proclamation declaring the office of Sheriff vacant, and such Sheriff shall not thereafter be eligible to either election or reappointment to the office. Provided, however, that such former Sheriff may within ten days after such lynching occurs file with the Governor his petition for reinstatement, and give ten days' notice of the filing of such petition. If the Governor upon hearing the evidence and argument, shall find that such Sheriff has done all within his power to protect the life of such prisoner then the Governor may reinstate the Sheriff and the decision of the Governor shall be final. This Bill passed both houses, was signed by Governor Deneen and became a law in 1905.

In the Springfield riot and lynching of two years later, the only parts of this law that were applicable were those providing punishment for the persons inciting rioting and lynching, and damages for the relatives of the victims of the mob. The men lynched then were not prisoners in the custody of the Sheriff, but peaceable, law abiding citizens whom the mob lynched at their homes for the fun of it. Because of the dangerous public sentiment, which says it is all right to kill so long as the victim is a Negro, no jury has been found in Springfield to convict any of those who were tried for that lynching and murder.

On the morning of November 11th last year, a double lynching was reported from Cairo, Ill.—a white man and a Negro. A white girl had been found murdered two days before. The bloodhounds which were brought led to a Negro's house three blocks away. A Negro who had stayed in that house the night before was arrested and sweated for twenty-four hours. Although the only clew found was that the gag in the girl's mouth was of the same kind of cloth as the handkerchief of the prisoner, threats of lynching him became so frequent that the Sheriff took him away from the city, back in the woods twenty-five miles away. When the mob had increased its numbers, they chartered a train, went after the Sheriff, brought him and his prisoner back to Cairo. A rope was thrown over Will James' neck, he was dragged off the train to the main business corner of the town. The rope was thrown over a steel arch, which had a double row of electric lights. The lights were turned on and the body hauled up in view of the assembled thousands of men, women and children. The rope broke before James was strangled to death and before hundreds of waiting bullets could be fired into his body. However, as many as could crowd around, emptied their revolvers into the quivering mass of flesh as it lay on the ground. Then seizing the rope the mob dragged the corpse a mile up Washington Street, the principle thoroughfare, to where the girl's body had been found. They were followed by a jeering, hooting, laughing throng of all ages and of both sexes of white people. There they built a fire and placed this body on the flames. It was then dragged out of the fire, the head cut off and stuck on a nearby fence post. The trunk was cut open, the heart and other organs were cut out, sliced up and passed around as souvenirs of the ghastly orgy and our American civilization. Having tasted blood, a voice in the crowd said, "Let's get Salzner." Away went the mob to the county jail. Salzner, a white man, had been indicted for wife murder and was in jail awaiting trial. The suggestion is said to have come from the brother of Salzner's murdered wife. The mob demanded that the Sheriff, who had repaired to his office in the jail when Will James had been taken for him an hour before—get Salzner for them. He begged them to go away, but when they began battering in the doors he telephoned the Governor for troops. The lynchers got Salzner, hanged him in the court yard in front of the jail, emptied their remaining bullets in his body and went away. When troops reached the scene six hours later, they found, as the leading morning paper said next day, that "the fireworks were all over."

In mass meeting assembled the Negro citizens of Chicago called on Governor Deneen to do his duty and suspend the Sheriff. Two days later the Sheriff's office was vacated. Ten days more and Sheriff Davis had filed his petition for reinstatement, and on December 1st, argument was had before Governor Deneen both for and against the Sheriff.

The Sheriff's counsel, an ex-state Senator, and one of the leading lawyers of Southern Illinois, presented the Sheriff's petition for reinstatement, which declared he had done all in his power to protect the prisoners in his charge. He read letters and telegrams from Judges, editors, lawyers, bankers, merchants, clergymen, the Mayor of the City, Captain of Company K, of the State Militia, his political opponents and even the temporary incumbent of the Sheriff's office himself—all wrote to urge Sheriff Davis' reinstatement. The petitions were signed by hundreds of citizens in all walks of life and the Catholic Priest of Sheriff Davis' Parish was present all day and sat at the Sheriff's side.

As representing the people who had sent me to Cairo to get the facts, I told of the lynching, of visiting the scenes thereof, of the three days' interview with the colored people of Cairo, and of reading the files of every newspaper in the city published during the lynching to find some account of the steps that had been taken to protect the prisoner. I told of the mass meeting of the Negroes of Cairo in which a resolution was passed declaring that from Tuesday morning when Will James was arrested, until Thursday night when he was lynched— the Sheriff had neither sworn in deputies to aid him in defending the prisoners, nor called on the Governor for troops. We said that a reinstatement of the Sheriff would be an encouragement to mobs to hang, shoot, burn and pillage whenever they felt inclined in the future, as they had done in the past.

Governor Deneen rendered his decision a week later, removing the Sheriff. After reviewing the case he said: "The sole question presented is, does the evidence show that the said Frank E. Davis, as Sheriff of Alexander County, did all in his power to protect the life of the prisoners and perform the duties required of him by existing laws for the protection of prisoners? The measure of the duty of the Sheriff is to be determined from a consideration of his power. He is vested in his County with the whole executive power of the State. He wields within his jurisdiction all the power of the State for the preservation and protection of the public peace. In this capacity it is within his power to call to his aid when necessary any person or the power of the County. The law has made it a criminal offense for any person over the age of eighteen years to neglect or refuse to join the posse comitatus. In case the preservation of the peace and good order of society of any community shall require it, the Sheriff has the power to summon and enroll any number of special deputies. Such deputies when enrolled, have all the powers of deputy sheriffs and are subject absolutely to the orders of the Sheriff. It is made a criminal offense to decline to be enrolled as a special deputy. The Sheriff has the power to arm such force of special deputies to suppress riot. After having commanded the riotous persons to disperse, the Sheriff or his special deputies are justified in taking life should such riotous persons refuse to disperse.

The Sheriff is the keeper of the jail and has custody of all persons confined therein. In case of mob violence, which the Sheriff and his deputies are unable to suppress, the Sheriff may call upon the Governor for troops.

Such being the tremendous power vested in the Sheriff, what are his duties with respect to the protection of a prisoner who has been committed to his keeping?

Upon this question the Legislature has spoken in such terms as not to be misunderstood. It has cast upon the Sheriff the very highest degree of care. The Legislature in the mob violence Act of 1905. has said that in case a prisoner is taken from the Sheriff and lynched, the Sheriff after having been removed from office, must before reinstatement, show that he did all in his power to protect the rear life of such prisoner the Legislature has in this Statute specifically defined the duty of the Sheriff. No part of his power can with safety be neglected. The very highest degree of care must be exercised for the protection of the prisoner. The Sheriff must take every precaution that human foresight can reasonably anticipate. In fact under this Statute, the Sheriff is practically the insurer of the safety of the prisoner.

The law guarantees to the prisoner a fair and impartial trial, not by mob violence, but by the orderly proceedings of duly constituted courts. To this the personal presence of the prisoner is necessary. To await his trial the State has deprived the prisoner of his liberty. By the Statute in question, however, the whole power of the State surrounds the prisoner and guarantees to him the protection of his life.

Measured with these standards it does not appear that Frank E. Davis, as Sheriff of Alexander County, did all in his power for the protection of the prisoners. The crime was of such a nature to excite great public indignation. Ordinary prudence would indicate that at such a time riots, turmoils and breaches of the peace might be expected. No attempt was made then, nor at any time, to summon or enroll special deputies. Not the slightest preparation was made to resist the mob. No showing is made that the jail in Alexander County would not have been safe for the confinement of the prisoner William James. The Sheriff knew some hours before taking William James into custody that mob violence was threatened. Knowing this he neither enrolled special deputies nor communicated with the Governor advising him of the fact and requesting the aid of troops, although two companies of State Militia were stationed in the City of Cairo. In the face of this the Sheriff took his prisoner almost without protection, outside the County. When the Sheriff left the train at Dongola, no attempt was made to communicate either with the Governor or with the Sheriff of Union County. While the Sheriff had the prisoner William James in custody, it does not appear from the evidence in my judgment, that reasonable precaution was taken for his protection.

After the execution of James the mob repaired to the County jail. Although cognizant of the temper of the mob, no effort what-ever was made to place additional guards about the jail. Neither the Sheriff nor his deputies made any showing of force. The most that was done was to ask for volunteers. Although it must have taken some time to beat down the cell door, yet the Sheriff is unable to identify a single person composing the mob, or to identify a single person whom he asked to aid him in suppressing the mob. After Salzner was taken from his cell, no effort was made to follow up the mob and rescue Salzner.

In view of these facts only one conclusion can be reached, and that is that the Sheriff failed to take the necessary precaution for the protection of his prisoners. Mob violence has no place in Illinois. It is denounced in every line of the Constitution and in every Statute. Instead of breeding respect for the law it breeds contempt. For the suppression of mob violence our Legislature has spoken in no uncertain terms. When such mob violence threatens the life of a prisoner in the custody of the Sheriff, the law charged the Sheriff, at the penalty of the forfeiture of his office, to use the utmost human. endeavor to protect the life of his prisoner. The law may be severe. Whether severe or not it must be enforced.

Believing as I do that Frank E. Davis, as Sheriff of Alexander County, did not do all within his power to protect the lives of William James and Henry Salzner, I must deny the petition of said Frank E. Davis for reinstatement as Sheriff of Alexander County, and the same is done accordingly."

Alexander County was one of the pivotal Counties, politically speaking, in the last election. Sheriff Davis belonged to the faction of the Republican party in Illinois, which gave Governor Deneen his re-election to the executive chair in 1908, by a smaller majority than four years before. It was believed that because of this the Governor was obligated to heed the wishes of Sheriff Davis' friends. But he had a higher obligation as Governor to protect the fair fame and uphold the Laws of Illinois. He had the highest obligation of protecting his friends from themselves, of enforcing their respect for the majesty of the law, and of aiding them to see beyond their passions and prejudices, "so they might rise on stepping stones of their dead selves to higher things."

It is believed that this decision with its slogan "Mob law can have no place in Illinois" has given lynching its death blow in this State. On three separate occasions since Sheriffs of other Counties in the State have checked the formation of mobs by calling at once on the Governor for troops, and in this way prevented the scheduled lynching.

But the people of Cairo were not convinced, besides they were in an ugly mood because of Sheriff Davis' retirement from office and they determined to try the metal of the new Sheriff, who had sworn to uphold the laws. During the first week in March, two months ago, two Negroes were in jail in Cairo, having been arrested on suspicion of pocket-book snatching. Sheriff Nellis, having heard threats of lynching, immediately swore in special deputies and strengthened his guard at the jail. When the mob appeared at eleven o'clock that night, the

Sheriff warned them not to cross the threshold. The warning was unheeded—a volley rang out, and one man—the leader of the mob—lay dead on the steps, and several more were wounded. No lynching took place that night and Sheriff Nellis had done what the Grand Jury of Alexander County, sitting for the whole month of December, had failed to do—found the leaders of a mob. The dead man was John Halliday, the son of a former Mayor of Cairo, and his uncle owns the leading hotel in Cairo—the Halliday House, which bears his name. The others who were wounded were men of like station. They have since been indicted by the Grand Jury and it rests with local public sentiment whether a jury can be found to convict them of attempted murder, and make their punishment so severe that the lesson will not soon be forgotten.

In this work all may aid. Individuals, organizations, press and pulpit should unite in vigorous denunciation of all forms of lawlessness and earnest, constant demand for the rigid enforcement of the law of the land. Nay, more than this, there must spring up in all sections of the country vigilant, aggressive defenders of the Constitution of our beloved land. South Carolina and her section have dominated this country to its hurt and sorrow from the beginning. When Payne wrote the Declaration of Independence, South Carolina refused to come into the Federation Colonies unless they struck out the clause abolishing slavery. She won, and slavery was fastened as an octopus upon the vitals of the land. She was responsible for the cringing, compromising, yielding attitude of Congress on the slavery question for the fifty years preceding the war. She fired on the flag of the United States and for the fifth time attempted to secede from the Union. She plunged the country into the most terrible Civil War the world has ever known. She has led in all the secession movements for the nullification of the constitution and for the abrogation of the 14th and 15th amendment. She has led in all the butcheries on the helpless Negro which makes the United States appear a more cruel government than Russia, for her deeds are not done under the guise of democracy and in the name of liberty.

2

N. W. EDWARDS

Fiat Justitia Ruat Caelum (*Christian Recorder,* August 1, 1895)

HISTORICAL CONTEXT

In practice, the foundational belief system of constitutional theological protectionism reflects a social-political consciousness. It is within this space that ministers like Rev. N. W. Edwards believe themselves responsible to be conscious of the political landscape around them, and they are led by their faith to contextualize and apply biblical teachings to the nuances of their environments. For Edwards, the issue at hand is lynching, and the solution includes a biblical encouragement to help support a proposed lynching law.

SERMONIC RESPONSE

MR. EDITOR:—In view of the startling fact of oppression and lynching now in operation in different sections of the United States, and especially in South Carolina, which is being heaped upon my race, I am called upon by conscience to pen a few words for publicity by way of condemnation. Allow me to ask, is it right in the light of Scripture, reason, law or humanity? Is it necessary for the good of the republic? If such is your conviction, then I say continue it orate sempre. If not, then I say to each and all, bring to bear all of your combined forces upon these awful imposing monsters, which are destined to hurl this nation into such a crevasse of immorality and sin. I am proud of our American form of government and code of laws, but shudder when I think of how they are enforced—enforced, yes, and that in the eyesight of our lawmakers of both State and United States. I sympathize with the "Irish movement," now in progress in Ireland, and would to God that we, the poor negro, especially of the South, had someone who could and would so arouse this nation with his Chief d'senore of eloquence until she would acknowledge us as human beings and grant us those rights which God has given us.

We do not seek or beg for favors or intermarriage. No, no, no. But we demand in the name of reason, law, humanity and God those rights decreed to us from the foundation of the world. We are deprived of our rights before the courts of so-called justice, which ought to hold out to every man equal balanced scales without regard to race, color, position, political opinion or previous condition. We are cheated out of our earnings and driven from our homes and made to wander from place to place as if we were vagabonds. We are taken from the custody of the sheriff and from our homes, from the bosom of a wife and the care of mothers, sisters and children and whipped, shot or hung to some tree without judge, jury or law. "In this day there is no judge in Israel." Yes, such is the state of affairs in South Carolina and other sections of the South—the "Solid South"—the "New South."

Ah! Do I hear the query from statesmen and others asking, "Where is your witness and proof of Judge Lynch's work?" If it was necessary I could produce them, yea, living ones, but I simply say to the sane mind and to that one who doubts my assertion, Si monumentum requiris circumspice.

May I ask what next? Our votes are gone, the "Seventh," or "Black District" is all but out of our hands and what next? Oh, slavery! Slavery! Slavery! If this be what the "Pilgrim Fathers" came to America for—if this be what the "Colonial Fathers" fought for—if this is the pearl of great price which caused the disunion and rebellion—if this is the freedom that our fathers spilt their life blood on the battle fields for—if this is the liberty which called forth those burning words of eloquence from the lips of the eminent Patrick Henry, Caeteris paribus, give me slavery. Yes, give me slavery. Imprimatur that I say give me slavery. I call upon ministers and statement to life their voices in Church and in the halls of congress, etc., against this greatest evil of the day, remembering that "righteousness exalteth a nation, but sin is a reproach to any people."

3

JOSEPH WESLEY SMITH

Opinions and Personalities (*Christian Recorder,* September 26, 1889)

HISTORICAL CONTEXT

Rev. Joseph Smith, a minister in the AME Zion denomination, exhibits a concern for President Harrison and his lack of support for the lynching law. Constitutional theological protectionism will often push one to identify civil liberties as a theological expression of *imago dei*—being made in the image of God.

SERMONIC RESPONSE

Several weeks have passed since I penned anything to your excellent paper. I come again I like to write for your journal when an opportunity presents itself. The fiery Bishop Turner, the able W. H. Heard and scholarly I. F. Aldridge write occasionally for the *Star of Zion,* of my denomination, therefore fair exchange is no robbery. Your liberal spirit in publishing letters from ministerial brethren on the other side of the fence, exemplifies a desire for "fraternal" union, at least between these two great bodies of African Methodism. Now to business.

   Notwithstanding a whole army of office seekers have been tired out waiting for the appointments that never came and have left for home, there are still enough of that class left in Washington to impart quite a lively appearance on the streets during the day. It is safe to say they are not admirers of Deer Park which has temporarily removed from their grasp the head of the nation. They stand about hotel lobbies and walk the streets, a disconsolate lot, and make calculations as to how soon their prey will be within their reach again.

The ruling passion is so strong in some of them that they can't keep away from the White House during the absence of the President. They flit in a post-like manner about the corridors of the deserted mansion and try to imagine that they are in that state of blissful anticipation which is so attractive to the place hunter when he is waiting for an audience. The angry expressions, the scowl on some faces and the poking of fun at their less contented companions, tell pretty plainly how they feel. Some have run short of money and can't get home. They don't care to take the pick and shovel and do a little work so as to get cash to travel back home. Their hands are too tender—feet also. Poor fellow: there are very few crumbs falling from the national crib. I am glad I am not an office seeker. I am waiting for the office to seek me—in politics I mean.

The sneaking Democrats of the South are actually crazy with rage over the defeat of Grover Cleveland, and to console themselves have gone to work within the last three weeks, to lynch and shoot down by the wholesale the colored citizens who dare to stand up for their rights. Rev. Dr. T. G. Steward, one of the brainy leaders of the A.M.E. Church, in an address delivered in the Presbyterian Church, Baltimore, September 17th, said: "The recent troubles grew out of the unsettled condition of the country there and was now specially fomented for political ends." How true!

Lynching colored people is now the crime of the South. It is a disgrace. There is no State in the Union in which lynching can be justified; it is simply murder and men who take part in such homicide are murderers, no matter what their social standing may be. If they are respectable citizens, their guilt is enhanced by the fact of their respectability; for their example is calculated to subvert law and order and throw society into a state of anarchy. Encouraged by the example of men of character and influence, the tougher elements of whites conclude that they may with impunity trample upon the laws. Can nothing be done to stop this wholesale murdering? Is the State powerless? Can't a national government do something? It better had. The table may turn by and by. If President Harrison would show back-bone and speak out in behalf of a race who helped to elect him, it would do good. If the Indians or Chinese were being murdered he would soon speak out. When Clayton was murdered in Arkansas for political reasons, the President expressed himself pretty freely. Why not do the same for the poor defenseless Negro? We are American citizens and he is President of the colored as well as the whites. He should make the South obey the laws as well as the other sections of the Union. Grant did it. It is time to call a halt to this "murder business" of the South. Forbearance is ceasing to be a virtue. Our race leaders should bring this matter to President Harrison and urge him to say something about it in his message to Congress.

Washington, D.C.

4

WILLIAM HENRY HEARD

Items on the Wing (*Christian Recorder*, **February 6, 1890**)

HISTORICAL CONTEXT

In the midst of pushing for a lynching bill, many AME preachers sought emigration back to Africa. Rev. William Heard's response in this letter accentuates the
paradigm of constitutional theological protectionism while maintaining Black
autonomy, arguing, "We will go to Africa as missionaries, pleasure-seekers
and gold hunters, but will never accept traveling expenses of the government,
only when in its services. We are too American to be trapped by this bill."

SERMONIC RESPONSE

Tuesday finds us in Washington, D.C., full of the grip, but at the post of duty
assigned us. We visited Mr. Blair's educational committee. He assured us that
President Harrison was ready to do anything to stop this lynching. Our visit
to the President proved the assertion of Senator Blair true, for the President
said he had always condemned the unjust treatment of colored citizens in the
South and felt our agitation and organization was the very thing to bring about
a better public sentiment. He said there was an unrest that showed that even
those who lived in the South were not satisfied at the fraud and lynching going
on in South Carolina, Georgia and other States.

We also send you a letter from the *News and Courier* of Charleston, S.C.,
and our answer:

DEAR SIR:—In view of the action that will soon be taken by Congress on a proposal to aid the colored people to return to Africa, I would like very much to have the opinions of a number of the most intelligent leaders of the colored people on the subject. As I understand it, the proposal is to furnish free transportation and a small outfit to all colored residents of the Southern States who desire to return to the land of their fathers. I will be very much obliged if you will send me your opinion on this proposed exodus. I wish to publish it in The News and Courier and other leading newspapers.

Very truly;
JOHN LANGDON WEBER.
News and Courier, Charleston, S.C.

MR. JOHN L. WEBER—

SIR: In answer to your questions concerning the Afro-Americans being helped to Africa, I answer, I am opposed to any appropriation for the Negro as a Negro, for such recognizes a state of affairs that the constitutions of the States and United States do not recognize, that the Negro is an inferior to other citizens. I am of the opinion he should receive only what are given other citizens: free tuition in the public schools, just treatment on the public highways, accommodations paid for, recognition in the jury box and a fair trial by a jury of peers, the right to vote at any and all elections and to be voted for at the same, and have his vote honestly counted, the privilege to purchase and hold property, the protection of the city, county, state and national government and the opportunity to go to Africa, Europe or wherever he can pay his passage. This is the opinion of nine-tenths of the race. We know Messrs. Blyden, Hayne, Lee and Bishop Turner favor Senator Butler's bill; I take the high ground of an American citizen. We will go to Africa as missionaries, pleasure-seekers and gold hunters, but will never accept traveling expenses of the government, only when in its services. We are too American to be trapped by this bill.

5

ELISHA WEAVER

The Texas Holocaust (*Christian Recorder*, February 16, 1893)

HISTORICAL CONTEXT

The lynching of Henry Smith has been labeled the most gruesome in the history of Texas. Smith was found guilty of killing a three-year-old child and was lynched in Paris, Texas, on February 1, 1893. The child was the daughter of a local police officer, who had recently subdued Smith with vicious force.[11]

The lynching of Smith became notable for many reasons. First of all, the *New York Times* covered it, as it had become a national story even prior to the lynching. Second, the crowd in Paris had been estimated to be up to 15,000 strong, making it one of the largest public lynchings in American history. Finally, Smith was publicly tortured for more than fifty minutes, which included the mutilation of his body with strange objects, fire, and incisions.

A week later, Smith's stepson was also found hanging from a tree, his body riddled with bullets.[12]

SERMONIC RESPONSE

Had a white man been guilty of the dire deed for which the black man, Henry Smith was burnt alive at Paris, Texas a few days ago, it is said he would have shared a similar fate. Gross ignorance of our Southern situation, and its animus or a disposition to conceal the enormity of the crime for which that Parisian populace stands guilty is the only rational way of accounting for such a far fetched conclusion. True, had the fiendish deed been committed by a white brute upon a white child victim, in all probability vengeance would have been sure and swift had the perpetrator been caught. Even in that event however, though the deed were ever so diabolical and revolting, there would have been no savage course of revenge pursued by the community, much less winked at by those who constitute the law and order representatives of the community.

Supposing a white demon still the transgressor and a colored child the helpless and fatal victim of only a wild imagination would fancy the spirit of vengeance as taking such a turn and ripening into the malignity which marked the barberous tragedy at Paris. Unless the outraged parent or friends had taken the law in their own hands, supposing the boot upon a black foot the law would have been too slow to catch, much less punish, the pale faced sinner. As a rejoinder therefore to the gratuitous crumb of cold comfort affirming that a white man would have been thus dealt with we say it depends upon the value of the ox as well as the nature of the owner whether vengeance and how much of it would have ever overtaken the white man. Thus much however only as a preliminary to a higher observation and more serious view of the holocaust.

Far more in keeping with the dignity and responsibility of enlightened public opinion in this enlightened age would it be to divest the bloody deed of its racial or local aggravativeness and consider the danger and duty of civilization toward it. The seriousness of the affair is obvious in the fact that the chief instruments of public opinion and of civilization seem to be paralyzed and lifeless, in the failure of the state, press or pulpit of the land to record a protest or trumpet a note of warning against these organized evil-doers. If the law has any majesty, it is time at least for these advocates of public morality and acknowledged guardians of order and peace, to so declare. To remain silent when it is done, or openly endorse a mob's usurpation of the functions of the machinery of law, is a cowardice that breeds crime and culpability that society should and God will condemn.

To justify a community of murderers on the ground that it is natural for them to be revenged under trying circumstances, is madness, coupled with a vicious misconception of what is right. Of what use is the strong arm of law or the balance wheel of a reason but to suppress the animal and brute in an excited populace as well as in an enraged individual? To say that the law in such cases is too powerless to assert its supremacy, is an inference of guilt and self-condemnation, as inexcusable as the most deliberate deed of the foulest criminal. To plead the scalp taking practice borrowed from the Red Man is to go back to the dismal past and covet the vileness of a people that has never been able to rise above nature.

If the civilization of our land is to be arraigned thus, can the thing that passes for Christianity, not of the South alone, but of the whole country as well, hope to pass muster before Almighty Justice. Where and when has the Christianity of the land recorded its protest against mob violence, lynchings and race outrages? In some few conventions where individual responsibility would be felt to be so light that every one could afford to be a hero or imaginary martyr and forget it all on returning home. Unless the spirit of Wesley of Haven or Lovejoy or Beecher returns to America to pioneer its white Christianity, a thunderbolt from God is liable to drop at any time and blast its shallow form.

The formal part of the Texas holocaust is over now. No such a day was possibly ever witnessed in the town of Paris as that on which its assembled thousands witnessed the roasting alive of a human fiend, perhaps. The platform which furnished his temporary Tophet is perhaps taken down. The hot irons and angry hands and incensed rabble who were party to the execution by torture have all cooled down by this time.

With the exception of three Southern newspapers, to wit, the "Macon Telegraph," "Atlanta Republic," the press of the South has endorsed that outrage upon society, civilization and law. The same moulders of public thought and morals has doubtless endorsed the brutal lynching of the step-son of the burnt man and another innocent man who was killed by the infuriated mob who held him to fatal account because he was thought to resemble the real criminal. The viciousness of the Southern moral sense surely could not have been missed too far, when a white visitor to the scene of burning declared that the participants in the mob were no better than the victim they tortured, provided the part be taken as a sample of the whole South. Another outspoken champion of right, declared that it was not surprising that such products of degradation as the burnt Negro should disgrace Texas, judging by the wholesale manner with which that community plunged in the most revolting crime.

We may take our leave of the subject by commending the stand taken by the Governor of Texas. Unfortunately however, it was taken too late to save the name and credit of the State. It is better nevertheless that he has spoken though late than never. He must after all be somewhat of a leader to break with the public sentiment as represented by the press and his party and call upon the associate powers to assist him in maintaining the majesty of the law. Would that as much could be said in favor of the churches of Texas and of the South who are satisfied to follow rather than lead in the matter of moral reform and practical righteousness.

The Race Question, Mobs and Lynching
(*Christian Recorder*, August 10, 1899)

HISTORICAL CONTEXT

Rev. Elisha Weaver, like many constitutional theologians, had to acknowledge the need for a careful strategy when taking on lynching. Weaver's introduction of the lynching law to the African Methodist Episcopal Church is a wonderful glimpse into how the lynched community interpreted its political right to employ theological protectionism. In the later portion of this speech, Weaver includes a powerful shot against many of his peers who interpret lynching as an act of vigilante justice. This includes people who justify lynching due to Black criminality; this is as much a farce as it is demeaning, to Weaver. "Neither our ignorance or our poverty should be taken advantage of, for we are not responsible for either."

SERMONIC RESPONSE

Last week we clipped and published from the Boston Post and bill prepared by the Hon. Edward Everett Brown, one of the leading lawyers of our race, and the Secretary of the Massachusetts Citizen's Association, touching the lawless treatment of human beings in many sections of our country. The bill aims to make lynching a crime against the government and requires the government to take cognizance of it and punish the guilty. It is not the purpose of the proposed bill to reach the crime of lynching through an amendment to the Constitution, but by a law placed upon the statute books of the United States. The bill has been carefully drawn up, and if passed, and enforced, the crime aimed at would soon cease to be committed. Lynchings have become so frequent in this country that courts of law are beginning to be little thought of, but almost in every section the people, or rather the lower order of them are ready at a moment's notice to join in a mob and hang, shoot and burn the accused without a shadow of trial and not even wait to take any kind of evidence. I know ten thousand objects will be raised against the bill and many will say that Congress will not pass it and that it would not be enforced if it were passed, and that the Supreme Court would declare it unconstitutional, etc.; but it has not been tried. While the people of all race-varieties are interested in such a law, it cannot be gainsaid that we, more than any other variety, are sufferers from the mob-spirit and ought, without doubt, to be more earnest in our advocacy of the passage of this or some other law that would take from national authorities the least semblance of an excuse for not seeing that life is secure with us any and everywhere, and that if accused of a crime a trial shall come before the penalty is executed. The thousands of our poor helpless people who have been cruelly murdered cry this from the other world to take some steps towards our own lives.

There is no use talking about fighting; that is all the worst kind of nonsense. We have not got the guns, the ammunition, the leaders nor the disposition to fight, and if we had them all, we would find ninety per cent of the American people up in arms against us, for blood is thicker than water, and all we would get by attempting to raise up and fight would be annihilation. What we want is the right law and its rigid enforcement. Such a law is the one we are discussing. Let the race unite in an effort to get Congress to enact this bill into law and then rigidly enforce it. After it is passed and one of our people is accused of crime and is brought up for trial let us be just as ready as the other people to say when he is proven guilty, let the law be executed and the guilty punished, and not one of us to screen the guilty.

As a race we ought to try to do something and to insist upon our right to live and pursue our own course in trying to get on in this world, being always subject to the law. The fact is, we have never made a united effort for anything in the interest of the race. If we have effected an organization we have soon divided and turned it into a self-aggrandizement institution; but we can unite and we can do much toward self-help by uniting. Our race in this country has suffered torture enough. From the day of our landing on the banks of the James River down to to-day we have been most cruelly oppressed, and no people on earth have been more patient and submissive under it all than we. Our poor old mothers and fathers meekly bore all that was put upon them, and only went to Jesus on their knees and told Him about it. In due time, as God saw fit, relief, to a certain extent, came, but not then till "millions of broken yokes went floating down a river of blood." We are still praying, and for one, I believe in still praying and talking to God and we must do something else at the same time. If I meet a sick man I tell him to pray and put his trust in God, but that if he knows a good doctor of medicine get to him as quickly as possible and that God will be a good deal more apt to answer his prayer and restore him to health if he does make haste to get to the doctor. Let us stand just as close to God as we possibly can and at the same time let us find every Congress man we know and insist upon the United States Congress passing laws that will ensure our safety in a country which so many thousands of our fathers and brothers have died to save and make free. We did have a right to live until we forfeit our lives that any other people have or enjoy.

This talk about our being a race of criminals is false, as false as anything ever was or ever can be. We have our bad men and women just as every other race or people have, and our bad ones ought to be punished just as others are. But neither our ignorance or our poverty should be taken advantage of, for we are not responsible for either. The white man passed laws a few years ago to make it a criminal offense for us to be found with even the Bible in our hands, and now he will not allow us to join a labor union. As a matter of fact, it is just as easy for a colored man to be elected a member of Congress as it is for him to get the position of a motorman on a trolley car in the city of Philadelphia. I doubt whether one of the large stores in Philadelphia could be induced to employ a colored clerk even if the proprietor knew by so doing he could get all the trade of the forty thousand colored people in the city.

We are mistreated everywhere and in all parts of the land we have such a battle to fight as no other people ever had in the United States, and we must fight it. The one in question now is for our lives. The white people have always oppressed us and now they are killing us without law, judge or jury. This we must first get changed, and to do so let us without stopping to quibble over methods, try the one suggested and see what we can get the coming Congress to do. In the meantime let every colored man in the land resolve not even to look towards a white woman wherever and whenever it can possibly be avoided. Let us understand once for all that it does not make much odds whether we mean crime or not, the white people in many sections of the country have to get it into their heads that we mean to assault their women and they mean to take our lives if we even look toward them, therefore, let us keep our eyes in some other direction always and at all times. We have all the women of our own that we need or want. We have them of every hue and color and we need no other kind, color or class. We have them Black, brown, yellow and red, and if no other kind will do, we have them as white as any other race on earth. From them let us get our wives and our company keepers and leave alone, severely alone in every way, shape and form the women of every other race on earth. We may talk about our rights to choose whom we will, but this claimed right, if even hinted at, simply means death and ruin. Now, let it be well understood that I do not now and never have believed that one charge of a colored man attempting to keep company either lawfully or unlawfully with a white woman in ten thousand had the least particle of truth in it, but they had to lose their lives at the hands of blood thirsty mobs just the same as if all had been true. I know well enough that scores of our poor men have been accused to simply give a pretext to some enemy to get them out of the world and also know that at the great judgment day there will be fearful accounts to give, but at the same time nothing that we can say or do now will bring the victims back to life, so our work is to save the living. Let us do it by lawful means.

A New Way (*Christian Recorder*, September 28, 1899)

HISTORICAL CONTEXT

On September 16, 1899, Noah Finley of Pulaski, Virginia, was accused of way-laying and robbing a white man, one Major J. H. Darst, on a public highway. Finley went to trial in August, but the jury initially struggled to reach an agreement. When the jury was warned by an outside posse that they had until "10 o'clock this morning, or the Negro would be lynched," Finley was soon convicted and sentenced to hanging.[13]

SERMONIC RESPONSE

The outcry against the whole sale lynchings which have disgraced this country so long, is becoming so loud and pronounced that even the professional lynchers are tiring of the old and brutal methods. Lynchings do not cease but the methods are changing. In Virginia they have discovered an old law which permits the death penalty to be inflicted for such second class crimes as highway robbery, and the first to suffer under it, is, of course, a Negro.

Noah Finley of Pulaski, Va., was accused of waylaying and robbing a white man, one Major J. H. Darst. He was arrested and would have been lynched, but to save the disgrace of the state, this old and antiquated statute was brought to light. Under it, he was tried, convicted and executed. His body was exposed to the view of thousands of people, doubtless, to serve the double purpose of showing the organized lynchers of the state how easy it would be to give semblance of law to the execution of Negroes, and of showing to those Negroes that a legal way had been discovered to dispose of them which could not be effectually criticized even by their friends.

This is decidedly a new way and will doubtless commend itself to the murderers of other states. We know that under the present political regime in the South, any law, however absurd, which aims to oppress Negroes will find but slight opposition in any of the law-making bodies. No sane mind will believe that such a law will be impartially administered; that white men, as well as Black men, will be sentenced under it. This is additional weight to "The Black Man's Burden" and he must develop strength to bear it.

6

JAMES M. TOWNSEND

Dr. Townsend's Farewell Address
(*Christian Recorder*, November 12, 1891)

HISTORICAL CONTEXT

Rev. James M. Townsend was an AME minister and a state legislator in Indiana. He was a preeminent voice for Black political agitation in the late nineteenth century.

SERMONIC RESPONSE

Ladies and Gentlemen, Fellow Citizens:—I arise for the purpose of humbly and modestly thanking you for this exceedingly high and unmerited greeting which you pay me, an humble fellow citizen.

First of all, it is due, Mr. President, that I should sincerely thank the Blaine Invincible Club with its excellent president, that distinguished organizer and leader of men,—Col Carson. (Applause.)

It is mine also to thank you, my comrade soldiers, for the honor that you pay me in lending your presence. It is mine to most gratefully and humbly thank the distinguished gentlemen who have passed their glowing tributes, and their encomiums upon me, covering me with honors. I did not sleep any last night; I am sure I cannot sleep any to night, for I shall be thinking, thinking, thinking.—I shall think of the same when I remember that but a few years ago, I was a poor untaught, uneducated wood-sawer, a poor boy with patches on the knee and a brown straw hat just before Christmas.

In that condition, I was preparing to go to college with $22.50 in my pocket with which to pay current expenses of a college student for one year. Now I did not come here to say this, but it has come to me since I arose; but I am a quaker, that is to say, I go by the spirit.

What I say to-night, I say for a purpose. I desire, honored sir, that some young Afro-American may catch inspiration in this house to-night. There are those in this house who remember when I used to saw wood back of old Tappen Hall, that the other boys might have fire, and the next day I got a five cent loaf of bread, cut it into three pieces, and had bread and water one day; for a change, water and bread for the next.

And so the days passed on, and now, I find myself at the nation's capital, standing in the presence of this splendid audience, named as the distinguished gentleman of the occasion; well, Mr. President, it is simply wonderful, and all this only shows what are the possibilities of the boy; he may be a man. But enough; I am here to thank you sincerely.

I think this occasion, Mr. President, is calculated to inspire young men who are in this room, and to encourage them to seek such attainments as to make men truly noble and grand. While the Blaine Invincible Club, and the others who joined with them intended that this gathering should be complimentary to my humble self, I think that it is not so much to me personally as to the principles and convictions, the sentiments which I have in some small degree, been the representative.

Two years ago last May, I was distinguished by the President of the United States, in being appointed to an office that has proven one of importance and trust, and for which distinction Mr. Chairman, I am profoundly grateful, for it has lent me an opportunity.

I came among you, my fellow citizens, comparatively a stranger. You received me kindly, and from that hour to this, I have had your cordial treatment, and your kindliest greetings. That I have many friends is a source of rejoicing to me; that I have made a few enemies is evidence to my mind that I have tried to do something that was about right. (Applause.) And unless I am mistaken, I expect to do some more of the same kind. And so I came to you, I have lived with you for two years. In my social relations I have endeavored to be as broad as the extent of our population and as varied, possibly, as the classes or the groups which mark the large and advancing steps of our race civilization. I have visited some of the most cultured and refined homes among you and at the same time I have spent many pleasant hours among the lowly and the poor. (Applause.) At no time, Mr. Chairman, have I forgotten that I was a humble minister preaching God's word to dying men and women. Instead of spending my leisure at the boards of festive cards or sparkling wine, as some tell me a popular office holder must always do, I preferred to cast my lot with those who honor God, and choose to walk on planes of higher selection.

As an officer I have endeavored to be faithful, conscientious and just. In all my public life I have endeavored to keep three things distinctly in my mind: 1st, a respectful regard and cordial friendship for the administration under which I served; and, a loyal devotion to that party, which is the party of my choice and which is the party whose position and whose men are right—the Republican party. (Great applause and cheering); 3rd. above all things else, I have endeavored to look to that which was for the best interest of my people; best for their religion, best for their development, best for their enlightenment. At no time, Mr. Chairman, have I loved my party, its men, its principles less, at no time have I loved my country or its magnificent institutions less; because I have loved my people more. (Applause.) The man is yet to be moulded who is more devoted to the principles of his party than I am; yet when the rights of my people are in danger, as some one has said to-night, because my people need me more than my party does, I go to my people. (Applause.) I will always believe that the strong can take care of themselves. It is the weak whom we are to help. That is all.

Now you, my sir, (to Mr. Douglass), have been accused of some things recently. So have I. At one time somebody said: "Well, I believe Townsend is against the administration and against the party, and I would not be surprised if he turned out in league with the democrats for a while." Well, now, when it comes to the Democratic party, I am by it as Sheridan was by the State of Texas. When he was asked how he like Texas, he replied, "Well, if I owned Texas and owned hell, I would rent out Texas and live in hell." (Laughter). Now, there is no danger of my going over there.

Now, these things have been said simply because when I get religiously mad over the outrages which are perpetrated upon my people in certain sections of this land, and when I grow weary and sick and faint; when I say these things then somehow or another I feel like cursing, cursing, cursing, and to keep myself from cursing, I must get up and say some pretty bitter things about them.

I must say to the slanderers and vilifiers of my race, to the murderers of my people I must lay aside everything else and say to them, "By the Eternal, you must halt!" Now, that is my way of putting things. Then some modest preacher says, "Oh, well, Mr. Townsend is backsliding." Not the least so; for all of that that I was saying a minute ago, I have the approval of my conscience, I believe I have the respect of the party and more of the administration. (Applause.)

I do not retire from politics. Our cause is here, and possibly I shall be found contending for the principles which underlie good government, and for the rights of my people in this country, as I never contended before. Wherever I shall be, look for me well up in the line of battle, where the fight is up and where the smoke is ascending and the hurry and clash of arms are heard. Look for me there. (Applause.) While life lasts, expect to hear my weak voice mingled with that of this distinguished sire (Hon. Fred Douglass) with gray hairs, the prince enthroned in the hearts of his countrymen. (Applause.) Now, all of the small fry may try to dethrone him as much as they please, but he will reign.

Young men, if you want to get up to the top, it must be on your own merits; you will never get up by downing the man in front of you.

Expect, ladies and gentlemen, to hear my wear voice, but know that I am in harmony and concert with Langston and Pinchback, and Morris and Carson, and Green, and Scarborough, and Mitchell of Virginia. If you had more such men in the Southland, there would be less lynchings and hangings in that section; such men as Smythe and I say Fortune. We need some agitators for the race, and he is one of them. And all of that grand army of race loving young colored men, North, East, South and West, with them, expect to find me battling for the rights of my people, contending for good government, doing what I conceive to be right and leaving the results with God.

In conclusion, I want to say, my friends, that in the battle we will have, we must depend more largely upon ourselves than we have done in the past. We have been depending too much upon the President of the United States and upon that party, upon the legislatures and upon Congress. It was said in the olden time that the gods helped those who helped themselves.

I mean the men who would be free, themselves must strike the first blow. Now, then, I am depending upon nobody save God and my humble self. I hope you understand me. As a man of the race, I depend upon no political organization, no legislature, no Congress; but with my mallet and chisel in hand, with God's help, I will carve my way through. (Applause.) And the more we do for ourselves, the more we will be respected and helped by others. United, one and all, young and old, men and women, we must take hold of this problem and with Divine help, solve it.

You will excuse me, but I hold in my hands a pair of nickel shears. When I was out in Indiana, "making speeches against the administration" I visited Kokomo, Ind., up in the gas belt among the factories. After I had delivered my lecture, a gentleman came up to me and said: "Brother Townsend, a colored men is the foreman of the factory where these shears were made and if he leaves the factory, it must close down." Sir, I said, you have solved the problem in this quarter. What we want to do, what we must do, is to make ourselves indispensable in some way or other, so that when we stop, "the factory" must close down. We can do it religiously, in the business world, and I am sure we can in the political world. Any other people in this land that held the balance of power in themselves would bring somebody to time or there would be a rumpus in the gallery.

Now when I say these things, I do not mean leave the party nor anything of the kind.

I come back to the man with the shears. This is a colored man and the rest are white men; and they do not strike either. They are like government clerks—seldom resign in view of the salary that does not follow after resignation. This gentleman learned the trade from an Englishman from Sheffield, England. He knows the fourteen parts that are used in making of the shears and he is the only man who knows that much. Now, that man is solving the problem. Speeches are not going to do it; the legislatures are not going to do it, nor is Congress. We tried that last winter in the Elections Bill and before that in the Blair Educational Bill.

I want to call attention of our young men to the fact that, if our race ever comes and takes its place along with our fellow citizens, we have got to work our way to that place by our own volition and our own energy.

History does not record the fact where any people was living in the midst of a superior people and the superior ever reached down, took hold of the inferior one and raised it to a level with themselves. It is not according to nature.

Again, I repeat, we must fight our own battles if we would prevail, Now as one member of the race, I am going to do that.

I am going out West to take charge of a church. It is rather a strange coincidence. I have been called back to the pastorate of the first church I ever served as a minister, to the people among whom I have lived 16 years.

Now my friends, in conclusion, I say, hardly knowing why or how I did so, I came. Some of my friends regarded it as a grave mistake. From one point of view, perhaps it was. And now I leave you almost as mysteriously as I came. I scarcely know why I go but I go, and as I go, I feel that I carry with me your good wishes, your prayers, and your desire for my success. If I have this, I am satisfied.

Again, Mr. chairman, ladies and gentleman, members of the Blaine Invincible Club, one and all, I most devoutly thank you for this distinguished honor which you confer upon me, and bid you all farewell. (Applause and great cheering.)

7

WILLIAM H. NIMAR

Fortune Admonishes the Race to Wake Up to Their Sense of Duty
(Christian Recorder, August 9, 1894)

HISTORICAL CONTEXT

William H. Nimar's article on Ida B. Wells exposes how revered her voice
was against lynching during the Nadir era. Her reported work at Bethel AME
Church exhibits the relationship of theological protectionism with the social-
political figures of the time.

SERMONIC RESPONSE

Rev. J. S. Henderson, M.D. pastor of Bethel Church, Sullivan St., New York,
did not hold the regular Sunday night preaching service on Sabbath last, but
instead gave the entire evening to the discussions of that all important topic
now before the Afro-American League and our people in general. . . .

After handling the subject as probably no other person can, he introduced
Miss Ida B. Wells to the audience. She spoke without paper or notes of any
kind for about one hour and the vast audience was held spellbound by her
thrilling narrations. We are pleased to know that her mission abroad was
crowned with a marked degree of success. We regret we have not a hundred
more Ida B. Wells to proclaim and defend the truth. But where, oh where are
our leading men? Those who have spoken out on the subject are few and far
between. Men, women and children awaken from your lethargy; the time has
come when we must organize, agitate and support one or the other, for something must be done and quickly, too. The mere fact that we in the North are

not lynched as is our brother in the South is no reason why we should not sympathize with him. A Black man is but a Black man all the world over. We know there are good and bad among all the races, but our white brother will not admit of such an argument. The question then remains largely with us to be settled, but as long as there remains so strong a prejudice among ourselves just so much longer is our progress retarded. Yes, we are sorry to admit that there is a strong sectional feeling among us which we must wipe away instanter or else cease grumbling concerning the manner in which we are treated by the whites. I know whereof I speak and defy contradiction. The horrors to which our people have been subjected are well attested and Miss Wells in their depiction does not in the least distort the facts or exceed the truth. It is right time that good citizens of all sections regardless of color should rise up in protest against the revolting outrages constituting one of the few dark stains upon our country's honor which survived the war and perpetrate the curse of slavery. Let us continue then to hold each Sunday meetings as was held at old Bethel. There were seated around the chancel President fortune, Revs. J. M. Henderson and Anderson, Dr. Hamilton Williams, Hon. H. C. Astwood, Dr. Morton, C. Sims, Miss Lyons, Revs. James M. Carter, chaplain of the League and the writer, who is Secretary of the League.

8

O. J. LEBOEUF

A Moving Time in the Thibodeaux District
(*Christian Recorder*, August 5, 1897)

HISTORICAL CONTEXT

In Franklin, Louisiana, the AME Church Thibodeaux District exhibited bravery as it decided to host its meeting fifteen days after the lynching of Jack Davis. Davis, who also went by Buddy Jack, was said to have entered the residence of "Widow Marcot," a local white woman, and sexually assaulted her around midnight. It was said that this transgression took place at the home of a Dr. Percot, a local physician who was set to provide the Marcot family with medicine.[14] There are disputes about the story's reporting, as varying outlets reported that a Willis Jewell was also a participant. Attempting to run away, Davis was said to be chased following Marcot's screams. He soon was caught and was hanged on the day of the incident, July 22, 1897. Jewell, the said accomplice, was said to be severely whipped and forced out of town.[15]

SERMONIC RESPONSE

Whereas, The influence of lynch-law is spreading and fastening itself on the people of the country without regard to locality or section, and that should it be tolerated and countenanced much longer, will have a damaging effect on the advancement of the prosperity of the people, and in the eyes of the world, America will be looked upon as the home of savages and barbarians.

Resolved, That we, the officers and members of the A.M.E. Church Thibodeaux District Conference, convened in the town of Franklin, La., do earnestly protest against the common practice of lynching, and call upon the Christians and loyal people of the United States, and especially the Governors and President, to raise their voices in condemnation of the barbarous and inhuman practice of such crime, irrespective of race or color, and pray that the influence of the Higher Power will intervene, and stay the hand of the assassins. Revs. G. B. Billups, D. Burrell, L. E. Carter and Mr. L. Murphy, committee.

O. J. LEBOEUF

9

WILLIAM DAVID CHAPPELLE

Freedom (*Christian Recorder*, August 26, 1897)

HISTORICAL CONTEXT

William David Chappelle, president of Allen University and eventually a bishop in the AME Church, penned this outstanding retort to American exceptionalism and the nation's unconstitutional treatment of Black people. This methodological fight exhibits the tenets of theological protectionism.

SERMONIC RESPONSE

That all men are created free with certain inalienable rights no sane man will question. Among these are life, liberty and the peaceful pursuits of happiness. If then, all men are created free, freedom is a natural endowment from Almighty God and, therefore, inalienable freedom, says one, is the normal condition of the human soul; liberty of the normal condition of the human body.

It was the greatest principle of freedom that forced the Pilgrim Fathers to launch upon the turbulent Atlantic in search of a new home—a home upon whose soil they could kneel and worship the Great God who gave their being. They fled from despots and lords to the humble cottages upon the shores of our American continent and there implanted that principle of freedom which has floated through all the annals of American history, and will go down to the latest generations upon this continent, whether black or white, because freedom is taught at the fireside of every home and cemented by the prayers and baptismal vows of our mothers and fathers; it is printed in our books, taught in our schools and sung in our churches. This principle of freedom and the recognition of human rights have permeated the great North Maine, Massachusetts, New York, Pennsylvania, Illinois, with Indiana, the District of Columbia and Kentucky, have acknowledged the endowment of freedom by our Creator.

Freedom is a right, a natural right from God we must admit then that this carries with it a corresponding obligation. Right and obligation are reciprocal—that is, whenever there is a right in one person, there is a corresponding obligation upon others. If one man has a right to an estate, others are obligated to refrain from it. If parents have a right to reverence from their children, their children are obligated to reverence parents and so in all other instances.

Moral obligation depends, as we have seen, upon the will of God. Right, which is correlative to it, depends upon the same. Right therefore, signifies consistency with the will of God.

We conclude therefore, that it is God's will to have created us free, then it is the corresponding right of others to protect the freedom of their fellows, and if this is not done an obligation to Almighty God is violated and an unpardonable wrong is perpetrated upon your fellows.

Let us stop upon the very hilltop of Christian civilization and in the shadows of the nineteenth century and enumerate some of the wrongs, and their dire consequences, which are the direct results of broken obligations and cowardice. For instance, the holding of human flesh as slaves, the disfranchisement of a free man by fraud and intimidation. The proscription of the Negro race from our institutions of learning and that blackest and most cowardly of all crimes, the lynching of a defenceless Negro without judge or jury; and this, too, right under the shadow of the stars and stripes, that great symbol of the "land of the free and the home of the brave,"

We have read of George III, who usurped English liberty, but he had his Cromwell; we have read of Julius Caesar, who usurped Roman freedom, but he had his Brutus; we have read of Napolean, who made France tremble beneath his frowns of vengeance, but he had his Waterloo; we have seen the British lion bearded in the American waters and the colonies set as liberty; and now, under the American eagle, with the stars in one claw and the stripes in the other, blending the two, we have the mighty symbol of freedom, which is farce. Using Mr. Ingersoll's terms, "Any flag which does not protect her citizens is a filthy rag and pollutes the very air in which it floats." Freedom in general means that intellectual, moral and religious development which equips one for every emergency in life.

Intellectual training is the eye through which we see the condition in which we are placed by the side of other races, and traces in splendor the rising star of an infant race. Fellow classmates, we are charged with a great responsibility, of emancipating our people from that slavish chain of ignorance, vice and immorality. We assume that responsibility today of carrying the torchlight of Christian education in the foremost ranks of the race, and it is for us to prove ourselves worthy of so great a responsibility.

It is clear, then, that before this right can be universally exercised, the integral whole must be made to know its rights, and then to claim them. The United States Government, it seems, is awaiting such a development, but she forgets that she is committing a crime in allowing that black demon of race-prejudice to stay the above-mentioned results. Take the barriers out of our pathway and throw about us the common protection of the law and we ask nothing more; thereby guiding us while we lift our people from the straw press of immorality, the slush hods of indecency and the horrible pit of ignorance.

We are not praying for help, but for protection. When we commit crime, whether it be larceny, arson or the nameless crime, let the pure sunlight of investigation shine upon us before an unbiased jury, and we ask nothing more.

I do not think the race is as bad as it is made to appear by the press of the country. We are about as the other race, all things considered. Place about us the same environments and protection, lynch every white man who insults a colored woman, make all the jurors black, make all the constables black, make all the sheriffs black, make all the judges black, make all the lawyers black, make seventy-five per cent of the white people paupers as the Negroes are, let their women wait on Negro men, let them be hired on Negro farms, let them nurse Negro babies, let them be owned by the Negro babies, let them be owned by the Negro race and let this condition of affairs extend over a period of two hundred and fifty-three years, would they not be in the same condition? Is not this enough to brutalize, subjugate and, in short, destroy the last vestige of manhood in any race regardless of color. This done, what is necessary? Protection under the law, and not prostitution of the law. Let those in authority rise up in their manhood and sense of right and proclaim from the sacred rostrum human freedom. Let the majesty of the law proclaim human freedom, let the United States government protect human freedom in all of its phases and aspects. When this is done, and not until then, let the American people sing: "My country 'tis of thee, Sweet land of liberty," etc.

10

C. T. SHAFFER, H. T. JOHNSON, AND J. H. BEAN

Resolutions: By the AME Preachers' Meeting on the Georgia-Newnan Lynching (*Christian Recorder*, April 27, 1899)

HISTORICAL CONTEXT

Samuel Hose was lynched April 23, 1899, in Coweta County, Georgia. This particular lynching became a national story, as the image of Hose's mutilated and burned body became popularized on a postcard. Hose was said to have engaged in an argument over wages with employer Alfred Cranford. When the argument escalated, it was said, Cranford drew a gun to kill Hose. In self-defense, Hose threw an ax and killed Cranford. Although Hose tried to flee the county, he was caught on the train by a local posse.

The mob refused to give Hose over to the local officials, and the group of two thousand publicly tortured and killed Hose in one of the most gruesome lynching exhibitions of the era. It was said that some of Hose's remains were "toured," including the display of fingers and knuckles in a butcher shop window in Atlanta. In defense of their lynching, many began to float rumors that Hose also had a history of rape. These rumors were unfounded.[16]

After the fact, it was brought to national attention that Hose was posthumously found innocent and acting in self-defense. It was also brought to national attention that there was no rape charge attached to Hose, and that lynching apologists had created this rumor to justify his death.

SERMONIC RESPONSE

Whereas, we have read the harrowing account of the butchery and burning of a colored man went yesterday at Newnan, Georgia, and

Whereas, the alleged crimes for which the victim suffered is one worthy of the strongest denunciation of all law abiding and decent people and deserving of the severest penalty of the law, and

Whereas, we have no toleration for that class of deprived creatures among us, who are equally reckless in their invasion of the divine rights of priceless life in sacred virtue, and who have done more to place the race in universal disfavor, if not contempt, than anything with the exception of the monster curse of slavery itself, and

Whereas, the detection, prosecution and punishment of Negro criminals and offenders need never be questioned through legalized channels, since the machinery of law, superior power and prowess are all on this side of the dominant race, hence the infliction of mob penalties and lynch lawlessness is the more to be condensed and without the slightest justification. Therefore be it

Resolved, that the horrible mutilation and burning of the alleged murderer and rapist at Newnan, Georgia, one yesterday, in the light of the foregoing observations and surrounding facts, maybe more fearful because of its occurrence on God's holy day.

Resolved, that this flagrant contempt for law and order in the outrageous desecration shown for the present a situation far more deplorable than that which caused our nation to interpose in behalf of the Cuban or its armies and navy in Philippine waters or on the Philippine shores.

Resolved, that the situation of Palmetto and Newnan, Georgia, invokes and abundantly justifies the presence and services of Mission armies armed with the Spirit and worth of God more urgently than Chinese idolaters, African hotten tots or Fiji Islanders.

Resolved, that we appreciate our sole dependence on Almighty Justice under existing conditions and lawlessness and encourage our helpless people who suffer alike from all sides of lawlessness affecting the race.

Resolved, that we pray that God's gospel light may reach these regions of lawlessness and that justice and law may be dispensed to all citizens without regard to race, color or previous condition.

C. T. Shaffer, H. T. Johnson, J. H. Bean

11

GEORGE F. RICHINGS

Personals (*Christian Recorder*, May 4, 1899)

HISTORICAL CONTEXT

George Richings's letter is an additional response to the Hose lynching. It also includes a brief statement concerning a personal near-death experience, as he mentions "being mobbed" just a few miles from the church meeting. Perseverance and diligence in the cause of antilynching is exhibited in this letter.

SERMONIC RESPONSE

Dear Brother Johnson, I do not often trouble you for space in your paper, but I will be very thankful if you will give room for a few lines enclosed . . .

I need not tell you that the people here in a fastball over the South, feel keenly the awful lynching in Georgia. The whites, and I suppose some of the colored people, will censure Bishop Walters for what he said at Jersey City. But I tell you, I am of the opinion that we have reached the point in the history of lynchings and mob violence where something must be done. The better class of people down here say they are opposed to mob law, but they do not take any steps to prevent it. I have written to Miss Impey, of England and if I can get her cooperation again, I think a little newspaper agitation from England might have some reflex action on this country that would be helpful, and especially since we have just gone to war with Spain to free the poor people in Cuba. As I write this I am reminded that I'm only a few miles from where the white people mobbed me, and left me for dead. But, despite all these awful things

I'm hopeful, and I fully believe that the colored man has a great future in the country, and will play a prominent part in its development.

Yours truly,
G. F. Richings

12

WILLIAM ARNETT

Colored Ministers on Southern Legislation
(*Christian Recorder*, May 9, 1901)

HISTORICAL CONTEXT

This published retort from AME bishop William Arnett aligns well with the respectability politics of Booker T. Washington. Arnett, in contrast to his cohorts in their report, found political maneuverability by identifying lynching as an individual response to "vigilante justice" rather than a system of caste and racial violence. His indication of persons lynched as criminal rapist also speaks volumes to the plurality of Black religious consciousness within theological protectionism.

SERMONIC RESPONSE

Resolutions Adopted by the A.M.E. Conference at Frederick—Criticism of President McKinley, Appointments Made For The Year.

Frederick, Md., April 30th.—The Baltimore conference of the African M.E. Church, which convened last Thursday in Quinn's Church, completed their work tonight, and after announcing the appointments adjourned to meet in Waters Chapel, Baltimore, Md., next year.

The committee on the state of the country, involving the Negro problem, made their report today and evoked a general discussion. The report, in part, said:

"The tendency in certain sections of the South is to humiliate and downgrade the Negro and weaken him by the enaction of discriminating laws by which to deprive him of his vote, and the introduction of the separate car law. It is not against the enactment of qualification law that we complain, but against the mode of applying it so that the brother in white is ever and the brother in black is never qualified to exercise the right of franchise.

We do not complain against the separate cars for the races, but against being compelled to pay the same price that others pay without receiving the same accommodations, comforts and privileges, and all of this in the face of the constitution of the United States.

The butchering and resulting burning alive of human beings has more the appearance of degeneracy of a once great people than it has of the relics of the dark ages of the world. The silence of the white pulpits and press, and the silence of the judicial and executive departments of the country, both in the states and in the nation, the absence of mass meetings by the good white people in our large cities to right the wrong, and of the most deplorable state of human society. We most earnestly plead with the people of this country to adopt speedy measures to put an end to and forever stamp as a thing of the past the lynching of persons charged with crime. We do not want to evade the law, nor do we want the guilty to escape punishment, but we want that punishment meted out by law."

Camp meetings and excursions were condemned by the committee, and the attention of the conference was called to the fact that President McKinley had failed in his inaugural address and his message to Congress to speak of the outrages against the American Negro.

Bishop Arnett said: "What is the use of complaining about race discrimination. If you are refused a glass of soda water it means that you should establish a fountain of your own. So, save up your money and go into business." Speaking of the lynch clause in the report, he said that resolutions of vituperation should be passed on lawlessness. He had no faith in a man who would assault womanhood and declared that he was a dangerous character.

13

R. S. QUARTERMAN

How Lynchings Can Be Stopped (*Christian Recorder*, May 4, 1893)

HISTORICAL CONTEXT

R. S. Quarterman's sermon references an event that took place March 14, 1891, when eleven Italian Americans were publicly executed in New Orleans. The lynching was over the murder of police chief David Hennessy, and a mob broke out in violence when some of the men were acquitted at trial. Due to a growing belief that Italian Americans were establishing organized crime syndicates, alongside a growing political relationship with the Democratic Party, this lynching sought to put the race back in its place. Interestingly enough, although thousands of people surrounded the parish prison, the lynchings were spontaneous and isolated. Those who conducted the execution were city leaders, including lawyers, politicians such as Mayor Walter C. Flower, businesspeople, and John C. Wickliffe, editor of the *New Delta* newspaper.[17]

SERMONIC RESPONSE

There is not a newspaper in these United States, I venture to say, that has not had something in its columns about lynch law. Some of the leading men of this country have come out through the columns of the newspaper and condemned lynchings, and still it goes on.

Now I ask the question, what will stop it? Will class legislation? No. Will party affiliation? No. Then what will stop it? Public sentiment or public opinion. And this can only be brought about by the Pulpit and Bar associations of the different States and districts. Having had conversations with some of the leading men of the South, I am convinced that if the ministers of both races would preach against this evil it would end. Justice, so far as this law is concerned, is bridled; the judges and governors are muzzled, they can't carry out the law's request. Why? Because public opinion is against them. They may condemn the lynchers and offer a reward for their conviction, but what good can or will that do, when sometime a part or all of the county officials are in sympathy with the mob who are so auspicious to take human life.

History will sustain us in saying, that you cannot suppress any great evil until the pulpits do their duty. To meet in our conferences, associations and assemblies and pass a series of resolutions condemning lynch law and there, it will do no good. We must reach the masses, and this can only be done by appealing to their reason from the pulpits. Let the ministers of both, or all races in this country go to their pulpits and from time to time preach against this evil; show their congregations that it is a sin and disgrace to civilization, not to any particular race, but to a supposed civilized country, and to lynch will never rid us of the evil—two wrongs will never make one right. Let these bar associations and the ministers of all colors come out and take a bold stand for the right, and then liberty will come to this country. The law can't stop it because public sentiment or public opinion is in favor of lynching. To prove what I have said, please consider this one fact—two wrongs will not make one right. These mobs were first organized to put down rape, since then they lynch for stealing, political prejudice, wife beating, debt and at last, for nothing. This sin is raging in this country because the colored and white ministers are afraid to preach against it. I do not write this article because I am so afraid of race-war, as it is so often called in the newspapers, but because the time is near upon us when the people of this nation will be called on to protect the flag of the nation, and it will be on account of this evil—lynching. We were threatened a few years ago by the lynching at New Orleans. I am sure if the colored and white ministers of this country would take this matter to their people and agitate it from time to time, and lynching would soon be a thing of the past.

Orlando, Fla.

NOTES

INTRODUCTION

1. Tolnay and Beck, *Festival of Violence;* Seguin and Rigby, "National Crimes." See also "Lynching in America."

2. For religious studies that highlight the development of Black liberation theology and its sociopolitical consciousness, see Montgomery, *Under Their Own Vine and Fig Tree;* Swift, *Black Prophets of Justice;* Washington, *Frustrated Fellowship;* Wilmore, *Black Religion.*

3. Fulop, "Future Golden Day," 77, 79.

4. For early twentieth-century social science research on lynching, see Cutler, *Lynch Law;* Dollard, *Caste and Class;* Shay, *Judge Lynch;* Brown, *Strain of Violence;* Rosenbaum and Sederberg, *Vigilante Politics.*

5. For research that highlights the role religion played in American lynching, see Ehrenhaus and Owen, "Race Lynching"; Bailey and Snedker, "Practicing What They Preach?"; Baker, Steed, and Moreland, *Religion and Politics in the South.*

6. Hall, *Revolt Against Chivalry.* See also Hall, "Mind That Burns in Each Body," 328–49; Zangrando, *NAACP Crusade.* For a case study of a northern lynching, see Downey and Hyser, *No Crooked Death* and *Coatesville and the Lynching of Zachariah Walker.* On profound generational shifts in southern historiography, especially in approaches to violence, gender, and race, see Thelen, "What We See and Can't See"; Williamson, "Wounds Not Scars," 1221–53; Harris, *Exorcising Blackness.* For another interpretation of lynching, emphasizing race and ritual, see Patterson, *Rituals of Blood,* 169–231.

7. Fulop, "Future Golden Day," 75–76.

8. Miller, *Elevating the Race,* xviii.

9. "Lynching Project."

10. For historiographical research on lynching, see Pfeifer, "At the Hands of Parties Unknown?," 832–46; Brundage, *Under Sentence of Death,* 1–23; Zangrando, *NAACP Crusade.*

11. Delgado and Stefancic, *Critical Race Theory,* 16–17, 20.

12. For historical studies that highlight the relationship between the antilynching campaign and the Black church, see Fortune, *T. Thomas Fortune;* Marrs, *Life And History;* Wells, *Memphis Diary.*

13. Wilmore, *Black Religion;* Cone, *God of the Oppressed.*

14. "Bishop Turner's Wail," July 18, 1896.

15. Tolnay and Beck, *Festival of Violence;* Senechal de la Roche, "Sociogenesis of Lynching."

16. Johnson and Jersild, *"Ain't Gonna Lay My 'Ligion Down."*

17. Beck and Tolnay, "When Race Didn't Matter."

18. Dickerson, *African Methodist Episcopal Church,* 559

19. Pfeifer, *Rough Justice,* 106, 112.

I. RADICAL THEOLOGICAL PROTECTIONISM

1. Johnson and Jersild, *"Ain't Gonna Lay My 'Ligion Down,"* 45–47.

2. Raboteau, *Slave Religion,* 290.

3. *TCR,* June 13, 1895.

4. *TCR,* October 19, 1893.

5. *TCR,* May 25, 1893.

6. Ibid.

7. *TCR,* December 5, 1895.

8. *TCR,* July 3, 1902.

9. *TCR,* June 29, 1893

10. *TCR,* April 24, 1884, copied from the *Richmond Planet.*

11. *TCR,* August 9, 1888.

12. *Evening Star,* March 11, 1878.

13. *Old Commonwealth,* March 14, 1878.

14. *Alexandria Gazette,* March 11, 1878.

15. *Charlotte Observer,* April 27, 1893.

16. Brundage, *Under Sentence of Death,* 261–62; "The Brooks County War Is Ended"; "Seven Lives for One."

17. "Loftin Resigns His Office."

18. Finnegan, *Deed So Accursed.*

19. "State and County Officers Investigating Church Fire."

20. Walters, *My Life and Work.*

21. "Rev. D. A. Graham."

22. "Talk of War on Whites at Negro Conference."

II. PIOUS THEOLOGICAL PROTECTIONISM

1. Beck and Tolnay, "When Race Didn't Matter," 9.

2. *TCR,* August 16, 1894.

3. *African Methodist Episcopal Church Hymnal,* 137.

4. *TCR,* January 22, 1885.

5. *TCR,* November 7, 1889.

6. *TCR,* August 3, 1893.

7. *TCR,* September 16, 1897.

8. *TCR,* January 3, 1895

9. Adeleke, *UnAfrican Americans,* 152.

10. *TCR*, August 1, 1895.

11. *TCR*, September 7, 1893.

12. *TCR*, March 18, 1897.

13. *TCR*, June 1, 1899.

14. *TCR*, August 8, 1895.

15. *TCR*, July 1, 1897.

16. *TCR*, February 25, 1897.

17. *TCR*, January 9, 1890.

18. *TCR*, July 4, 1889.

19. Raboteau, *Slave Religion*, 75, 283.

20. *TCR*, August 24, 1893.

21. *TCR*, March 30, 1899.

22. *TCR*, May 18, 1899.

23. *TCR*, May 18, 1899.

24. Brundage, *Under Sentence of Death,* 152; Tolney and Beck, *Festival of Violence,* 29, 134–35; Rivers and Brown, *Laborers in the Vineyard of the Lord,* 50.

25. *TCR*, July 22, 1897.

26. Tolnay and Beck, *Festival of Violence,* 254.

27. *TCR*, September 16, 1897.

28. *TCR*, December 1, 1898

29. *TCR*, January 15, 1891.

30. *TCR*, November 2, 1893.

31. *TCR*, December 31, 1891.

32. *TCR*, August 7, 1902.

33. "Appendix: 'The Great Long National Shame,'" 1165–77.

34. *Manning Times,* January 1, 1890.

35. *Wilkes-Barre Times Leader,* December 30, 1889.

36. *Dallas Morning News,* July 29, 1893.

37. Konhaus, "I Thought Things Would Be Different There," 13

38. *Daily Gazette,* August 1, 1894.

39. Brown, *Strain of Violence,* 97.

40. *New Orleans Daily Picayune,* July 17, 1902; Elizabeth, "Death at the Hands of Persons Unknown."

41. *Mena Star,* March 23, 1899.

42. *Houston Daily Post,* 6; "War of Races"; "Wholesale Lynching," 5.

43. Elizabeth, "Death at the Hands of Persons Unknown," 160.

44. Wells, *Red Record: Tabulated Statistics.*

45. *New Orleans Times-Picayune,* September 18, 1893.

III. CONSTITUTIONAL THEOLOGICAL PROTECTIONISM

1. Blum, "There Won't Be Any Rich People in Heaven," 372, 375.

2. Wood, *Lynching and Spectacle,* 6, 9; Waldrep, *Lynching in America,* 45.

3. *TCR,* August 3, 1893.

4. *TCR,* August 9, 1894.

5. *TCR,* October 6, 1898.

6. *TCR,* August 5, 1897.

7. *TCR,* May 4, 1899.

8. *TCR,* August 10, 1899.

9. *TCR,* May 9, 1901.

10. Wood, *Lynching and Spectacle,* 261.

11. Osofsky, *Burden of Race,* 181–84.

12. Wells, *Red Record: Lynchings.*

13. "Colored Man Hang For Robbery."

14. *St. Joseph Weekly Gazette,* July 23, 1897, p. 2; *New Orleans Times-Democrat,* July 21, 1891, p. 1.

15. *Topeka Daily Capital,* July 23, 1897, p. 2.

16. Ray, "Lynching of Sam Hose."

17. Wall et al., *Louisiana: A History.*

NOTES TO PAGES 185–233

BIBLIOGRAPHY

PRIMARY SOURCES

Digital and Manuscript Collections

"Lynching in America: Confronting the Legacy of Racial Terror." Equal Justice Initiative, https://eji.org/reports/lynching-in-america.
"The Lynching Project." Lynching Violence Website, https://sites.uw.edu/lynching.
Sadie Tanner Mossell Alexander Papers. University Archives & Records Center, University of Pennsylvania, Philadelphia.

Newspapers

Alexandria Gazette, Virginia
The Call, San Francisco, California
Charlotte Observer, North Carolina
Christian Recorder, Nashville, Tennessee
Daily Gazette, Charleston, West Virginia
Dallas Morning News, Texas
Evening Star, Washington, DC
Florence Morning News, South Carolina
Houston Daily Post, Texas
Los Angeles Herald, California
Manning Times, South Carolina
Mena Star, Arkansas
New Orleans Daily Picayune, Louisiana
New Orleans Times-Democrat
New York Times, New York
Old Commonwealth, Harrisonburg, Virginia
Richmond Planet, Virginia

Times-Picayune, New Orleans, Louisiana
Topeka Daily Capital, Kansas
Wilkes-Barre Times Leader, Pennsylvania

SECONDARY SOURCES

Adeleke, Tunde. *UnAfrican Americans: Nineteenth-Century Black Nationalists and the Civilizing Mission.* Lexington: University Press of Kentucky, 1998.
African Methodist Episcopal Church Hymnal. 7th printing. Nashville: African Methodist Episcopal Church, 2006.
"Appendix: 'The Great Long National Shame': Selected Incidents of Racial Violence in the United States." *Counterpoints* 163 (2001): 1165–77.
Bailey, Amy Kate, and Karen A. Snedker. "Practicing What They Preach? Lynching and Religion in the American South, 1890–1929." *American Journal of Sociology* 117, no. 3 (November 2011).
Baker, Tod A., Robert P. Steed, and Laurence W. Moreland, eds. *Religion and Politics in the South: Mass and Elite Perspectives.* New York: Praeger, 1983.
Beck, E. M., and Stewart E. Tolnay. "When Race Didn't Matter: Black and White Mob Violence Against Their Own Color." In *Under Sentence of Death: Lynching in the South,* ed. William Fitzhugh Brundage, 132–154. Chapel Hill: University of North Carolina Press, 1997.
"Bishop Turner's Wail." *Cleveland Gazette,* July 18, 1896.
Blum, Edward J. "'There Won't Be Any Rich People in Heaven': The Black Christ, White Hypocrisy, and the Gospel According to W. E. B. Du Bois." *Journal of African American History* 90, no. 4 (Autumn 2005): 368–86.
"The Brooks County War Is Ended: Videttes Find Everything Peaceful and Return to Their Homes—Lynching Generally Condemned." *New York Times,* December 26, 1894.
Brown, Richard Maxwell. *Strain of Violence: Historical Studies of American Violence and Vigilantism.* New York: Oxford University Press, 1975.
Brundage, William Fitzhugh, ed. *Under Sentence of Death: Lynching in the South.* Chapel Hill: University of North Carolina Press, 1997.
"A Colored Man Hang for Robbery." *Black Virginia: The Richmond Planet, 1894–1909,* https://blackvirginia.richmond.edu/items/show/1702.
Cutler, James Elbert. *Lynch-Law: An Investigation into the History of Lynching in the United States.* New York: Longmans, Green, 1905.
Delgado, Richard, and Jean Stefancic. *Critical Race Theory: An Introduction.* New York: New York University Press, 2001.

Dickerson, Dennis C. *The African Methodist Episcopal Church: A History.* Cambridge: Cambridge University Press, 2020.

Dollard, John. *Caste and Class in a Southern Town.* 1937. Madison: University of Wisconsin Press, 1989.

Downey, Dennis B., and Raymond M. Hyser. *Coatesville and the Lynching of Zachariah Walker: Death in a Pennsylvania Steel Town.* Charleston, SC: History Press, 2011.

———. *No Crooked Death: Coatesville, Pennsylvania, and the Lynching of Zachariah Walker.* Champaign: University of Illinois Press, 1991.

Ehrenhaus, Peter, and A. Susan Owen. "Race Lynching and Christian Evangelicalism: Performances of Faith." *Text and Performance Quarterly* 24, no. 3–4 (2004): 276–301.

Elizabeth, Mary. "Death at the Hands of Persons Unknown: The Geography of Lynching in the Deep South, 1882 to 1910." PhD diss., Louisiana State University, 1992.

Finnegan, Terence. *A Deed So Accursed: Lynching in Mississippi and South Carolina, 1881–1940.* Charlottesville: University of Virginia Press, 2013.

Fortune, Timothy Thomas. *T. Thomas Fortune, the Afro-American Agitator: A Collection of Writings, 1880–1928.* Ed. Shawn Leigh Alexander. Gainesville: University Press of Florida, 2008.

Fulop, Timothy E. "'The Future Golden Day of the Race': Millennialism and Black Americans in the Nadir, 1877–1901." *Harvard Theological Review* 84, no. 1 (1991): 75–99, http://www.jstor.org/stable/1509831.

Hall, Jacquelyn Dowd. "'The Mind That Burns in Each Body': Women, Rape, and Racial Violence." In *Powers of Desire: The Politics of Sexuality,* ed. Ann Snitow, Christine Stansell, and Sharon Thompson, 328–49. New York: New York University Press, 1983.

———. *Revolt Against Chivalry: Jessie Daniel Ames and the Women's Campaign Against Lynching.* New York: Columbia University Press, 1993.

Harris, Trudier. *Exorcising Blackness: Historical and Literary Lynching and Burning Rituals.* Bloomington: Indiana University Press, 1984.

Johnson, Alonzo, and Paul Jersild, eds. *"Ain't Gonna Lay My 'Ligion Down": African American Religion in the South.* Columbia: University of South Carolina Press, 1996.

Konhaus, Tim. "'I Thought Things Would Be Different There": Lynching and the Black Community in Southern West Virginia, 1880–1933. *West Virginia History* 1, no. 2 (Fall 2007): 25–43, https://dx.doi.org/10.1353/wvh.2008.0015.

"Loftin Resigns His Office: Negro Postmaster of Hogansville, Ga., to Have a Place in Washington." *New York Times,* October 4, 1987, p. 1.

Marrs, Elijah P. *Life and History of the Rev. Elijah P. Marrs.* Louisville, KY: Bradley & Gilbert, 1885.

McGovern, James R. *Anatomy of a Lynching: The Killing of Claude Neal.* 1982. Updated ed. Baton Rouge: Louisiana State University Press, 2013.

Miller, Albert G. *Elevating the Race: Theophilus G. Steward, Black Theology, and the Making of an African American Civil Society, 1865–1924.* Knoxville: University of Tennessee Press, 2003.

Montgomery, William E. *Under Their Own Vine and Fig Tree: The African-American Church in the South, 1865–1900.* Baton Rouge: Louisiana State University Press, 1995.

Osofsky, Gilbert. *The Burden of Race.* New York: Harper & Row, 1967.

Patterson, Orlando. *Rituals of Blood: Consequences of Slavery in Two American Centuries.* New York: Basic Civitas, 2006.

Pfeifer, Michael J. "At the Hands of Parties Unknown? The State of the Field of Lynching Scholarship." *Journal of American History* 101, no. 3 (December 2014): 832–46.

———. *Rough Justice: Lynching and American Society, 1874–1947.* Urbana: University of Illinois Press, 2004.

Raboteau, Albert J. *Slave Religion: The "Invisible Institution" in the Antebellum South.* Oxford: Oxford University Press, 2004.

Ray, Janine. "The Lynching of Sam Hose." *Clio: Your Guide to History,* May 29, 2016, https://theclio.com/entry/22714.

"Rev. D. A. Graham, 'Some Facts About Southern Lynchings.'" 1899. *Black Past,* January 29, 2007, https://www.blackpast.org/african-american-history/1899-reverend-d-graham-some-facts-about-southern-lynchings.

Rivers, Larry E., and Canter Brown. *Laborers in the Vineyard of the Lord: The Beginnings of the AME Church in Florida,1865–1895.* Gainesville: University Press of Florida, 2001.

Rosenbaum, H. John, and Peter C. Sederberg, eds. *Vigilante Politics.* Philadelphia: University of Pennsylvania Press, 1976.

Seguin, Charles, and David Rigby. "National Crimes: A New National Data Set of Lynchings in the United States, 1883 to 1941." *Socius* 5 (May 6, 2019), https://doi.org/10.1177/2378023119841780.

Senechal de la Roche, Roberta. "The Sociogenesis of Lynching." In *Under Sentence of Death: Lynching in the South,* ed. William Fitzhugh Brundage, 48–76. Chapel Hill: University of North Carolina Press, 1997.

"Seven Lives for One." *Los Angeles Herald,* December 24, 1894.

Shay, Frank. *Judge Lynch: His First Hundred Years.* New York: Biblo and Tannen, 1969.

"State and County Officers Investigating Church Fire." *Florence Morning News,* October 7, 1955.

Swift, David E. *Black Prophets of Justice: Activist Clergy Before the Civil War.* Baton Rouge: Louisiana State University Press, 1989.

"Talk of War on Whites at Negro Conference: Bitter Anti-lynching Speeches at Afro-American Council," *New York Times,* October 10, 1906.

Thelen, David. "What We See and Can't See in the Past: An Introduction." *Journal of American History* 83, no. 4 (1997): 1217–20, https://doi.org/10.2307/2952898.

Tolnay, Stewart E., and E. M. Beck. *A Festival of Violence: An Analysis of Southern Lynchings, 1882–1930.* Urbana: University of Illinois Press, 1995.

Waldrep, Christopher, ed. *Lynching in America: A History in Documents.* New York: New York University Press, 2006.

Wall, Bennett H., Light Townsend Cummins, Judith Kelleher Schafer, Edward F. Haas, and Michael L. Kurtz, eds. *Louisiana: A History.* 5th ed. Wheeling, IL: Harlan Davidson, 2008.

Walters, Alexander. *My Life and Work.* Wilmore, KY: First Fruits, 2016.

"A War of Races Rages in Arkansas." *The Call,* March 24, 1899, p. 1

Washington, James Melvin. *Frustrated Fellowship: The Black Baptist Quest for Social Power.* Macon, GA: Mercer, 1986.

Wells, Ida B. *Crusade for Justice: The Autobiography of Ida B. Wells.* 2nd edition. Edited by Alfreda M. Duster. Chicago: University of Chicago Press, 2020.

———. *The Memphis Diary of Ida B. Wells.* Ed. Miriam Decosta-Willis. Boston: Beacon, 1995.

———. *The Red Record: Lynchings in the United States: 1892–1893–1894.* Pamphlet. Chicago: Donohue & Henneberry, 1894.

———. *A Red Record: Tabulated Statistics and Alleged Causes of Lynchings in the United States, 1892–1893–1894.* Chicago, 1895.

Williamson, Joel. "Wounds Not Scars: Lynching, the National Conscience, and the American Historian." *Journal of American History* 83, no. 4 (March 1997): 1221.

Wilmore, Gayraud S. *Black Religion and Black Radicalism: An Interpretation of the Religious History of African Americans.* Maryknoll, NY: Orbis, 1998.

Wood, Amy Louise. *Lynching and Spectacle: Witnessing Racial Violence in America, 1890–1940.* Chapel Hill: University of North Carolina Press, 2011.

Young, Kevin W. *The Violent World of Broadus Miller: A Story of Murder, Lynch Mobs, and Judicial Punishment in the Carolinas.* Chapel Hill: University of North Carolina Press, 2024.

Zangrando, Robert L. *The NAACP Crusade Against Lynching, 1909–1950.* Philadelphia: Temple University Press, 1980.

INDEX